CULTS IN
AMERICA

A Reference Handbook

Other Titles in ABC-CLIO's
CONTEMPORARY
WORLD ISSUES
Series

Books in the Contemporary World Issues series address vital issues in today's society such as terrorism, sexual harassment, homelessness, AIDS, gambling, animal rights, and air pollution. Written by professional writers, scholars, and nonacademic experts, these books are authoritative, clearly written, up-to-date, and objective. They provide a good starting point for research by high school and college students, scholars, and general readers as well as by legislators, businesspeople, activists, and others.

Each book, carefully organized and easy to use, contains an overview of the subject, a detailed chronology, biographical sketches, facts and data and/or documents and other primary-source material, a directory of organizations and agencies, annotated lists of print and nonprint resources, a glossary, and an index.

Readers of books in the Contemporary World Issues series will find the information they need in order to better understand the social, political, environmental, and economic issues facing the world today.

CULTS IN
AMERICA

A Reference Handbook

James R. Lewis

CONTEMPORARY
WORLD ISSUES

ABC-CLIO

Santa Barbara, California
Denver, Colorado
Oxford, England

Library of Congress Cataloging-in-Publication Data

Lewis, James R.
    Cults in America : a reference handbook / James R.
Lewis.
        p.   cm. — (Contemporary world issues series)
    Includes bibliographical references and index.
    ISBN 1-57607-031-X (alk. paper)
    1. Cults—United States.   2. Sects—United States.
3. United States—Religion.   I. Title.   II. Series :
Contemporary world issues.
    BL2525.L486   1998
    291—dc21   98-29089
                                                      CIP

02 01   10 9 8 7 6 5 4

ABC-CLIO, Inc.
130 Cremona Drive, P.O. Box 1911
Santa Barbara, California 93116-1911

This book is printed on acid-free paper ∞.
Manufactured in the United States of America

Contents

Preface

The cult controversy is an issue that periodically explodes into public consciousness, dominates the TV networks and newspapers for a time, and then disappears as reporters turn their collective attention toward newer, fresher scandals and disasters. The impression this sporadic coverage may create is that our society is filled with innumerable weird groups capable of breaking out into some form of sociopathic behavior at any moment. This picture is not accurate. In this book I hope to supply some of the pieces that are missing in order to present a more balanced image.

Scholars have studied this conflict since the 1970s. These collective findings produce a picture of the controversy profoundly at odds with popular stereotypes. While I have attempted to allow competing points of view to find expression in the following pages, this volume's orientation to the issue derives from the consensus of the mainstream academic viewpoint.

Chapter 1 presents an overview of the controversy. The two major competing points of view are delineated, particularly with respect to the brainwashing debate. This chapter also provides some historical background, a brief overview of the role of the media, an analysis of what people find attractive about membership in minority religions, and a discussion of the characteristics of truly dangerous groups.

Chapter 2 is a chronology of the controversy. Because this issue is in some ways an extension of earlier cycles of religious conflict, particularly in the legal arena, this time line begins in the American colonial period.

Nontraditional religions are quite diverse. Chapter 3 presents an overview of many of the groups and movements that have been involved in the conflict. This survey has been incorporated into the present volume in lieu of the biographies normally included in this series.

Because of church-state separation issues, the primary battleground for the controversy has been the courts. Chapter 4 surveys the history of this conflict. A number of recent decisions have defeated the cultic mind control argument in the courts and weakened the anticult movement.

Chapter 5 presents a sample set of primary documents on the controversy from the 1970s as well as some statistical data derived from a wide variety of social scientific studies. Chapter 6 surveys relevant organizations and Chapter 7 covers bibliographic resources on the conflict.

Introduction

1

A Tale of Two New Religions

The cult controversy is a complex social issue that has engendered an emotional and often mean-spirited debate. At the center of this debate is a wide variety of diverse groups that often have little in common. While some are political organizations or psychological movements, the great majority are religious groups. Most embrace belief systems at odds with the Judeo-Christian mainline, although some are quite orthodox. And, although they are usually relatively small and new organizations, almost all have roots in older, larger traditions.

Decades of social conflict have left their impress on the term "cult," which, to the general public, indicates a religious group that is false, dangerous, or otherwise suspect. Because of these connotations, mainstream scholars and other neutral observers who have studied the controversy prefer to talk in terms of "new religious movements" or "minority religions" instead of "cults."

The controversy has tended to polarize participants into extreme positions, making it difficult to find a middle ground from which to approach the issue. Hence, rather than tackling the problem directly, we will work our way into the debate indirectly, through the stories of two contrasting religious groups that will serve to highlight some of the dilemmas associated with the controversy. The story of Heaven's Gate, the UFO group that committed suicide in 1997, will be used to exemplify the concerns that anticultists bring to the controversy. The Island Pond raid—involving Northeast Kingdom, a less well known Christian group—will, on the other hand, be used to exemplify the concerns of religious libertarians.

Heaven's Gate

Getting Off the Planet

On March 26, 1997, the bodies of thirty-nine men and women were found in a posh mansion outside San Diego, all victims of a mass suicide. Messages left by the group indicate that they believed they were stepping out of their "physical containers" in order to ascend to a UFO that would be arriving in the wake of the Hale-Bopp Comet. They also asserted that this comet, or parts of it, would subsequently crash into the earth and cause widespread destruction. In a taped message, their leader further noted that calendars were off—that the year 1997 was really the year 2000—and that the world would end precisely two millennia after the time of Jesus. The death of Heaven's Gate members embodies a sinister aspect of apocalyptic religiosity, one that propels group members to engage in radical acts of preemptive violence as a way of invoking the final end.

Heaven's Gate—formerly known as Human Individual Metamorphosis (HIM)—originally made headlines in September 1975 when, following a public lecture in Waldport, Oregon, over thirty people vanished overnight. For the next several months, reporters produced stories about glassy-eyed cult groupies abandoning everyday lives to follow the strange couple who alternately referred to themselves as "Bo and Peep," "the Two," "Do and Ti," and other bizarre monikers.

Bo and Peep founded one of the most unusual flying saucer religions ever to emerge out of the occult-metaphysical subculture. Bo (Marshall Herff Applewhite) and Peep (Bonnie Lu Nettles) met in 1972 in a Houston hospital where Bo was receiving psychiatric treatment in connection with a sexual problem that was causing him emotional and employment difficulties. In 1973, they had an experience that convinced them that they were the two witnesses mentioned in Revelation 11 who would be martyred and then resurrected three and a half days later—an event they later referred to as the Demonstration. Preaching an unusual synthesis of occult spirituality and UFO ideology, they began recruiting in New Age circles in the spring of 1975. Followers were required to abandon friends and family, detach themselves completely from human emotions as well as material possessions, and focus exclusively on perfecting themselves in preparation for a physical transition (i.e., beaming up) to the next kingdom (in the form of a flying saucer)—a metamorphosis that would be facilitated by ufonauts.

Applewhite and Nettles further taught that aliens had planted the seeds of current humanity millions of years ago and were coming to reap the harvest of their work in the form of spiritually evolved individuals who would join the ranks of flying saucer crews. Only a select few members of humanity would be chosen to advance to this trans-human state, the rest being left in the spiritually poisoned atmosphere of a corrupt world.

Applewhite would later teach that after the elect had been picked up by the space brothers, the planet would be engulfed in cataclysmic destruction. When, in 1993, under the name of Total Overcomers Anonymous, the group ran an advertisement in *USA Today,* their portrayal of the post-rapture world was far more apocalyptic than Applewhite and Nettles had taught in the 1970s: "The Earth's present 'civilization' is about to be recycled—'spaded under.' Its inhabitants are refusing to evolve. The 'weeds' have taken over the garden and disturbed its usefulness beyond repair" (Balch 1995, 163).

For followers of the Two, the focus of day-to-day existence was to follow a disciplined regime referred to as the overcoming process or, simply, the process. The goal of this process was to overcome human weaknesses—a goal not dissimilar to the goal of certain spiritual practices followed by more mainstream monastic communities.

The group developed quietly until the media interest evoked in the wake of the Waldport, Oregon, meeting. It subsequently canceled a planned meeting in Chicago and split the group into a number of autonomous "families" consisting of a dozen or more individuals. Another change was the subsequent announcement that the Demonstration had been canceled because the followers had not been making rapid enough progress in the overcoming process. Rather than focusing on the time when members would be taken up by the saucers, they would each concentrate on individual development.

This seminomadic period ended within a few years when two followers inherited a total of approximately $300,000. The group rented houses, initially in Denver and later in the Dallas–Fort Worth area. Each house, which members called a "craft," had the windows covered to prevent neighbors from watching activities inside. Followers adhered to a strict routine. Immersed in the intensity of their structured lifestyle, the teachings of the Two became more and more real to members.

The group's strict segregation from society was suddenly altered in 1983 when many followers visited their families on Mother's Day. However, these members dropped out of contact as soon as they left. It was during these visits that they communicated to their families that they were learning computer technology. Another change took place in 1985, when Nettles died of cancer. The group surfaced again in 1994 when, thinking the lift-off would begin in a year or two, members held another series of public meetings. It was as part of this new cycle of missionary activity that the *USA Today* ad appeared.

Details about how the group came to attach apocalyptic significance to the Hale-Bopp Comet are scanty. The prediction that a giant UFO was coming to earth, "hidden" in the wake of Hale-Bopp, appeared on the Internet. When Heaven's Gate retrieved this information, Applewhite took it as an indication that the long-awaited pick-up of his group by aliens was finally about to take place. The decision that the time had come to make their final exit was most likely made not more than a few weeks before the mass suicide.

The idea that the group might depart via suicide had emerged in Applewhite's thinking only in the previous few years. The earlier idea was that the group of individuals selected to move to the next level would bodily ascend to the saucers in a kind of "technological rapture." Applewhite may have begun to rethink his theology after Nettles's death because, in his thinking, in order to be reunited with Nettles, her spirit would have had to acquire a new body aboard the spacecraft. While the death of Nettles may or may not have been the decisive influence, he later adopted the view that Heaven's Gate members would ascend together spiritually rather than physically.

The Anticult Movement: A Response to the Antisocial Actions of Extreme Groups

The deaths of Heaven's Gate members are the latest in a series of dramatic incidents involving minority religions. Other incidents include the Jonestown murder/suicides (1978), the ATF/FBI raid on the Branch Davidian community (1993), the Solar Temple suicides (1994), and the Tokyo subway poison gas attack (1995). In the wake of these events, the mass media sought out a variety of cult experts in an effort to make sense of seemingly irrational behavior. Most of these commentators offered the public an explanation in terms of the notion of cultic mind control, colloquially known as brainwashing. The seemingly crazy actions of cult members were not difficult to explain, many claimed, as long as one understands that megalomaniacal cult leaders like Applewhite are able to control the thought processes of their followers: Under the influence of mind control, cult members are capable of anything because they have given up their wills to the leader.

According to spokespeople for cult watchdog groups, our society is populated by hundreds—perhaps even thousands—of cult groups, many of which are capable of extreme actions. In addition to mind control and the imputation of sinister motives to the leaders, cults are accused, among other things, of deceptive recruiting practices, financial and sexual exploitation, food and sleep deprivation of members, various forms of illegal activities, child abuse, and ritual abuse. Because of the interest the mass media have taken in this issue, this stereotype has become widely accepted in contemporary society.

There are or have been groups for which some of these accusations are or were appropriate. In particular, children have been abused within a few religious communities. Members of certain organizations have been financially and/or sexually exploited by the leadership. A handful of minority religions have taken the law into their own hands. And at least one group consciously deceived potential recruits by systematically hiding the identity of the group until after workshop attendees had become de facto members.

There are, however, obvious dangers in applying these stereotypes of cults to all strange or different religious groups. The problems that can be generated by jumping to the conclusion that unusual religious communities must be guilty of misdeeds simply because former members level accusations against them are well exemplified in the raid against the Northeast Kingdom.

Northeast Kingdom

The Island Pond Raid

The Northeast Kingdom Community Church began in the foothills of Tennessee around 1972, when an independent preacher, Elbert Eugene Spriggs, built a loyal following of believers into a model New Testament community church. Spriggs called his group the Light Brigade and spent most of his early ministry pulling drug addicts and alcoholics off the streets of Chattanooga. The name was changed to the Vine Christian Community Church and the ministry spread into surrounding communities.

The church members separated themselves from worldly pursuits and materialistic gains, supporting themselves with homegrown foods and necessities which they also sold to local area residents. One of the mainstays of financial support has been their delicatessen and takeout shop, which features natural foods. The church has always attracted the attention of the local residents, but most accepted the group members as different but nice. At first glance, the members of the church remind one of the Amish church members. The women wear kerchiefs on their heads, long dresses, little or no makeup, and the men usually wear beards, long hair, and overalls.

The Tennessee community grew to more than 400 residents and became a very successful example of the alternative communities that dotted the countryside during the early 1970s and 1980s. There was never any violence and very few confrontations with anyone outside of the community. There were a few marital disputes, but only a small number of divorces compared to a typical church of similar size. One of the few problems to surface during the Tennessee years laid a foundation for later controversy.

Clifford Daniels, a young man with a history of personal problems, joined the community and soon rose to a leadership position managing one of the business interests of the community. Problems developed with the church elders when Daniels borrowed some of the business funds and a church vehicle without authority. When the indiscretion was discovered and he appeared before the church Board of Elders, he became violent and attempted to attack one of the leaders with a tire iron.

He was banished from the community. Daniels eventually became acquainted with another former resident of the area, Ted Patrick. Patrick had migrated to southern California but was still connected to the Tennessee foothills where his family and friends continued to live. It was the mid 1970s and Patrick had gained some notoriety as a "deprogrammer"—a term he coined for his practice of abducting young people from controversial spiritual groups and attempting to compel them to recant their religious beliefs. Patrick's methods were quickly gaining him wide recognition among relatives of adult children who had joined the religious versions of the hippie revolution. They were more than willing to hire him to return their adult children to them.

Daniels became a contact for Patrick, as the members of Sprigg's church provided excellent potential for Patrick's enterprise. Daniels soon became a deprogrammer himself. Many of the kidnapping incidents were perpetrated by the deprogrammers as a means to gain custody of children who were still in the church when one of the parents had left or were previously deprogrammed. Some of these would end up in court where the non-custodial parent would seek a new custody hearing by recounting stories by deprogrammed former members about child abuse. A campaign of letters and charges to various officials attempted to build their cases. At one point, several families were charged with truancy for failing to send their children to a public school instead of home schooling or because their children were in the church school. These charges were dropped for lack of evidence.

In spite of the negative publicity stirred up by Patrick and Daniels against the church to support their kidnapping activities, the church continued to grow and prosper. In 1976, the church had an opportunity to move onto land they had acquired in northern Vermont. It offered the perfect haven for their lifestyle and the vision that Spriggs saw for his church.

A self-appointed cult watchdog group eventually joined the campaign against the church from Tennessee. Vermont is a rural state, and the Vermonters easily accepted the wild accusations and charges levied against these outsiders from Tennessee. The network of deprogrammers, anticult activists, and deprogrammed former members pursued a campaign against the church. The campaign included town hall meetings where dramatic stories of abuse—including such wild allegations as killing babies—were proffered with vivid details. Letters of protest and allegations of abuse flooded the offices of the Department of Social Services, the Department of Education, congressmen, senators, governor, and every law enforcement agency that could be found. Even Immigration, the Internal Revenue Service, and the State Department were petitioned.

The allegations and protests were peppered with supposed atrocities from other states that involved similar local churches that had to be addressed by government officials. The charges were even embellished with overtones drawn from publicity surrounding the Jonestown incident. Finally, Governor Richard Snelling and Attorney General John Easton became convinced that there were enough allegations and testimonies to take serious action against the community of believers.

At 6:30 A.M. on Friday, June 22, 1984, a caravan of state police officers, social service workers, sheriff deputies, and an assortment of other officials arrested 110 adults and took 112 children of all ages into custody. They loaded the 222 men, women, and children into separate buses, separating crying children from their distraught and bewildered parents with little or no explanation.

While the Northeast Kingdom Community members were huddled in a gymnasium that served as a makeshift detention center, the state attorney requested a blanket detention order from the district court so that a full-scale investigation could be conducted. The judge refused, holding that "the state failed to present any specific evidence of abuse," and ordered all of the children to be released. After a thorough examination by the social service caseworkers, no evidence of any abuse of any kind could be found.

Religious Libertarianism: A Response to the Persecution of Minority Religions

Concern generated by incidents such as the Island Pond raid led to the emergence of an alternative school of opinion opposed to the anticult perspective. This opposing group is composed of a diverse group of religions, religious liberty organizations, and scholars of minority religions. While not seeking to defend organizations like Heaven's Gate, this school of thought asserts that the extreme actions of a few groups should not be taken as representative of all minority religions. Individuals associated with this opposition group see themselves as defending religious liberty.

Because the word "cult" has acquired negative connotations, the people and organizations who defend minority religions do not call themselves the "procult movement," and, further, would not accept the label "cult apologists," which anticultists sometimes seek to give them. In fact, this group would reject the use of the term cult altogether, instead referring to such organizations as new religious movements (the preferred term among academics), alternative religions, nontraditional religions, or minority religions. Recognizing its problematic status, the term cult will be avoided when referring to a specific religion throughout this book. It is, nevertheless, still useful to talk about the cult *controversy*, and, where appropriate, the term will be used when discussing the stereotype associated with minority religions more generally.

The anticult movement in North America can be subdivided into two wings, secular anticultists and conservative Christian anticultists. While these two wings share certain traits and in the past have occasionally cooperated with each other, the target of much Christian anticultism is a minority religion's deviation from traditional doctrine—a concern most secular anticultists do not share. Also, Christian anticultists tend not to be involved in the controversial practice of deprogramming—one of the hallmarks of the secular anticult movement. When discussing the anticult movement, this book refers to the secular wing of this movement, unless otherwise noted.

As with other social conflicts, opponents in the cult controversy have become polarized into extreme positions. Many anticultists have come to adopt an attitude of suspicion toward a broad spectrum of religions, ready to portray almost any unusual group as a potential Heaven's Gate, and almost any charismatic religious leader as a potential David Koresh. Defenders of the rights of minority religions, on the other hand, have tended to downplay all issues except the issue of religious liberty. The result of this polarization is an ongoing and frequently bitter debate that periodically finds expression in books, articles, court cases, and, more recently, in official reports issued by European governments.

While the current controversy has certain unique aspects, it is, in many ways, an extension of earlier religious conflicts. As a way of providing a background for our discussion of the cult controversy, we will look briefly at the anti-Catholic and anti-Mormon movements of the nineteenth century.

Religious Persecution in Nineteenth-Century America

On the evening of July 28, 1834, Edward Cutter, a resident of Charlestown, Massachusetts, was startled by the sudden appearance of a hysterical woman at his doorstep. She was clad only in a nightgown and delirious from a combination of stress, high fever, and the sweltering heat of a Boston summer. Elizabeth Harrison's closely cut hair indicated that she was a resident of Mount Benedict, the nearby Ursuline convent. A nun of some thirteen years as well as an accomplished music teacher at the convent school, Harrison had undergone a partial breakdown as a result of overwork. Not knowing quite what to do, Cutter took her to a friend's place in nearby Cambridge. As soon as the delirium passed, she returned to the convent.

The news of this unusual but otherwise minor incident somehow filtered out into the surrounding Protestant community—a community hostile to the Catholic presence. While contemporary Americans accept Catholicism as a natural part of the religious landscape, in the early nineteenth century, Popery or Papism, as it was popularly called, was an object of contempt, not unlike the way

Moonies are regarded in the late twentieth century. The nunnery itself—a new structure directly across from Bunker Hill—attracted attention comparable to the attention a Hare Krishna temple would draw if it were to appear in rural Nebraska. In the words of Louise Whitney, who, at the time, was a student at the nunnery school, "the whole establishment was as foreign as the soil whereon it stood, as if, like Aladdin's Palace, it had been wafted from Europe by the power of a magician" (Whitney 1969, 2).

Harrison's story was changed and exaggerated into a sensational tale in which pursuing Catholics recaptured an escaping nun and compelled her to return to the convent against her will. The nuns, it was said, had not only driven the American lady to madness, but had incarcerated her. Following her escape attempt, they had then, with the approval of the bishop, actually tortured her to death.

Certain particulars of this rumor seemed to follow the plot of a tale that was being circulated at the time by another "escaped nun" from the Ursuline convent, and it is reasonably certain that the Harrison tale was shaped, to a greater or lesser extent, by the Rebecca Theresa Reed story. Reed, who had worked at the convent for a few months as a servant, had, for several years, been propagating the story (later published as *Six Months in a Convent*) that she had aspired to be a nun but had escaped from the convent after witnessing unspeakable immorality. One of the themes of the anti-Catholic literature of the time was the abuse of young females in Catholic nunneries. The Reed story and the Harrison rumor appeared to reinforce each other as well as to give substance to Protestant fears about what was going on behind the benign public face of the local nunnery.

In the midst of this potentially explosive state of affairs, the famous minister Lyman Beecher came to town, and on Sunday, August 10, delivered an impassioned anti-Catholic sermon in three different churches on the same day. This sermon, published later as *Plea for the West*, pictured Catholics as in a state of mental bondage—a "brainwashed" state, in the idiom of the late twentieth century: "If they dared to think for themselves, the contrast of protestant independence with their thraldom would awaken the desire for equal privileges and put an end to arbitrary clerical dominion over trembling superstitious minds" (Beecher 1835, 118). Although the oft-repeated charge that Beecher was directly responsible for ensuing events is unlikely, his stormy denunciations of Rome could not have helped the situation.

Afraid of what might happen if they did not act, city officials inspected Mt. Benedict the next afternoon. They were given a complete tour by Elizabeth Harrison, the very nun who was being featured as a tormented prisoner. Finding nothing amiss, they returned home to compose a report that was to appear in the next morning's paper.

However, around eight o'clock that evening—only a few hours after the selectmen had left—a mob arrived in front of the Ursuline convent and demanded that they be shown the nun whom they supposed was being held there against her will. Rather than attempting to reason with them, the mother superior gave in to feelings of exasperation. Indignant that a mob of workingmen should issue demands after having just proven Mt. Benedict's innocence to city officials, she responded with threats of her own, such as, "the Bishop has twenty thousand Irishmen at his command in Boston, and they will whip you all into the sea!" This unwise response only infuriated the crowd, which, after a short delay, began to force its way in. Nuns and schoolgirls fled into the back garden and eventually escaped through a back fence with the aid of their neighbor, Mr. Cutter. It is unlikely that the schoolgirls, many of whom were from Protestant homes, would have been hurt by the attackers, but some of the nuns, and particularly the mother superior, might well have come to harm.

The assault on the convent was motivated, in part, by the misguided but nevertheless genuine desire to free "imprisoned" inmates. The genuineness of this motivation is evident in extant documents. It is particularly clear that the mob's initial purpose was to release Elizabeth Harrison, whom they still believed was being held against her will. The rescue operation, however, quickly degenerated into a riot. After failing to discover dungeons and engines of torture, the mob began to run through the abandoned nunnery, looting and destroying as they went. The convent was finally torched, and, intoxicated by the boldness of their actions as well as by rum, the mob turned to the looting and destruction of surrounding buildings. The bishop's house and library were put to flame. The mausoleum in the school's garden was broken into, its coffins opened, and the remains of the dead mutilated. Firefighting teams from Charlestown and from the surrounding communities appeared but were turned back by the crowd.

The following evening the mob returned and burned down fences, trees, and everything else they could find on the grounds. Only the presence of troops guarding Edward Cutter's home kept them from destroying a nearby Catholic church. For the rest of the week, nightfall found club-wielding mobs roaming the streets looking for trouble. The last act of destruction occurred on Friday night when a shack that served as a home to thirty-five Irish laborers was torched.

Although the public's first reactions to the incident were shock and outrage, anti-Catholic feelings quickly overcame this initial response. While some Protestants expressed outrage over the convent burning, for many others the event was an inspiration for stepped up anti-Catholic activity. For example, within a week of the Charlestown incident, two new anti-Catholic newspapers began publication: *Downfall of Babylon* (Philadelphia) and *American Protestant Vindicator* (New York). Of the thirteen persons indicted for arson, all were eventually released, acquitted, or pardoned. The state was empowered to reimburse victims for loss of property due to civil disorders, but public opinion frustrated every effort of the Ursulines to recover their losses. The nuns themselves eventually moved to Canada.

Although immigrant and native-born laborers had scuffled with each other for years, the burning of the Ursuline convent was the first major act of violence in a long series of incidents that were to reach a peak in the Philadelphia riots of 1844. The anti-Catholic crusade did not, however, really die down until after the nation's passions had been redirected into the slavery issue and the Civil War.

When we look back on certain themes in nineteenth-century anti-Catholic literature from the perspective of the late twentieth century, it becomes clear that the Catholic church was portrayed in much the same way as new religious movements are portrayed today. Convent schools like the one in Charlestown were, for example, often viewed as covert tools ("cult front groups") for converting unwitting non-Catholics. Anti-Catholics explained the conversion of these young Protestant women in terms of flattery and devious indoctrination designed to influence impressionable young ladies to take the veil. In the words of Edith O'Gorman, another former nun and author of the anti-Catholic potboiler *Convent Life Unveiled:* "My confessor flattered me in my delusion, telling me that the Lord had endowed my soul with His highest gifts, and He had designed me from all eternity to become a great saint. . . . At the same time he urged me to hasten my entrance into a Convent, because, if I delayed long in the world, God would withdraw from me those heavenly gifts. As a natural consequence of these false teachings, I soon became puffed up with my own self-righteousness, and was led to regard myself as better than others" (O'Gorman 1881, 55–56). Once inside the convent, according to O'Gorman, inmates were convinced to remain by subtle, psychological pressure, such as fear of hell and the belief that any doubts were inspired by Satan. Reed described this in the following words: "The Bishop said the Devil would assail me, as he did Saint Theresa, and make me think I ought to go back to the world; and make me offers of worldly pleasures, and promise me happiness. In order to prevent this, I must watch and pray all the time, and banish entirely worldly thoughts from my mind" (Reed 1835, 89). This passage could easily have been taken from a contemporary account of cult brainwashing.

Although anti-Catholicism was a major phenomenon of nineteenth-century American life, we have conveniently forgotten this ignoble chapter in our national life because it does not fit our self-image as tolerant lovers of freedom. Catholics were, however, not the only religious group to be vigorously persecuted in North America. In the colonial period, Quakers were regularly hung in Puritan Boston. In the late nineteenth century, the federal government forbade American Indians from practicing their traditional religions and divided up the reservations among the various denominations in an effort to Christianize them. The prohibition against traditional Indian religions was not overturned until the 1930s.

Among the candidates for the most-persecuted religious group in American history, one of the most deserving is the Church of Jesus Christ of Latter-Day Saints, popularly called Mormons. In addition to their founder-prophet being murdered by a mob (after he had given himself up peacefully to authorities), the Mormons have the distinction of being the only religious group in American history to be the subject of an openly declared extermination campaign: In Missouri in 1838, then governor Liburn W. Boggs declared that "the Mormons must be treated as enemies, and must be exterminated or driven from the State if necessary, for the public peace" (Corrill 1939, 41). The militia was called up to enforce this declaration. Among other atrocities, the militia raided Haun's Mill, a small Mormon settlement near Far West, Missouri, on October 30, 1838, killing seventeen men, women, and children. Twelve others were wounded, some of whom died later. An old man who was wounded and lying on the ground was shot through the heart and then his body hacked and mutilated. A young boy of nine, found hiding in a blacksmith shop, was shot in the head with the comment, "Nits will make lice" (Roberts 1930, 474).

The Mormon church, like the Catholic church, became the subject of numerous atrocity tales built around the same themes of captivity and abuse. In anti-Mormon literature, polygamous wives played essentially the same role that nuns played in anti-Catholic literature, and apostate (those who renounce the faith) Mormon females composed similar captivity narratives. However, a certain conceptual problem emerged in Mormon apostate stories: How could one make the case for a state of bondage in a situation where the alleged captive was apparently free to walk out at any time? Nunneries could be portrayed as prisons, but Mormon women were obviously not so confined. Thus, in addition to the "deluded follower" theme used to characterize Catholic bondage, one finds the first theory of "hypnotic mind control" in anti-Mormon literature. For example, in the totally fabricated apostate tale, *Female Life among the Mormons*, Maria Ward described her "capture" in terms of mesmerism (the original term for hypnosis, also termed "animal magnetism"):

> At the time I was wholly unacquainted with the doctrine of magnetic influence; but I soon became aware of some unaccountable power exercised over me by my fellow traveller. His presence seemed an irresistible fascination. His glittering eyes were fixed on mine; his breath fanned my cheek; I felt bewildered and intoxicated, and partially lost the sense of consciousness, and the power of motion. . . . I became immediately sensible of some unaccountable influence drawing my sympathies toward him. In vain I struggled to break the spell. I was like a fluttering bird before the gaze of a serpent-charmer. (Ward 1855, 12)

The Mormon apostate tales, like the Catholic apostate stories, were loosely connected accounts containing crudely crafted descriptions of violence. The violence in anti-Mormon tales was often quite vivid. For example, in the totally fictional apostate tale, *Boadicea: The Mormon Wife*, Alfreda Eva Bell describes the following cold-hearted murder: "'Will you go with me?' asked he. 'No,' answered the dying woman. 'Then you are done for,' said Yale; and deliberately, before my very eyes, in spite of my wild screams for his mercy, he fired at her and scattered her brains over the floor" (Bell 1855). Like anti-Catholic stories, anti-Mormon tales were capable of evoking violent, vigilante-style activity—as is evident in such events as the murder of Joseph Smith—and governmental intervention—as witnessed by such actions as the 1857 invasion of Utah by federal troops.

Today, the notion of brainwashing or cult mind control has become the center, rather than a subsidiary theme, in the debate over religious groups. The link with notions from earlier eras is quite evident, especially in more popular tales. For example, compare the following passage from Chris Edwards' *Crazy for God*

(Edwards is an ex-member of the Unification church) with the description of Mormon mesmerism cited earlier: "She took my hand and looked me straight in the eyes. As her wide eyes gazed into mine, I felt myself rapidly losing control, being drawn to her by a strange and frightening force. I had never felt such mysterious power radiate from a human being before . . . touching something within me that undermined thought itself" (Edwards 1979, 60). Like nineteenth-century counterparts, former members of minority religions recount the same stories of deception and exploitation, which in turn evoke public outrage.

Emergence of the Contemporary Cult Controversy and the "Brainwashing" Debate

Cultic Mind Control

The origins of the contemporary cult controversy can be traced to the early 1970s when many new religions arose out of the counterculture to succeed elements of the youth movement of the 1960s. In an attempt to understand these new groups, observers sometimes concluded that the founders and leaders of these groups had discovered a special form of social control that enabled them to recruit their followers by short-circuiting their rational, questioning minds by keeping them locked in special trance states. A handful of professionals, mostly psychologists and psychiatrists associated with the anticult movement, attempted to provide scientific grounding for this notion of cultic brainwashing/mind control.

There are issues of abuse, exploitation, and undue influence associated with at least some minority religions. But the debate over new religions has focused on the notion of cultic mind control. Rather than viewing the social pressures found in minority religions as extensions of social influence, anticult professionals argue for the existence of a unique form of influence confined to these alternative religions. Viewing the argument as a form of special pleading with potentially grave implications for religious liberty, mainstream academics focused their responses on criticizing the idea of cultic mind control. By the mid 1970s the debate was set and would continue for the next two decades.

Social scientists have asked: How does one distinguish cultic brainwashing from other forms of social influence—forms of social influence like advertising, military training, or even the normal socialization routines of the public schools? Some have theorized that members of minority religions are in an ongoing, quasi-hypnotic state; others assert that the ability of cult members to process certain kinds of information has "snapped." In other words, cult members are unable to exercise critical judgment—the critical faculty has broken down and snapped like a brittle piece of plastic.

But if cultic influences actually override the brain's ability to logically process information, then these members should perform poorly on I.Q. tests or, at the very least, manifest pathological symptoms when they take standardized tests of mental health; but, when tested, they do not. If anything, such empirical studies have shown that members of new religious movements are actually smarter and healthier than the average member of mainstream American society (e.g., Sowards et al. 1994).

Other studies have also failed to support the view that new religions rely upon some exceptional form of social influence to gain and retain members. For example, if new religions possess powerful techniques of mind control that effectively override a potential convert's free will, then everyone—or at least a large percentage—of attendees at recruiting seminars should be unable to avoid conversion. However, sociologist Eileen Barker, in her important study, *The Making of a Moonie,* found that only a small percentage of the people attending seminars sponsored by the Unification church eventually joined. Furthermore, of those who joined, more than half dropped out within the first year of their membership. In another important 1984 study, Canadian psychiatrist Saul Levine found that, out of a sample of over 800 people who had joined controversial religious groups, more than 80 percent dropped out within two years of membership. These are not the kind of statistics one would anticipate in groups wielding powerful techniques of mind control.

In the face of these and other empirical studies, social scientists have further asked: Given the lack of empirical support, where does the brainwashing notion originate? and, What is the real nature of the conflict that these stereotypes obfuscate? David Bromley and Anson Shupe's book-length study *Strange Gods: The Great American Cult Scare* postulates that the principal source of the controversy is a parent-child conflict in which parents attempt to reassert parental control by marshaling the forces of public opinion against the religious bodies to which their offspring have converted. This conflict is then exacerbated by mass media accounts. An industry is established that generates profit (the rescue of entrapped cult members, i.e., deprogramming) and special interest groups are created that have a vested interest in promoting negative stereotypes of alternative religions by scaring parents with stories of what will happen to their adult child if they fail to have her or him deprogrammed. In this manner, many well-meaning parents are recruited into the controversy.

Deprogramming and the Anticult Movement

In the early 1970s, opposition to minority religions was organized around deprogrammers—individuals who forcibly abducted individuals from nontraditional religions. Members were abducted off the street and locked up in houses or motel rooms. Relatives and deprogrammers then attempted to convince the member of the falseness of the religion in an effort to convince her or him to leave the group.

Deprogramming began more or less accidentally when a son and a nephew of Theodore Patrick, Jr., considered joining the Children of God, a so-called Jesus freak organization. In 1971, Patrick was then governor Ronald Reagan's special representative for community relations in southern California, working as a kind of ombudsman. On the fourth of July, he and his family were staying at a hotel on Mission Beach in San Diego. When his son Michael and a nephew failed to return from a fireworks display, he called the police. The boys showed up as he was dialing, but he was struck by what seemed to be a strange look on Michael's face. They then related an encounter with the Children of God (COG). Alarmed at first, Patrick and his family gradually forgot about the incident.

In his job as ombudsman, however, he began to hear other complaints about the Children of God. In Chula Vista, California, William Rambur's daughter dropped out of school in order to move to a COG ranch in Thurber, Texas. Unable to persuade her to leave the group, Rambur began a personal crusade to warn other parents about the danger of the group. Eventually he met Ted Patrick, and together they formed the first anticult organization. The name of this group, Parent's Committee to Free Our Children from the Children of God, was later shortened to Free the Children of God, and popularly referred to as FREECOG.

Increasingly frustrated by the authorities' refusal to do anything about COG, Patrick began to consider more desperate approaches. As he studied the matter, he found that kidnapping charges would be difficult if not impossible to make stick if parents were involved at every stage of such an operation. In cooperation with other parents, he began to experiment with the tactic of abducting members, confining them, and then questioning their religious choices and trying to convince them that they had been brainwashed and manipulated by their religious group. In 50 percent or more of the cases, the members did leave their new faith. Thus the practice of deprogramming was born.

Initially, Patrick did not pursue deprogramming for personal enrichment. Gradually, however, he found the demand high enough that he could turn his attention to deprogramming full-time and began to ask compensation for his time. In response to critics, Patrick has softened his description of deprogramming by asserting that "all he does is talk to people." But in his book *Let Our Children Go!* it is described as follows: "Deprogramming is the term, and it may be said to involve kidnapping at the very least, quite often assault and battery, almost invariably conspiracy to commit a crime, and illegal restraint" (Patrick 1976, 63). "I believe firmly that the Lord helps those who help themselves—and a few little things like karate, Mace, and handcuffs can come in handy from time to time" (Patrick 1976, 70).

Other anticult organizations began springing up, with Citizen's Freedom Foundation (later renamed Cult Awareness Network) becoming the national umbrella group. The support for deprogramming by anticult organizations evoked criticism. As early as 1974, for example, the National Council of Churches passed a strong resolution against the practice. Deprogrammers diversified kidnapping activities to include Evangelical Christians, a move that brought criticism from Christian groups that opposed these alternative religions but who, by the late 1970s and early 1980s, withdrew from this alliance with secular anticultists. Walter Martin, the most prominent Christian anticultist, asserted in 1980: "I cannot stand behind such practices. It is true that cultists have been blinded by the 'god of this age,' but it is also true that they have the right to make up their own minds, and we should not stoop to un-Christian tactics to accomplish God's ends" (cited in Melton 1992, 349).

These and other criticisms influenced the secular anticult movement to rethink its stance on deprogramming. In 1981, for example, Citizen's Freedom Foundation (CFF) issued a statement that read, in part, that "CFF does not support, condone, or recommend kidnapping or holding a person against his will." CFF did, however, continue to voice support for voluntary deprogramming (i.e., counseling situations where members are free to break off the conversation and leave at any time), referred to as "exit counseling."

Most deprogrammers have little or no background in psychological counseling. They are, in fact, often deprogrammed members. Advocates claim that deprogramming does nothing more than reawaken cult members' capacity for rational thought, but an examination of the process reveals that the technique of deprogramming involves directly assaulting a person's belief system. The deprogramming process consists of the following:

1. A breakdown in insulation from the outside world, accomplished by physically removing the member from her or his group.
2. A highlighting of the inconsistencies between group ideals and the actions of leaders, as well as internal inconsistencies *within* the group's belief system.
3. The pull of family ties. Deprogrammings are almost invariably paid for by other family members who then participate in the sessions.
4. The presentation of an alternative belief system. Deprogrammers often attempt to convert deprogrammees to conventional religion or, more often, to the secular mainstream.
5. Offering an alternative explanation for the individual's recruitment and membership—the familiar deception/mind control ideology.

These five steps are usually effective in disrupting the religious beliefs of the individual. Success is not, however, guaranteed, as the high failure rate of deprogramming—between one-third and one-half return to their respective movements—demonstrates.

Examination of the attitudes of deprogrammed former members of minority religions provides understanding of the contemporary controversy. Groups opposed to such religions base much of their criticism on the testimony of deprogrammed former members who often relate tales of manipulation and abuse. However, studies contrasting the attitudes of former members who left their movements voluntarily with former members who had been deprogrammed reveal a systematic difference that calls the objectivity of such testimony into question. It was found that most voluntary defectors were ambivalent or even positive about their former religion, often characterizing their membership period as a beneficial learning experience. In sharp contrast, people who had been involuntarily removed described their membership and their former religion in terms of popular negative stereotypes. Perhaps deprogramming is not a therapeutic intervention after all, but is, rather, an intensive indoctrination process in which the abductee's religious faith is systematically destroyed and replaced with anticult ideology. While this does not mean that there is nothing to be criticized in certain minority religions, a careful consideration of this finding might cause a hesitation before accepting the more extreme accusations proffered by anticultists. Those who have been kidnapped out of their religion should be especially suspect as being less than neutral witnesses. Rather than forming generalizations based on a broad range of data, the anticult movement generates its own data from a select number of individual cases and then finds evidence for its ideology in the testimony of these same individuals.

Deprogrammed former members play roles in the controversy in a number of other ways. In court battles, ex-members recruited by opponents of minority religions give testimony against their former movements, such as in child custody cases where one of the parents is a group member and in cases where governmental agencies need evidence for violations of laws. The testimony of a deprogrammed Branch Davidian was, for example, part of the evidence used to obtain a search warrant before the assault on the Davidian community. And, finally, at the level of basic research, these former members are interviewed in pseudoscientific surveys designed to substantiate such claims as that brainwashing techniques induce mental illness in their members and that child abuse is widespread in alternative religious groups. One of the more significant attempts to empirically document the effects of supposed mind control is the set of studies on the cult withdrawal syndrome, sometimes referred to as "information disease."

The Cult Withdrawal Syndrome

Because members of controversial religious groups fall within the normal parameters of objective tests of intelligence and social adjustment, attempts to demonstrate the negative effects of cultic brainwashing scientifically have tended to focus on the psychological problems former members encounter after leaving their religion. This postinvolvement syndrome, sometimes referred to as "information disease"—a term coined by Flo Conway and Jim Siegelman in their book *Snapping: America's Epidemic of Sudden Personality Change*—is described as a unique mental illness, caused by prolonged exposure to mind control techniques.

This appears to be an attempt to psychologize—to medicalize—a controversy that is actually an ideological controversy. Some sociologists of religion who have studied the controversy have suggested that the core of the controversy is parent-child conflict (e.g., Bromley and Shupe 1981; Lewis 1989). It often happens that parents become concerned about their offspring when they adopt eccentric lifestyles and beliefs. Such parents are literally unable to understand their adult children's rejection of secular career goals and conventional family life and as a consequence readily believe that their offspring have been brainwashed.

But the recruitment and indoctrination techniques of nontraditional religions are not demonstrably more deceptive or manipulative than such socially approved activities as advertising or military recruitment and training. Also, if members of new religions had truly undergone radical personality changes, if their minds had "snapped," and if they were actually victims of ongoing trances (all fairly standard accusations leveled against nontraditional religions), then such pathological mental states should show up as some kind of irregularity when standardized psychological tests are administered. However, as both defenders and critics of alternative religions will agree, members of such groups fall within the range defined as healthy on objective tests.

Anticultists have thus focused their attention on the syndrome that former members experience following removal from their religious communities. This syndrome is described in various ways, depending on the source, and usually includes such symptoms as poor attention span, "floating" in and out of altered states, amnesia, hallucinations, suicidal tendencies, guilt, fear, violent outbursts, and lack of a sense of directedness. Anticult researchers assert that this psychological disorder is specifically the result of exotic mind control techniques, parading under the guise of religious practices—praying, meditating, and Bible-reading—to which members have been subjected. Concentration on the postinvolvement period characterizes the empirical work of such anticult researchers as Flo Conway and Jim Siegelman, Margaret Singer, and John Clark.

Of these studies, the one that conveys the most substantial appearance to casual readers is Conway and Siegelman's survey of 400 ex-members of controversial religions that was reported in a 1982 article, "Information Disease: Have Cults Created a New Mental Illness?" In this piece, Conway and Siegelman presented data on seven symptoms—floating/altered states, nightmares, amnesia, hallucinations/delusions, "inability to break mental rhythms of chanting," violent outbursts, and suicidal/self-destructive tendencies—for which respondents reported "long term mental and emotional effects." More particularly, Conway and Siegelman claimed that "the psychological trauma cults inflict upon their members is directly related to the amount of time spent in indoctrination and mind control rituals" (Conway and Siegelman 1982, 92).

The greatest weakness of the information disease notion—and it should be noted that Singer and Clark do not use the term information disease, although the same basic notion of a cult withdrawal syndrome is implicit in their work—is that this supposedly new and unique syndrome bears symptoms similar to those of the traumatic stress response. There are a number of syndromes—from bereavement to the mourning symptoms that follow divorce—with which information disease can be compared. While any of these disorders could be used to point out the parallels between information disease and responses to traumatic stress, it is easiest to make a case for the connection between the cult withdrawal syndrome and what the *Diagnostic and Statistical Manual of Mental Disorders* (the psychological profession's standard diagnostic reference) calls post-traumatic stress disorder (PTSD). The manual describes the cause of PTSD as any "psychologically traumatic event that is generally outside the range of usual human experience," such as assault, military combat, natural disaster, or an accident. The trauma of deprogramming, particularly a classic deprogramming involving a violent kidnapping, clearly fits the category of a stressful event outside the range of normal human experience. And, because two-thirds to three-fourths of the samples used by anticult researchers were deprogrammed (71 percent in Conway and Siegelman's information disease study), it is reasonable to hypothesize that the difficulties these individuals experienced could be partially—if not entirely—a response to traumatic stress. The symptoms of PTSD—nightmares, guilt, memory impairment, difficulty concentrating, phobic response, explosive outbursts, suicidal tendencies, and so forth—parallel those of deprogrammed members of these groups. Even some of the more bizarre symptoms of the postinvolvement syndrome, such as hallucinations and the tendency to slip into dissociated states, are also components of PTSD.

The manual describes another symptom as "recurrent and intrusive recollections," and as the "sudden acting or feeling as if the traumatic event were reoccurring," which in some instances is experienced as "dissociativelike states, lasting from a few minutes to several hours or even days." This intrusive recalling of the traumatic event—which can be experienced either as waking flashbacks or as unpleasant dreams—is a central symptom of PTSD. This symptom is probably also related to the experience of "floating" described by former cult members.

Finally, the other characteristics of the postinvolvement syndrome reported by anticult researchers—indecisiveness, a sense of meaninglessness, blurred mental acuity, and so forth—are symptomatic of a major depressive disorder that the *Diagnostic and Statistical Manual of Mental Disorders* notes regularly accompanies PTSD. This analysis rather forcefully demonstrates that information disease symptoms are either exact parallels to PTSD, or, where the parallel is weak, can be explained in terms of the influence of anticult indoctrination. It is thus highly probable that "information disease" is the direct result of the traumatic transition out of a nontraditional religion rather than the result of anything experienced while in such a group. This hypothesis has been supported by empirical research on former members of controversial religious movements (e.g., the 1987 Lewis and Bromley study summarized in Chapter 5).

The discussion up to this point has demonstrated that—while the ordinary forces of socialization and conformity are necessarily at work in every human group—a unique form of social influence corresponding with the popular idea of "cultic brainwashing" lacks scientific substance. We have, furthermore, noted that the primary source of this conflict lies in tensions between parents and their adult children. We should examine what the other forces are that are at work in society that help to shape the cult controversy in the minds of the general public. As the first step in analyzing these forces, it will be useful to examine some relevant social scientific findings that have arisen from the study of stereotypes.

Stereotypes and Public Perceptions of the Cult Issue

Stereotyping Cults

Several decades ago, sociologist Tom Robbins observed that if someone at a previously unknown vegetarian community died from being squashed by a giant cabbage, tomorrow's headline news story—splashed sensationally across the front page—would be a report on an act of cult violence. The incident would be used as an example of "what these awful groups are capable of." Robbins's observation seemed particularly appropriate in the wake of the Mt. Carmel incident. Prior to the ATF attack, the Branch Davidians had been a little-noticed group on the outskirts of Waco. Although some of the people familiar with the community had found it to be somewhat eccentric, it was rarely mentioned in the same breath as Moonies, Hare Krishnas, and so forth.

The reasoning at work here is the same illogic of stereotyping from which many minorities have suffered. Stereotypes portray certain, most often derogatory, traits as being characteristic of a whole group of people, and then explain or excuse social problems in light of these traits. Stereotypes are also usually held rigidly, in that we tend to ignore or to dismiss evidence that flies in the face of our generalization. Such rigidity indicates that our stereotype in some way protects our self-esteem or shields us from facing some unpleasant fact.

One of the more widely accepted dictums of sociology is that societies need enemies, particularly societies that are going through a disturbing period of change (e.g., Durkheim and the many sociologists influenced by his work). External threats provide motivation for people to overcome internal divisiveness in order to work together as a unit. Having an enemy one can portray as evil and perverse also provides support for the normative values and institutions of one's society: "They" are communists; "we" are capitalists. "They" are totalitarian; "we" are democratic. And so forth and so on.

So in situations where external enemies no longer threaten, a society will often find groups or individuals from within that it can construe as threatening and evil. Such enemies become particularly important to communities passing through a crisis in which fundamental values are being called into question; in the words of Albert Bergesen, from his important study, *The Sacred and the Subversive*, "a community will commence to ritually persecute imaginary enemies—conduct a witchhunt—to manufacture moral deviants as a means of ritually reaffirming the group's problematical values and collective purposes" (Bergesen 1984, vii). This notion has been effectively supported by certain social historical studies. For example, in an interesting and creative study of New England witchcraft, *Entertaining Satan*, John Demos demonstrated that the persecution and execution of "witches"—usually unsocial, crabby little old ladies—abated during periods of war and reappeared after peace had returned. This sheds light on our current social situation.

Communism has largely diminished as a potent international threat. The only significant remaining communist power is China, and the Chinese are more interested in cooperating with the West than in challenging it. Other threats, such as Iraq, flare up and pass rather quickly. The lack of pressing external enemies, in combination with our current, ongoing social crisis, might indicate that our culture will seek out groups within society to take the place of these adversaries.

Unless there are groups that are consciously antisocial or criminal, like organized crime or like gangs, the deviations from the norm that a community chooses to perceive as threatening are somewhat arbitrary. The groups that our culture has traditionally construed as deviant have been racial, ethnic, or sexual orientation minorities. In recent years, however, it has become increasingly socially unacceptable to persecute these traditional groups. This leaves few groups of any significant size to persecute. One of the few minorities that liberals have been slow to defend are nontraditional religions. This is due to a number of different factors, including the resistance of traditionally conservative religions to liberal change.

Groups of people experienced as threatening frequently become screens onto which a society projects its anxieties. If, for example, a culture is troubled by sexual issues (as is often the case), then its enemies are perceived as perverse and sexually deviant. This was a theme in nineteenth century anti-Catholic and anti-Mormon literature. Contemporary nontraditional religious groups suffer from the same projection.

In the classical formulation of psychological projection, Freud, who was especially concerned with sex and violence, viewed projection as a defense mechanism against unacceptable inner urges. Thus, in a society with strict sexual mores, an individual constantly keeping a lid on his desires might perceive rather ordinary dancing, let us say, as sexually suggestive and might then attempt to have all of the dance halls in town closed down. This hypothetical individual's inner struggle is being projected outward to provide a script for an outer struggle (i.e., internally he is repressing his desires while symbolically battling the same desires in the outer world). The same process is at work in the collective mind of society, perceiving marginal groups as sexually deviant. For instance, the stereotype of the sexually abusive cult leader, routinely forcing devotees to satisfy his or her sexual whims, perfectly captures the fantasy of many members of our society who desire to sexually control any person he or she wishes.

The same kind of thing happens with repressed aggressive urges. We live in a society with strict sanctions against overt violence; simultaneously, violence is glorified in the entertainment media. This sets up a cultural contradiction that is projected onto enemies and deviant groups, with the result that minorities are often perceived as violent and belligerent. This accusation is also regularly projected onto nontraditional religions. In particular, the radical actions of a tiny handful of alternative religions is mistakenly taken to indicate a widespread tendency among all such groups.

We can generalize beyond Freudian psychology's emphasis on sex and aggression to see that many other cultural anxieties/ contradictions are projected onto minority groups. For instance, our society gives us contradictory messages about the relative importance of money and possessions. On the one hand we are taught that economic pursuits are supposed to be secondary to social and spiritual activities. On the other, we receive many messages from the surrounding society that the single-minded pursuit of wealth is the be-all and end-all of life. This self-contradiction is projected onto alternative religions, as represented in the stereotype of the money-hungry leader who demands that her or his followers lead lives of poverty while the leader wallows in riches.

Similarly, the child abuse accusation and contemporary society's seeming obsession with child abuse flows out of another cultural contradiction. Our cultural heritage as well as many modern psychologists hold out the ideal of a child who is constantly under the wing of a loving parent, usually the mother. Current economic conditions, however, often require both parents to work full time, which usually entails leaving young children in the care of strangers. This results in a good deal of guilt, which is easily displaced onto such "deviant" groups as nontraditional religions. Like the accusation of violence, the radical actions of a tiny handful of alternative religions that have abused children is mistakenly taken to indicate a widespread tendency among all such groups. Despite the outcry against the Branch Davidians, for example, our best current information is that, while strict, the Davidians did not abuse their children. However, the readiness of people to buy into the stereotype of child-abusing cultists convicted David Koresh and sentenced him to death before he was able to receive a fair hearing.

One of the more important cultural contradictions that gets projected onto alternative religions is tied up in the brainwashing/ mind control notion that is the core accusation leveled against such groups. Discourse that glorifies American society usually does so in terms of a rhetoric of liberty and freedom. However, while holding liberty up as an ideal, we experience a social environment that is often quite restrictive. We often work in highly disciplined jobs where the only real freedom is the freedom to quit. Also, we are bombarded by advertising designed to influence our decisions and even to create new needs. Our frustration with these forms of influence and control is easily displaced and projected onto the separated societies of alternative religions, where the seemingly restricted flow of information offers a distorted reflection of the situation we experience as members of the dominant society.

The components of the cult stereotype that have been enumerated above, and others that could be mentioned, explain certain themes in anticult discourse as well as why this stereotype is attractive to members of present-day society. Without this pre-existing disposition to construe nontraditional religions negatively, the anticult movement would have little or no social influence. However, while the anticult movement has relatively little direct social power, the stereotype it has helped to shape has taken on a life of its own, independent of organized anticultism.

Self-Fulfilling Stereotypes

Once a stereotype is in place, a variety of different kinds of studies have shown that it becomes self-fulfilling and self-reinforcing. Directly relevant to the case at hand is an important article by Jeffrey E. Pfeifer, "The Psychological Framing of Cults," reporting the results of a similar study that compared responses to a biography in which a fictitious student, Bill, dropped out of college to enter a Catholic seminary, join the Marines, or join the Moonies. The short biography incorporated elements of indoctrination often attributed to cults: "While at the facility, Bill is not allowed very much contact with his friends or family and he notices that he is seldom left alone. He also notices that he never seems to be able to talk to the other four people who signed up for the program and that he is continually surrounded by [Moonies, Marines, Priests] who make him feel guilty if he questions any of their actions or beliefs." When given a choice of describing Bill's indoctrination experience, subjects who thought Bill had joined the Catholic priesthood most often labeled his indoctrination "resocialization"; those who were told that he had joined the Marines most frequently labeled the process "conversion"; and those who were under the impression that he had become a Moonie applied the label "brainwashing." On various other questions regarding the desirability and fairness of the indoctrination process, subjects who were told that Bill had joined the Moonies consistently evaluated his experience more negatively than subjects who were under the impression that Bill had joined either the Marines or a priestly order.

The implications of this research for the cult controversy is that the minority religions lose their chance for a fair hearing as soon as the label "cult" has been successfully applied. After that, the mass media selectively seeks out and presents information about the group that fits the stereotype. It is then only a matter of time before the media completely "demonizes" a particular group, as it did in the case of Koresh and his followers.

Cults and the Media

Less than a week after the ATF attack on the Branch Davidian community, the Rev. Mike Evans, who in 1986 had published a popular book about the end of the world, publicly pronounced that David Koresh was demon-possessed. The Waco confrontation had already begun to settle into the routine of an uneventful standoff, and the media was searching around for colorful news—hence the decision to feature a story on the Texas evangelist. "Satan is alive and well on planet earth," claimed Evans in the words of a popular book title. "The spirit that is in Koresh and his followers needs to be exorcised."

He offered his services to the authorities: "If it would save innocent lives, I would be willing to go in there one on one with him and cast that demon out." While he said that he "would prefer going in there and laying hands on him and rebuking the demons in him," Evans also noted that the next best thing to a personal exorcism would be to repeat a prayer through a loudspeaker, "rebuking the demon spirits in Koresh and commanding them to come out in the name of Jesus. Turn it up so loud that Koresh will not have a moment of rest 24 hours a day."

The fact that the media saw fit to give sideshows like Rev. Evans that sprung up around the Davidian siege as much coverage as the siege itself reflects a salient characteristic of the contemporary news media, which is that—because of the intense competition among different news agencies—the media seeks to *entertain* consumers of news, sometimes at the cost of *informing* them. The same drive to increase viewer/reader ratings is evident in the media portrayal of the Branch Davidians. While Rev. Evans had recommended casting out demons, and while the FBI tried to provoke Koresh's inner devils, the media took a somewhat different approach and proceeded to demonize the Davidian leader. In addition to the usual generic accusations about evil cult leaders and comparisons with Jim Jones, reporters dutifully repeated every allegation made about Koresh and the Davidians, whatever the source. Clearly the intention was to appeal to readers/viewers with sensationalism rather than to produce a balanced picture of the Branch Davidians.

In the case of new religious movements, newspeople sometimes tend to report those facets that seem to be strange, exploitative, dangerous, totalitarian, or sensational, possibly, part of the time, because this kind of reporting sells. But this kind of reporting contributes to the perpetuation of the cult stereotype. In the words of British sociologist James Beckford in "The Media and New Religious Movements,"

> Journalists need no other reason for writing about any particular NRM [new religious movement] except that it is counted as a cult. This categorization is sufficient to justify a story, especially if the story illustrates many of the other components which conventionally make up the "cult" category. This puts pressure on journalists to find more and more evidence which conforms with the categorical image of cults and therefore confirms the idea that a NRM is newsworthy to the extent that it does match the category. It is no part of conventional journalistic practice to look for stories about NRMs which do *not* conform to the category of cult. (Beckford 1994, 146)

Another important factor is the marked tendency of the mass media to report on a phenomenon only when it results in conflicts and problems. To again cite from Beckford's paper, "The Media and New Religious Movements," "NRMs are only newsworthy when a problem occurs. Scandals, atrocities, spectacular failures, 'tug-of-love' stories, defections, exposes, outrageous conduct—these are the main criteria of NRMs' newsworthiness. . . . And, of course, the unspectacular, unsensational NRMs are permanently invisible in journalists' accounts" (Beckford 1994, 144-145).

The different media vary somewhat in their tendency to produce imbalanced reports. "TV tabloids" such as *20/20* and *Hard Copy* that have to compete with prime time TV programming tend to be the most imbalanced. Rather than attempting to produce programs that examine the complex ramifications of issues, news shows usually present melodramas in which guys in white hats are shown locked in conflict with other guys in black hats. On the opposite extreme are the major newspapers, such as the *Los Angeles Times* and the *Washington Post,* which tend to do the best job of attempting to present balanced articles on controversial subjects. Such "balance," however, usually only means finding the space for opposing views. The journalist appears to be objective when her or his story is two-sided rather than one-sided. The news magazines such as *Time* and *Newsweek* tend to fall somewhere in between.

One of the more unusual aspects of the Waco standoff was the decision of NBC to create a "docudrama" about the Branch Davidians and the events leading up to the original ATF assault *before* the siege ended. The title of this made-for-TV movie, "Ambush in Waco," seemed to evoke images from the quasi-mythical past of frontier Texas, when sinister savages ambushed noble lawmen. Television, as we have already mentioned, is the least suitable medium for coming to grips with complex moral issues. In the case of "Ambush in Waco," the ATF agents were dressed in white hats and David Koresh in a black hat. It was, as might be expected, a shallow, rambling production built around a disconnected framework of accusations made against Koresh. The ATF was portrayed as a group of noble-minded public servants—not a single question was raised about the propriety of the ATF's actions. The filming of "Ambush" was still in process when the FBI attacked Mt. Carmel. The docudrama was a commercial success.

In an important article on the docudrama trend, "From Headline to Prime Time" (published in *TV Guide*), David Shaw observes that "fact based movies are suddenly the Hula-Hoop, the skateboard, the nintendo of the '90s." He further points out that most such movies are based on disasters and notes that "the instant dramatization of real tragedy has become a kind of video fast food, drama McNuggets." Shaw's conclusion is worth citing at length:

> Using the powerful and intimate medium of television to pander to the viewer's base instincts is not new, but this rush to do so is the latest step down a very dangerous road. Where will it all end? Will the next David Koresh be able to sit in his compound and watch his own dramatized death on television—and maybe figure out how to kill the cops instead? . . . Will producers decide that, rather than risk waiting until dramatic events actually take place before they begin costly bidding wars for the dramatic rights of the players, they should open negotiations with soldiers of fortune, jilted lovers, and putative terrorists *before* they do their dastardly deeds . . . perhaps even suggesting a traumatic twist or two in the ultimate execution to jack up the asking price? (Shaw 1993)

The Appeal of New Religions

Up to this point, the discussion has been focused on the cult controversy, and on how that controversy has been misperceived and misrepresented. We now turn our attention to understanding the sources of spiritual innovation as well as understanding the appeal of new religions. In successive sections we will examine the real issues—and, in some cases, the real dangers—associated with certain minority religious groups.

There have been a variety of historical periods during which religious innovation has flourished. In Europe, there was a proliferation of new religions in the late classical period, as well as in the wake of the Reformation. In the United States, historians have noted a recurring pattern of religious awakenings.

The most general observation we can make is that periods of renewed spiritual activity tend to occur in the wake of disruptive social and economic changes: The established vision of "how things work" no longer seems to apply, and people begin searching for new visions. In previous cycles of American religious experimentation, innovative forms of Protestantism often formed the basis for these new visions. As revivalist fervor died down, new or reinvigorated Protestant denominations became the pillars of a new cultural hegemony.

The most recent period of American religious innovation occurred in the decades following the demise of the 1960s counterculture. However, unlike previous cycles of revival, the religious explosion that occurred in the 1970s and 1980s has not provided a basis for a new spiritual and cultural synthesis. There has been a growth in conservative Protestant denominations during this period (a growth parallel to the pattern of earlier awakenings), but there has also been a marked growth in metaphysical religion. The most visible manifestation of this latter strand of spirituality has been the New Age movement, which offers a vision of the world fundamentally different from that of traditional Christianity. Thus, during this most recent cycle of religious enthusiasm, Protestantism has failed to reestablish its traditional hegemony over American culture.

Other factors inhibiting the formation of a new cultural synthesis have been the growing power of secularization and the influx of new immigrants from non-Protestant (and even non-Christian) countries. In the West's new, pluralistic society, Hindus, Buddhists, Muslims, and others represent a growing segment of the culture—a segment for whom neither Protestantism nor the New Age exercises much appeal. Also, a trend toward secularization that was set in motion in the preceding century has shaped yet another important segment of contemporary society, one alienated from religion altogether.

Lacking the power to generate a new basis for cultural synthesis, the current proliferation of new religious movements can be seen as a factor contributing to the disintegration of modern life. It is the very disconnectedness of the contemporary experience that contributes to the attraction of religions not in the mainstream. Many alternative religions hold out the possibility of life-transforming experiences—experiences that, to a greater or lesser extent, help one to drop the burden of the past and be reborn into a new and more whole life.

The mainstream Protestant denominations—Methodist, Baptist, and Presbyterian—once offered the seeker life-transforming experiences in the context of revivals and camp meetings. But as these religious bodies settled down into comfortable accommodation with the surrounding (largely secular) society, they lost their intensity. One result of this accommodation was that revivals and camp meetings—and the accompanying intense religious experiences—were relegated to a quaint and mildly embarrassing chapter in denominational histories.

Those happily adjusted to the social-cultural mainstream often have a difficult time understanding intense religiosity. Academics have not been exempt from this tendency. If, however, we attempt to really look at what might attract someone to an alternative religion, such involvement is not really difficult to understand. What if we actually could let go of the burden of our past and be reborn as new people? Such transformation may or may not be attainable, but the attractiveness of the possibility is certainly understandable. Many religions—conservative Christian sects included—hold out the promise of such life-changing experiences.

Many people become involved in a religious group in the wake of a spiritual experience. This factor was particularly emphasized in older academic literature about religious conversion. In this body of literature, the suddenness of the experience is stressed. The model is the Damascus Road experience, in which the apostle Paul was knocked off his horse by a bolt out of the blue, confronted by Jesus, and converted on the spot. Contemporary studies only rarely document such experiences. Rather, in most cases, individuals just gradually "drift" into a religious group until they cross a barely perceptible line between outsider and insider, undergoing a series of mini-conversions en route.

Religious experience is, however, only one aspect of the spiritual life, and only one of the factors that attract individuals to deeper religious involvement. Among the many approaches to religious studies, one of the older, yet still useful, scholarly analyses was articulated by the influential historian of religion, Joachim Wach. The heart of religion, according to Wach, is religious experience. Religious experience, in turn, is expressed in at least three ways:

- In a community (church, ashram, et cetera)
- In a doctrine (theology, worldview, ideology)
- In a "cultus" (ritual, ceremony, gathering)

Wach's analysis should give us a basic feel for the fundamental constituents of religion. In outline form, these constituents are:

- Spiritual experience
- Community
- Doctrine/idea system
- Gatherings/rites

Each of these four components sheds light on how individuals become involved in religious groups. We have already discussed the role of spiritual experiences. Often the community dimension of any religious group is the key element in initially attracting new members. We live in a society that would be alien to our ancestors. Surrounded by masses of people, we often do not know the names of our closest neighbors. In traditional societies everyone in a particular village knew everyone else, and took care of everyone else: If, for instance, you saw someone have an accident, you did not call 911; instead you ran over and helped out as best you could. Some churches and most alternative religions recreate this kind of community—a community comparable to an extended family.

The family metaphor is particularly apt. In modern society, our families are not the close emotional units they were in traditional societies. A small religious group many times recreates the sense of belonging to a family. If one has never experienced the closeness of a traditional family, it is easy to understand how the sense of belonging to a family unit would be attractive and even healing.

Something similar can be said about worldviews. In a traditional society, beliefs about the ultimate nature of the universe are largely taken for granted. In contemporary society nothing can be taken for granted except death and taxes. We are taught to be "nice" by our school system, but this moral teaching is not grounded in an ultimate source of value. We are also instructed in the basic skills necessary to operate in society, but public school teachers are often quiet about the greater questions of death, purpose, and the meaning of life.

We may place a positive or a negative evaluation on this relativistic education, but in any case we have to acknowledge that our culture's ambiguous approach to socialization departs radically from the socialization strategies of earlier societies. Our choices are always varying shades of gray, rather than black and white/good and bad.

The results of this ambiguity may be liberating to some people, but to others it is confusing. Without some kind of ultimate grounding, this is necessarily the case.

Nontraditional religions are often criticized for offering their followers the "easy" answers that come with black-and-white thinking. However, to many of the people who belong to such religions, the seeming narrowness of such thinking can be a liberating experience: Once one has stable criteria for what is good and true, this clarity and stability can then free one to go about the business of working, loving, and living life without debilitating anxieties about transcendent meaning and value. This is not, of course, to advocate a rigid belief system, but rather to point out why such a system is attractive without depreciating adherents as being somehow weak or defective.

In summary, we may say that people join alternative religions for the same sorts of reasons one would join any other religion, namely fellowship, a satisfying belief system, and so forth. When these needs are no longer being fulfilled in an acceptable manner, people leave.

Social Influence in Genuinely Dangerous Religions

The Nature of "Cultic" Influence

While we can dismiss the notion of a unique form of influence exerted by minority religions over their followers, it is nevertheless still clear that the members of any group—particularly a tightly knit spiritual community—experience various forms of social influence. Social pressure, conformity, and attitude change are bread-and-butter issues for social psychology, and small group dynamics are ideal situations in which to study such processes. However, the garden-variety group influences examined by social psychologists rarely find their way into the cult debate. On the one hand, they do not serve the purposes of anticultists who are intent on making the case for cultic mind control. On the other hand, defenders of religious liberty are so focused on demonstrating the presence of free will among members of controversial religions that they tend to gloss over the question of the other, less noble social dynamics found within such groups.

In discussing these dynamics, it should be noted that somewhat different factors are involved in recruitment as opposed to the ongoing maintenance of commitment to a group of any type. Proponents of the brainwashing theory have tended to ignore this particular distinction. At an earlier stage of the cult controversy, anticultists, particularly deprogrammers, tended to portray recruitment as a kind of "spot hypnosis" that was able to override the will of the recruit. This perspective ignored the obvious, which was that not everyone was susceptible to proselytizers—indicating that factors other than an irresistible hypnosis technique were at work in the recruiting situation. In particular, more objective observers noted that the great majority of individuals who joined high demand religions were unattached young people—people with few responsibilities who were thus relatively free to experiment with an alternative lifestyle.

Another point infrequently emphasized in anticult literature is that comparatively few nontraditional religions are as demanding as the Moonies or the Hare Krishna movement. In fact, the great majority of alternative religions are more like mainstream churches and synagogues in that they do not require members to leave their families or their jobs and move into an isolated communal facility. Recruitment to such groups thus tends to take place quite differently—through family, friend, and employment networks—and more gradually than the Pied Piper syndrome that is a cornerstone of the stereotype of cult recruitment.

It is not difficult to understand the initial attraction of such communities. Intensive religious groups provide participants with a ready-made fellowship, a stable worldview, and clear ethical guidelines that sharply contrast with the ambivalence and ambiguity of life in contemporary mass society.

Once one joins a religious group, the ordinary forces of social conformity come into play to further socialize the recruit into the mores of her or his new community. In Berger and Luckmann's classic study of the sociology of knowledge, *The Social Construction of Reality*, the authors make the case that the plausibility of any given idea is dependent upon the people one is in conversation with on a day-to-day basis. Thus if all of one's acquaintances are Republicans, even someone who had previously been a Democrat tends to convert to Republicanism, and vice versa. Similarly, the notion that Rev. Moon might be the new messiah seems silly to non-Moonies. But if one was to live in a community in which all of one's conversation partners held this belief, it would not be long before one would begin to entertain the idea as a plausible option.

The motive in such situations is the natural human desire to be accepted and the socially learned value of not wanting to disagree with others. These motives can actually alter the manner in which we perceive the world, as demonstrated in a classic experiment designed by social psychologist Solomon Asch. In the Asch experiment (1956), a subject was asked to judge which of three sample lines a given line was closest to in length. Unknown to the subject, however, the other seven people in the room were only pretending to be experimental subjects. Instead, they had been instructed to falsely identify a different line—one that was obviously unequal in length. When it came the subject's turn—who was always the last person to speak—he or she was thus faced with the dilemma of listening to his own senses or to the group judgment. A full 80 percent of the subjects in Asch's original experiment were influenced by the group to go against the evidence of their senses at least some of the time.

If the social forces influencing people to conform can have this high success rate with a group of strangers, imagine how such forces must be amplified within a group of friends—or, to take the case at hand, within a close-knit religious fellowship. The desire to conform, in combination with the ongoing conversation that gives a belief system much of its plausibility, influences group members to become convinced of ideas that seem odd or nutty to outsiders. It is unnecessary to posit a special form of social influence conforming to the popular notion of "cultic brainwashing" in order to explain such behavior.

In most cases, the results of these forces of social influence are benign. There are, however, situations in which the very same forces can be put to socially undesirable ends. In a different series of experiments, psychologist Stanley Milgram demonstrated how, in the right circumstances, ordinary individuals could be manipulated into obeying orders to torture and even kill other human beings. (No one was actually harmed; instead, experimental subjects were tricked into believing they had tortured and murdered someone.) While the implications of these experiments are frightening, at the same time they shed light on such apparently crazy acts as the Jonestown and the Heaven's Gate suicides: Under the right circumstances, people can be led to undertake extreme actions—even mass suicide. Once again, it should be noted that it is unnecessary to invoke ad hoc notions of cult mind control to explain such events.

If, however, the forms of social influence at work within minority religions are not distinctive enough to allow one to distinguish a dangerous group from a healthy group on the basis of socialization routines, then, how can we distinguish the Solar Temples, Jonestowns, Heaven's Gates, and AUM Shinrikyos from benign religious organizations? While any simple criterion for making such a distinction is likely impossible, there are a few guidelines that could function as early warning signs for a religion that has gone or is going "bad."

Cults or Bad Religion?

While the majority of minority religions are innocuous, many have been involved in social conflicts. A handful of these conflicts have made national and even international headlines, from the siege of the Branch Davidian community to the group suicide of Heaven's Gate members. One consequence of these highly publicized incidents is that they have served to reinforce unreflective stereotypes about "cults" and "cult leaders" that are appropriate for some—but certainly not the majority of—minority religions. Unfortunately, such stereotyped information is often the only "data" readily available to the media and law enforcement at the onset of such conflicts.

Putting aside the technical discourse of sociologists, in ordinary language people talk as if there is an objective category of groups call "cults" that can be distinguished from genuine religions. In this commonly accepted view, cults are by definition socially dangerous false religions, led by cynical cult leaders who exploit followers for their own gain.

This stereotype is, however, deeply flawed, and for more than one reason. In the first place, as we have already seen, "cult" is a socially negotiated label that often means little more than a religion one dislikes for some reason. To certain conservative Christians, for example, a cult is any religion that departs from a certain traditional interpretation of scripture. Alternately, ultraconservative Christians who take a strictly fundamentalist approach to scripture often appear "cult-like" to many mainline Christians. In other words, one person's cult is another person's religion.

In the second place, the founders of new groups are—despite whatever personal flaws some might have—almost always sincerely religious. Part of the problem here is that most people unreflectively assume that religion is always something "good." If, therefore, a given religious body does something "bad," then ipso facto it must not be "real" religion. Instead, it must be a false religion, created for no other reason than the founder/leader's personal gain. This attitude is, however, naive. The ancient Aztecs, to take an extreme example, regularly tortured and sacrificed other human beings as part of their religious rites. These practices were, in fact, a central aspect of the Aztec religion. But, however much we might be able to explain and even to understand why the Aztecs engaged in such practices, no contemporary person would defend these rites as "good."

The proper question to ask, then, is not whether some particular group is or is not a cult (in the sense of a "false religion"), but, rather, whether or not the social-psychological dynamics within a particular religion are potentially dangerous to its members and/or to the larger society. Unfortunately, once we get beyond such actions as torturing and murdering other human beings, the criteria for what one regards as harmful can be quite subjective. It has been seriously asserted, for example, that requiring "cult" members to be celibate and to follow vegetarian diets are harmful practices. Similarly, requiring followers to engage in several hours of meditation per day plus discouraging the questioning of "cult" doctrine have often been portrayed as parts of a group's "brainwashing" regime designed to damage one's ability to reason properly.

Once again, the problem with such criteria is that they are naive. If celibacy was harmful, for example, then how does one explain the lack of more-than-ordinary pathology among monks and nuns? Also, if certain mental practices actually damaged the brain, then why do members of intensive religious groups perform so well on I.Q. tests and other measures of individual reasoning ability? Such critical criteria also reflect an abysmal ignorance of traditional religious practices: Many traditional religions have promoted celibacy, restricted diets, prescribed lengthy prayers and meditations, discouraged the questioning of group ideology, etc. Clearly, if one wants to delineate serious criteria for determining "bad religion," then one must avoid focusing on traits that embody little more than the observer's ethnocentric attitudes.

To begin with, making a radical lifestyle change as part of joining a religious group should not, in itself, be taken to indicate that the individual has therefore become involved in something harmful. Friends and family members may feel that an individual is making a mistake to quit a job or to drop out of school—actions that, by the way, very few contemporary new religions would actively encourage—but a free society means nothing if one is not also free to make mistakes.

If one wishes to develop objective criteria for distinguishing harmful or potentially harmful religious organizations from harmless religions, one needs to place oneself in the position of a public policymaker. From this perspective, religions that should raise the most concern are those groups that tangibly, physically harm members and/or nonmembers, or engage in other antisocial/illegal acts. However, a public policymaker might well respond that this post facto criterion is too little, too late, and that what is needed are criteria that could act as early warning signs—criteria indicating that a previously innocuous group is potentially "going bad." In the following discussion we will attempt to develop such criteria, with the caveat that the presence of the less serious factors listed below in any given group does not automatically mean they are on the verge of becoming the next Heaven's Gate.

Early Warning Signs

As part of this discussion, we shall be referring to a few false criteria for distinguishing a healthy from an unhealthy religion. In the first place, the mere fact that a group is headed up by a charismatic leader does not automatically raise a red flag. This is because new religions are much like new businesses: new businesses are almost always the manifestation of the vision and work of a single entrepreneur. In contrast, few if any successful businesses are the outgrowth of the work of a committee.

Also, to found a religion, a leader usually makes some sort of claim to a special insight or to a special revelation that legitimates both the new religion and the leader's right to lead. The founder may even claim to be prophet, messiah, or avatar. While many critics of alternative religions have asserted that the assumption of such authority is in itself a danger sign, too many objectively harmless groups have come into being with the leader asserting divine authority for such claims to be meaningful danger signs.

Far more important than one's claim to authority is what one does with the authority once he or she attracts followers who choose to recognize it. A minister or guru who focuses her or his pronouncements on the interpretation of scripture or on other matters having to do with religion proper is far less problematic than a leader who takes it upon her or himself to make decisions in the personal lives of individual parishioners, such as dictating (as opposed to suggesting) who and when one will marry. The line between *advising* and *ordering* others with respect to their personal lives can, however, be quite thin. A useful criterion for determining whether or not this line has been crossed is to examine what happens when one acts against the guru's advice in such matters:

If one can respectfully disagree without suffering negative consequences as a result, then the leadership dynamics within the group are healthy with respect to authority issues.

One of the clearest signs that a leader is overstepping his or her proper sphere of authority is when this leader articulates certain ethical guidelines that everyone must follow *except for* the guru or minister. This is especially the case with a differential sexual ethic that restricts the sexual activity of followers but allows leaders to initiate liaisons with whomever they choose.

Perhaps the most serious danger sign is when a religious group places itself above the law, although there are some nuances that make this point trickier than it might first appear. Many of us, in some sphere of life, place ourselves above the law, when we go a few miles per hour over the speed limit or fudge a few figures on our income tax returns. Also, almost every religion in the world would be willing to assert that divine law takes precedence over human law—should they ever come into conflict. Hence a group that, for example, solicits donations in an area where soliciting is forbidden should not, on that basis alone, be viewed as dangerous to society. Exceptions should also be made for groups or individuals who make a very public protest against certain laws judged as immoral, as when a conscientious objector goes to jail rather than be drafted into the military.

On the other hand, it should be clear that a group leader who consistently violates serious laws has developed a rationale that could easily be used to legitimate more serious antisocial acts. Examples that come readily to mind are Marshall Herff Applewhite, founder/leader of Heaven's Gate, who regularly ducked out on motel bills and who was once even arrested for stealing a rental car, and Swami Kirtananda, founder of the New Vrindavan community, who was caught authorizing the stealing of computer software before being arrested for ordering the murder of a community critic. Documentable child abuse and other illegalities committed within the organization are also covered by this criterion.

Another misconceived criterion is perceiving groups as dangerous because of apocalyptic theologies. Almost every religion in the larger Judeo-Christian-Islamic tradition has an apocalyptic theology, even the traditional peace churches that forbid members from participating in the military. Thus, contrary to the assertions of some contemporary critics of alternative religion, having an apocalyptic theology does not, in itself, raise a red flag. This is because in most apocalyptic scenarios it is God and his angels who fight the final battle, not flesh-and-blood human beings. The human role is spiritual, and the "saved" fight a spiritual war, not a literal, physical war.

An apocalyptic theology is only dangerous when individual followers believe they are going to be called upon to be foot soldiers in God's army and prepare themselves by stocking up on weapons and ammunition. Groups that come to mind here are some of the Identity Christian churches who see themselves as preparing to fight a literal war with God's enemies. On the other hand, a community's possession of firearms—in the absence of such a theology of physical confrontation—is probably not dangerous, if no other danger signs are present. If the simple possession of firearms by members was a significant danger sign, then the Southern Baptist Convention would be the most dangerous "cult" in the nation.

Another false, yet frequently voiced criterion is that religious groups that see only themselves as saved and the rest of the world as damned are dangerous. Like apocalypticism, this trait is far too widespread among traditional religions to constitute an authentic danger sign. A more meaningful characteristic should be how a religion actually treats nonmembers.

Another criterion is a group's relative isolation. This trait is somewhat more complex than the others we have examined. On the one hand, there are abundant examples of traditional religions establishing communities or monastic centers apart from the larger society that have posed no danger to anyone. On the other hand, some of the worst abuses have taken place in the segregated (usually communal) societies of certain minority religions. From the suicidal violence of People's Temple to the externally directed violence of AUM Shinrikyo, it was the social dynamics found in an isolated or semi-isolated community that allowed such extreme actions to be contemplated.

In order to flag this characteristic while simultaneously avoiding stigmatizing every religion that sets up a segregated society as being potentially dangerous, it might be best to invert this trait and state it as a counterindicator. In other words, rather than asserting that any religion with a partially isolated community is potentially dangerous, let us instead assert that the relative *lack* of such boundaries indicates that the group in question is almost certainly *not* dangerous.

A final early warning sign is a group's readiness to deceive outsiders (and, to a lesser extent, the systematic deception of insiders). Some critics have said that a recruiter who invites a potential convert to a dinner without identifying the sponsoring church is deceptive. Others have criticized religions possessing a hierarchial system of knowledge to which only initiates are privy. These kinds of criticisms are trivial. But it is clear that when a guru publicly asserts that his organization does not own any guns and police later find a small arsenal in his basement, *that* is deception.

To summarize, the traits we designated above as early warning signs of "bad religion" are:

1. The organization is willing to place itself above the law. With the exceptions noted earlier, this is probably the most important characteristic.
2. The leadership dictates (rather than suggests) important personal (as opposed to spiritual) details of followers' lives, such as whom to marry, what to study in college, etc.
3. The leader sets forth ethical guidelines members must follow but from which the leader is exempt.
4. The group is preparing to fight a literal, physical Armageddon against other human beings.
5. The leader regularly makes public assertions that he or she knows is false and/or the group has a policy of routinely deceiving outsiders.

Finally, we noted that, while many benign religions constitute semisegregated communities, socially dangerous religions are almost always isolated or partially isolated from the larger society.

With the exception of placing the group's actions above the law, none of these characteristics, taken by themselves, are necessarily cause for alarm. On the other hand, a group possessing more than one or two of the above traits might well bear closer scrutiny. As a corollary to this line of analysis, minority religions possessing none of the above traits are, from a public policy standpoint, almost certainly harmless.

References

Account of the Conflagration of the Ursuline Convent, An. Boston: "printed for the publisher," 1834.

Arrington, Leonard J., and Davis Bitton. *The Mormon Experience.* New York: Vintage, 1980.

Asch, Solomon E. "Studies of Independence and Conformity: A Minority of One against a Unanimous Majority." *Psychological Monographs.* 1956.

Balch, Robert W. "Waiting for the Ships." In James R. Lewis, ed. *The Gods Have Landed: New Religions from Other Worlds.* Albany, NY: State University of New York Press, 1995.

Barker, Eileen. *The Making of a Moonie: Brainwashing or Choice?* Oxford: Basil Blackwell, 1984.

Beckford, James. "The Media and New Religious Movements." In James R. Lewis, ed. *From the Ashes: Making Sense of Waco.* Lanham, MD: Rowman and Littlefield, 1994.

Beecher, Lyman. *Plea for the West.* Cincinnati: Truman and Smith, 1835.

Bell, Alfreda Eva. *Boadicea: The Mormon Wife.* Baltimore: Arthur R. Orton, 1855.

Berger, Peter L., and Thomas Luckman. *The Social Construction of Reality.* Garden City, NJ: Doubleday, 1966.

Bergesen, Albert. *The Sacred and the Subversive.* Storrs, CT: SSSR Monograph Series, 1984.

Bromley, David G., and Anson D. Shupe, Jr. *Strange Gods: The Great American Cult Scare.* Boston: Beacon Press, 1981.

Charlestown Convent, The: Its Destruction by a Mob on the Night of August 11, 1834. Boston: Patrick Donahoe, 1870.

Conway, Flo, and Jim Siegelman. "Information Disease: Have Cults Created a New Mental Illness?" *Science Digest* 90, no. 1. January, 1982.

———. *Snapping: America's Epidemic of Sudden Personality Change.* New York: Lippincott, 1978.

Corrill, John. *A Brief History of the Church of Latter Day Saints (Commonly Called Mormons).* St. Louis: Printed for the Author, 1839.

Demos, John Putnam. *Entertaining Satan.* New York: Oxford University Press, 1982.

Edwards, Chris. *Crazy for God.* Englewood Cliffs, NJ: Prentice-Hall, 1979.

Levine, Saul. *Radical Departures: Desperate Detours to Growing Up.* New York: Harcourt Brace Jovanovich, 1984.

Lewis, James R. "Apostates and the Legitimation of Repression: Some Historical and Empirical Perspectives on the Cult Controversy." *Sociological Analysis* 49:4 (Winter 1989): 386–396.

Lewis, James R., ed. *From the Ashes: Making Sense of Waco.* Lanham, MD: Rowman and Littlefield, 1994.

———. *The Gods Have Landed: New Religions from Other Worlds.* Albany, NY: State University of New York Press, 1995.

Lewis, James R., and David G. Bromley. "The Cult Withdrawal Syndrome: A Case of Misattribution of Cause?" *Journal for the Scientific Study of Religion* 26:4 (December 1987): 508–522.

Martin, Walter. *The New Cults.* Santa Ana, CA: Vision House, 1980.

Melton, J. Gordon. *The Encyclopedic Handbook of Cults in America,* 2d ed. New York: Garland, 1992.

Milgram, Stanley. *Obedience to Authority.* New York: Harper and Row, 1974.

O'Gorman, Edith. *Convent Life Unveiled*. London: Lile and Fawcett, circa 1881; orig. publ. in United States circa 1871.

Patrick, Ted, with Tom Dulack. *Let Our Children Go!* New York: E. P. Dutton, 1976.

Pfeifer, Jeffrey E. "The Psychological Framing of Cults: Schematic Representations and Cult Evaluations." *Journal of Applied Social Psychology* 22 (1992): 531–544.

Reed, Rebecca Theresa. *Six Months in a Convent*. Boston: Russel, Odiorne and Metcalf, 1835.

Roberts, Brigham Henry. *A Comprehensive History of the Church of Jesus Christ of Latter-Day Saints: Century I*. 6 volumes. Salt Lake City: Deseret News Press, 1930.

Robertson, George. "Island Pond Raid Begins New Pattern." In James R. Lewis and J. Gordon Melton, eds. *Sex, Slander and Salvation*. Stanford, CA: Center for Academic Publishing, 1994.

Rothenberg, Paula. "The Prison of Race and Gender: Stereotypes, Ideology, Language, and Social Control." In Paula Rothenberg, ed. *Racism and Sexism*. New York: St. Martins, 1988.

Shaw, David. "From Headline to Prime Time." *TV Guide*. 1993.

Sowards, Bruce A., Michael J. Walser, and Rick H. Hoyle. "Personality and Intelligence Measurement of the Church Universal and Triumphant." In James R. Lewis and J. Gordon Melton, eds. *Church Universal and Triumphant in Scholarly Perspective*. Stanford, CA: Center for Academic Publishing, 1994.

Wach, Joachim. *Sociology of Religion*. Chicago: University of Chicago Press, 1944.

Ward, Maria. *Female Life among the Mormons*. New York: J. C. Derby, 1855.

Whitney, Louise Goddard. *The Burning of the Convent*. New York: Arno Press, 1969; orig. publ. 1877.

Chronology 2

The contemporary cult controversy did not get under way until the early 1970s. But there are clear links between this debate and earlier periods of religious controversy, although certain themes such as the emphasis on brainwashing are unique to the current debate. As we saw with the burning of the Charleston convent, even the portrayal of Catholics in early nineteenth-century America bears certain strong parallels to the manner in which minority religions are viewed in the present period. The following chronology takes note of these parallels by describing some key events in the persecution of minority religions in the United States prior to the 1970s.

The key historical event that set the stage for the debate over religious liberty in North America was the Reformation. The impact of the Reformation in England was to stimulate the formation of groups like the English Puritans and Quakers, as well as to implant a deep distrust of Catholicism in English culture. Puritans, Quakers, and Catholics all founded colonies in North America where they could worship as they wished without persecution or government interference.

Religious controversy did not, of course, end in the colonies. The theocratic colony of Puritan New England, for example, hung "witches" and itinerant Quaker preachers and ejected independent thinkers like Roger Williams. (Williams went on to found the colony of Rhode Island.) Later, an important series of controversies was set in motion by the so-called Great Awakening of the early 1740s—a cycle of religious revivalism that touched religious bodies in all of the colonies.

By the nineteenth century, the principal targets of persecution in the United States were Catholicism and Mormonism. Other minority religions, such as Shakerism and Native American religions, were also persecuted. In the twentieth century prior to 1970, members of Jehovah's Witnesses entered into conflict with the American mainstream.

The following chronology focuses on religious conflicts in the United States that were raised by the presence of minority religions. The cult controversy of the late twentieth century certainly occurs in other countries; the controversy became prominent in Japan and in Western European countries after the Solar Temple murder-suicides and the AUM Shinrikyo poison gas attack. Certain key developments overseas are mentioned toward the end of the chronology.

1740   The Great Awakening sweeps through the American colonies.

1774   Mother Ann Lee, a former Quaker, leads her group of persecuted Shakers to America. The group, which accepted celibacy as a sign of following Christ, becomes an object of scorn during the Revolution because of its pacifism. Despite the controversy, the Shakers begin to grow after the Revolution and establish a number of important communities in the early nineteenth century.

1791   The Bill of Rights are adopted as the first ten amendments to the Constitution. The First Amendment forbids the federal government from restricting the free exercise of religion and further prescribes that the government shall not establish any particular sect as the "official" religion of the United States.

1799   Handsome Lake, a Seneca clan leader, begins a movement that leads to the revitalization of traditional Iroquois religion.

The Great Revival, also referred to as the Second Great Awakening, begins, creating new conflicts within the major Protestant denominations.

1802   Thomas Jefferson pens an oft-cited letter to the Danbury, Connecticut, Baptist Association in which he interprets the nonestablishment clause of the First Amendment as "building a wall of separation between church and state." As president, Jefferson also breaks with the earlier practice of proclaiming national days of prayer, again referring to the authority of the nonestablishment clause as the basis for his decision.

1806   Tenskwatawa, Shawnee prophet, initiates the first pan-Indian religious movement—a movement that encourages Native Americans to oppose Anglo-American intrusion. The movement is later crushed by the United States military.

1831   William Miller begins preaching. Millerism becomes a wildly popular movement that soon evokes harsh criticism from the established churches. While the movement comes to an end in 1844 with the Great Disappointment (when the predicted end of the world failed to occur), remaining members of the movement found the Adventist church.

1834   The Ursuline Convent in Charleston, outside of Boston, is attacked and burned to the ground by a Protestant mob.

1837   Kenekuk, Kickapoo prophet, begins his ministry.

1838   The governor of Missouri declares that "the Mormons must be treated as enemies, and must be exterminated or driven from the State if necessary, for the public peace." The state militia raids Haun's Mill, a small Mormon settlement, initially killing seventeen men, women, and children, with some of the wounded dying later.

1844   Joseph Smith is assassinated while in protective custody at the county jail in Carthage, Illinois. Mormon residents of Illinois subsequently abandon their homes and flee westward under the leadership of Brigham Young.

1844   Violent anti-Catholic riots disrupt civil order in Philadel-
(cont.)   phia. The riots leave several dozen people dead and a
          number of Catholic churches in the city burned to the
          ground.

1848   The Hydesville, New York, "spirit" rappings take place
          at the home of the Fox sisters out of which modern Spiri-
          tualism originates.

1853   Brigham Young announces the doctrine of plural marriage,
          a tenet that scandalizes the rest of the nation and sets the
          stage for further persecution of the Church of Jesus Christ
          of Latter-Day Saints (LDS or Mormon church).

1858   The so-called Utah War of 1858 takes place in which fed-
          eral troops are sent to Utah to establish non-Mormon
          rule over Mormons.

1870   Wodziwob, a Paiute prophet, founds the first Ghost
          Dance movement, the influence of which is largely con-
          fined to Western tribes.

          President Ulysses S. Grant institutes a policy whereby
          different Christian denominations are given control of
          various Indian reservations.

1875   The Theosophical Society is founded in New York City.

1878   The *Reynolds* v. *U.S.* case reaches the Supreme Court. The
          Court decides against polygamy, asserting that, while
          the Congress cannot prescribe laws against what one may
          believe, it may legislate against actions.

1879   Christian Science is founded in Lynn, Massachusetts, by
          Mary Baker Eddy. Christian Science is controversial al-
          most from the very beginning. The church's stance
          against medical treatment will bring it into the spotlight
          again in the 1980s in a series of child endangerment cases.

1880   The Oneida Community, a highly successful religious
          communal experiment that had lasted for over three
          decades, dissolves. The community had survived fierce
          external criticism because of its controversial practice of

complex marriage, but it could not survive the disbelief of its second generation.

1882   Henry M. Teller, secretary of the interior, orders that all "heathenish dances" and ceremonies be ended because of their "great hindrance to civilization." Over the following years, this order—which basically forbids the practice of traditional Native American religions—is gradually implemented.

1887   Congress disincorporates the Mormon church in Utah, appropriating all church property not used for liturgical purposes. The church sues, but loses at the Supreme Court level in 1889 in *Mormon Church* v. *United States* and *Romney* v. *United States*.

The American Protective Association is founded, the largest and most active anti-Catholic organization of the late nineteenth century.

1889   The second Ghost Dance movement is initiated by Wovoka, another Paiute, and spreads eastward.

1890   More than three hundred peaceful Sioux Ghost Dancers—men, women, and children—are massacred at Wounded Knee by the U.S. military.

The Mormon church suspends its controversial policy of polygamy under intense pressure from the U.S. government.

1893   The World's Parliament of Religions is held in Chicago. This event is remarkable for giving Asian religions, particularly Buddhist and Hindu groups, a foothold in North America.

1918   Incorporation of the Native American Church takes place, the first formal organization representing a much earlier pan-Indian religion that, among other things, utilizes peyote to enhance religious experiences.

1924   Immigration barriers are raised against "non-Nordic" populations of Europe, which slows the immigration of

1924   Catholics into the United States. Jewish immigration
(cont.)   from Eastern Europe is also affected.

1932   Franklin D. Roosevelt appoints John Collier as Commis-
           sioner of Indian Affairs. Collier lifts prohibitions against
           traditional Native American religious practices.

1934   Elijah Muhammad becomes leader of the Nation of Is-
           lam, a Black Muslim group that was originally estab-
           lished in Detroit in 1930. The Nation of Islam will become
           famous with the emergence of Malcolm X as a public
           spokesperson.

1938   First important Supreme Court victory for the Jehovah's
           Witnesses in *Lovell* v. *City of Griffin* gives Witnesses per-
           mission to distribute literature despite an ordinance re-
           quiring a permit for such distribution.

1939   In England, Gerald B. Gardner establishes the beginnings
           of what will become the modern neopagan movement.

1940   A significant Supreme Court victory for the Witnesses
           in *Cantwell* v. *Connecticut* extends the freedom of religion
           clause to state governments and further serves to call
           into question the 1878 *Reynolds* decision giving govern-
           ment the power to regulate religious actions.

1942   The Way International, a Pentecostal, ultradispensational
           Christian group, is founded by Victor Paul Wierwille, a
           minister in the Evangelical and Reformed Church, as a
           radio ministry under the name of "Vesper Chimes," as-
           suming its present name in 1974. The Way remains rela-
           tively small until the Jesus movement of the early 1970s.

1943   Four cases involving the right of Jehovah's Witnesses to
           canvass door-to-door reach the Supreme Court. Three
           are decided in favor of the Witnesses (*Jones* v. *Oplika*,
           Murdock v. *Pennsylvania*, and *Martin* v. *Struthers*). The
           fourth case (*Douglas* v. *Jeannette*) is decided against the
           Witnesses, but on technical grounds.

           Another case involving the refusal of Witnesses to salute
           the flag, *West Virginia State Board of Education* v. *Barnette*,

is decided in favor of the Jehovah's Witnesses, overturning a related Supreme Court decision, *Minersville School District* v. *Gobitis,* made against the Witnesses in 1940.

1944   An important Supreme Court case involving the charge of mail fraud, based on the supposedly "ridiculous" nature of the group's religious beliefs, *U.S.* v. *Ballard,* is decided in favor of the "I Am" activity.

1947   The modern UFO era begins when Kenneth Arnold sights nine objects in the sky near Mount Rainier, Washington. The story of Arnold's sighting is reported in newspaper articles almost immediately. The term "flying saucers" is first coined by headline writers for this story. Religious significance is almost immediately attributed to UFOs, particularly in the wake of claims by George Adamski to have received communications from—and even to have ridden with—the "space brothers."

1949   Yogananda's *Autobiography of a Yogi* is published.

The Supreme Court dismisses *Bunn* v. *North Carolina* and rules that public safety outweighs concern for the free exercise of religion in a case involving the handling of poisonous snakes.

1950   L. Ron Hubbard's *Dianetics: The Modern Science of Mental Health* is published.

1951   Journalist Edward Hunter formulates the "brainwashing" model to explain Communist Chinese influence over American POWs during the Korean War in his popular book, *Brainwashing in Red China.*

1955   The Church of Scientology begins operations in Washington, D.C. Scientology has been involved in more religious liberty litigation than any other minority religion except Jehovah's Witnesses in the twentieth century in this country.

1958   Two former members of the W.F.L.K. (Wisdom, Faith, Love, and Knowledge) Foundation show up at the

1958
(cont.)
group's main building, confront the leader, Krishna Venta, and blow up the building, killing themselves, Venta, and seven others.

Mark L. Prophet, who had been active in two "I Am" splinter groups, founds the Summit Lighthouse in Washington, D.C. Elizabeth Clare Prophet becomes the Messenger after Mark Prophet's death in 1973, and Summit Lighthouse eventually expands to become Church Universal and Triumphant.

1961
The Supreme Court decides against Orthodox Jewish merchants protesting Sunday closing laws in Pennsylvania in *Braunfeld* v. *Brown.*

1963
In *Sherbert* v. *Verner,* a key case for what would become known as the "Sherbert-Yoder Test" for deciding free exercise of religion cases, the Supreme Court decides in favor of a Seventh-Day Adventist who had been denied unemployment benefits because she had not been able to accept work requiring work on Saturday.

1965
President Johnson rescinds the Asian Exclusion Act, a law that had prevented the large-scale immigration of Asians into the United States, thus allowing Asian spiritual teachers to enter the United States.

A. C. Bhaktivedanta Swami, founder of the Hare Krishna movement, journeys to the United States at the behest of his guru to establish Krishna consciousness in the West.

Malcolm X is assassinated by members of the Nation of Islam.

1966
Anton LaVey announces the formation of the Church of Satan. Highly theatrical but probably not dangerous, the Church of Satan provides a convenient target for conservative Christians with vague fears about the machinations of the Prince of Darkness.

1968
The Church of All Worlds, organized by Oberon Zell, is incorporated and in 1971 becomes the first neopagan

group to win federal tax-exempt status, the state ruling against it being overturned as unconstitutional.

Yogi Bhajan moves to Toronto and then to Los Angeles. The next year, 1969, he founds an ashram and the Healthy, Happy, Holy Organization (3HO) to teach kundalini yoga. Corporately, 3HO is later supplanted by Sikh Dharma.

1969   A benchmark U.S. Court of Appeals decision, *Founding Church of Scientology* v. *United States*, recognizes Scientology as a religion. This case marks a turning point in a conflict with the Food and Drug Administration that had begun dramatically in 1963 with an armed FDA raid during which Scientology literature and other materials were seized. In 1971, the Court orders the FDA to return the materials.

The Manson family murders take place, although Charles Manson is not arrested until 1971. The early anticult movement will use the actions of the Manson family as the most dramatic example of what cults are capable of, despite the fact that Manson and his followers are not a religion and present a very different sociological profile from the groups later stigmatized as cults.

1970   The cult controversy gets under way after the collapse of the 1960s counterculture. Rather than reengaging with mainstream society, many former counterculturists continue their quests for alternative lifestyles in a wide variety of religions. Hence the membership of many unusual religious groups that had existed quietly on the margins of American society suddenly explodes, laying the groundwork for the emergence of the cult issue.

1971   Ted Patrick begins the practice of deprogramming, which, along with the formation of the first anticult organization the next year, marks the emergence of the modern cult controversy.

Erhard Seminars Training, more commonly known as est, is begun by Werner Erhard. While not a church or religion, est will often be accused of being a "psychotherapy cult."

1971
(*cont.*)
Reverend Moon arrives in the United States. Although missionaries had been in this country since the 1950s, it is only with the arrival of Moon that the church begins to grow dramatically.

Guru Maharaj Ji, youthful leader of the Divine Light Mission, arrives in the United States.

1972
William Rambur and his wife, together with Ted Patrick and other concerned parents, establish the Parent's Committee to Free Our Sons and Daughters from the Children of God Organization (later shortened to FREECOG), the first modern anticult organization.

Richard Alpert (Baba Ram Das) publishes *Be Here Now*, regarded by some observers as signaling the beginning of the New Age movement.

Ervil LeBaron, founder of the polygamy-practicing Church of the Lamb of God, orders the murder of his brother, Joel LeBaron, founder and leader of the Church of the First Born of the Fullness of Times. More violence follows. In 1979, Ervil is arrested and convicted of murder.

In *Wisconsin* v. *Yoder*, a key case for what would become known as the "Sherbert-Yoder Test" for deciding free exercise of religion cases, the Supreme Court decides that a state law mandating high school education is an excessive burden on the Amish religion.

Marshall Applewhite and his partner, the founders of what eventually becomes Heaven's Gate, first attract national attention when 30 people abandon jobs, family, and possessions and pick up and depart with them after a lecture in Waldport, Oregon.

1973
The Divine Light Mission, a rapidly expanding religious group from India that had attracted considerable negative media attention, holds its Millennium '73 gathering at the Houston Astrodome. Too few people show up, and the Mission goes into debt. Although the movement continues, it never recovers its momentum.

1974   "Flirty fishing," the controversial practice of witness-
        ing that could involve sexual relations, is introduced
        by the Children of God. This practice is eventually
        abandoned, but not before it attracts extensive, nega-
        tive media attention.

        The Citizen's Freedom Foundation (CFF), a West Coast
        anticult organization, is established by William Rambur
        (one of the founders of FREECOG). CFF, which later
        changes its name to the Cult Awareness Network (CAN),
        grows to become the umbrella organization for anticult
        activity in the United States.

        The National Council of Churches issues a Resolution on
        Deprogramming that is highly critical of this practice.

1975   The Covenant of the Goddess (CoG) is established as a
        California nonprofit corporation on Halloween with the
        intention that it will serve the neopagan movement na-
        tionally as a legal church. It is the largest organization
        serving this purpose.

1976   Responding to a petition from his constituents, Senator
        Bob Dole holds hearings on the Unification church. The
        meeting is not a formal congressional hearing and leads
        to no governmental action.

        Ted Patrick's *Let Our Children Go!* is published, the first
        and only book on deprogramming.

1977   The FBI raids the Washington, D.C., and Los Angeles
        branches of the Church of Scientology and seizes many
        files of documents. The raid is declared illegal, but the
        documents remain in government possession, where
        they are open to public scrutiny.

        Katz v. *Superior Court*, also called the "Faithful Five/Faith-
        less Four" case (the principal cult conservatorship case),
        is decided in favor of parents seeking conservatorships
        for their five adult offspring who are members of the
        Unification church; the appeals court overturns the de-
        cision almost immediately. Four out of the five individu-
        als leave the church.

1977
(cont.)
JZ Knight, the most popular—as well as the most contro-versial—channel during the heyday of the New Age in the late 1980s, encounters Ramtha (he "appears" to her), a spiritual entity believed to have lived on earth approximately 35,000 years ago. Knight first publicly operates as a channel the next year.

1978
Jim Jones, leader of the Peoples Temple, orchestrates a "revolutionary suicide" at the communal agricultural settlement called Jonestown in the South American country of Guyana. Over 900 people—mostly black, some white—die from drinking a deadly poison. Almost overnight, the Peoples Temple replaces the Manson family as the primary examples of what in people's minds all "cults" are capable of doing.

Louis Farrakhan leaves the American Muslim Mission with several thousand followers and reestablishes the Nation of Islam as instituted by Elijah Muhammad.

An attorney suing the Synanon Church is bitten by a rattlesnake that had been placed in his mailbox by Synanon members.

The Parent-Teacher Association (PTA) officially adopts an "anticult" stance by issuing a "Resolution on Pseudo-Religious Cults" during its National Convention.

Flo Conway and Jim Siegelman's *Snapping* is published, a popular book presenting anecdotal evidence for "information disease," supposedly a unique mental illness caused by cultic mind control techniques.

The American Indian Religious Freedom Act is enacted, a measure intended to affirm traditional Native American religiosity. It is subsequently judged a failure, for lack of enforcement.

1979
A second unofficial hearing on the dangers of cults is sponsored by Senator Bob Dole. The testimony at this hearing is more extensive and volatile, but, in the end, it has no more effect than the first hearing (1976).

Publication of the first edition of Starhawk's *The Spiral Dance* and Margo Adler's *Drawing Down the Moon* that simultaneously document and further stimulate the expansion of the neopagan movement.

1980   A new concern about the possible presence of Satanism in the United States centers upon the sexual abuse of children in Satanic rituals and is initiated by the publication of *Michelle Remembers* by Michelle Smith and Lawrence Pazder.

1981   In *Thomas* v. *Review Board* the Supreme Court decides in favor of a Jehovah's Witness who had quit his job rather than work in an armaments factory and been denied unemployment benefits.

The Supreme Court supports the state's right to require solicitors to be confined to a booth rather than to wander about at the state fair in *Heffron* v. *International Society for Krishna Consciousness*.

1982   Rev. Sun Myung Moon is convicted and subsequently incarcerated on tax evasion charges. The Unification church decries the case as religious persecution.

In *Larson* v. *Valente* the Supreme Court decides in favor of the Unification church and against a solicitation law that targets new religious groups.

1983   An insurgent group of racial separatists, mostly Identity believers, known as the Order, or the Silent Brotherhood, begins a wave of crimes preparatory to the launching of attacks on the federal government. Between 1984 and 1986 members are captured and tried, and its leader, Robert Matthews, is killed in a shootout with the FBI.

Confrontations between law enforcement authorities and a North Dakota Posse Comitatus leader and Identity believer, Gordon Kahl, result in the deaths of two federal marshals.

1983   A young boy in the House of Judah, a Black Hebrew
(cont.)   group, is beaten to death, attracting national media at-
            tention. The mother of the boy is eventually sentenced
            to prison for manslaughter.

            American Family Foundation (AFF) begins publication
            of the *Cultic Studies Journal*, an academic journal pub-
            lishing research supporting the notion of cultic brain-
            washing. AFF, a latecomer anticult organization that
            came into being in the late 1970s, quickly establishes it-
            self as the scholarly wing of the anticult movement.

1984   The Island Pond raid occurs, in which the community's
            children are taken from the Northeast Kingdom in Ver-
            mont. They are almost immediately released, and there
            is no evidence of child abuse, as alleged.

1985   After years of controversial activity at Rajneeshpuram,
            his Oregon commune, Bhagwan Rajneesh (Osho) is
            charged with immigration fraud and deported back to
            India.

            Federal law enforcement authorities besiege and capture
            the commune of a heavily armed paramilitary Identity
            group in Arkansas, the Covenant, Sword and Arm of the
            Lord, with no loss of life.

            The Way International's tax-exempt status is revoked fol-
            lowing allegations of partisan political involvement and
            certain business activities at its New Knoxville, Ohio,
            headquarters. The ruling is reversed by the Supreme
            Court in 1990.

            The Local Church wins a libel case against authors who
            had accused the church of being a "destructive cult." The
            Spiritual Counterfeits Project, a Christian anticult group
            that published one of the books, was driven to bank-
            ruptcy in the face of an $11 million judgment.

            MOVE, a black communal group in urban Philadelphia,
            is fire-bombed by the city and destroyed. MOVE is sub-
            sequently labeled a "political cult."

1986   *Molko & Leal* v. *Unification Church* is decided in favor of
        the Unification church. This is one of the most impor-
        tant cases involving lawsuits brought against controver-
        sial religions by ex-members. The court decides in favor
        of the Unification church and against notions of coer-
        cive persuasion cited by the plaintiffs. However, three
        years later after a number of appeals, the case will be on
        the verge of being tried by the California Supreme Court.
        Rather than go through a new trial, the church finally
        settles out of court in November of 1989.

        The Vatican issues the "Vatican Report on Sects and New
        Religious Movements." World Council of Churches/
        Lutheran World Federation issues a parallel report,
        "Summary Statements and Recommendations."

1987   The city of Hialeah, Florida, enacts a ban against "ani-
        mal sacrifice" directly aimed at the growing Santeria
        community of the city. One Santeria house challenges
        the ban, and in 1993 the Supreme Court unanimously
        declares the Hialeah ordinance unconstitutional in
        Church of Lukumi Bablu Aye v. *City of Hialeah*.

        This is a year for growing media awareness of the New
        Age movement. Early in the year, Shirley MacLaine's
        miniseries, *Out on a Limb*, airs. In August, the media re-
        ports on the Harmonic Convergence gatherings. In the
        fall, *Time* magazine publishes an influential issue fea-
        turing a cover story on the New Age.

        The American Psychological Association rejects the re-
        port of the task force on "deceptive and indirect meth-
        ods of persuasion and control," a group of professionals
        with anticult leanings who had initiated the task force in
        an effort to win official support for the notion of cult mind
        control. This effort later backfires when the APA rejec-
        tion of the report is cited in the *Fishman* decision (see 1990).

1989   In an attempt to avoid negative publicity, two members
        of Church Universal and Triumphant attempt to acquire
        otherwise legal weapons in a nonpublic, illegal manner.
        The result is a public relations disaster.

1989   Bodies discovered on the grounds of a ranch near
(cont.)   Matamoros, Mexico, not far from the Texas border, make
              headlines. The murders, which are associated with a
              drug-smuggling operation, are immediately linked to
              Satanic worship.

1990   Members of Church Universal and Triumphant from
              around the world gather in Montana because of the pre-
              dicted possibility of an atomic catastrophe. Montana is
              flooded by reporters from around the world eager for
              sensationalist stories on a "doomsday cult."

              The Supreme Court rules against the right of Native
              American Church members to use peyote in *Employment
              Division* v. *Smith.*

              After a detailed review of their "coercive persuasion"
              ideas, the U.S. District Court, in *U.S.* v. *Fishman,* rejects
              Dr. Margaret Singer and Prof. Richard Ofshe as expert
              witnesses on mind control. This is a benchmark case,
              which is subsequently used to disqualify Singer and
              Ofshe from testifying in other cult cases.

1991   *Time* magazine publishes a front-page story critical of the
              Church of Scientology. The next year, the church files a
              major lawsuit against *Time* after discovering that the
              maker of Prozac—a psychiatric drug that Scientology had
              been active in opposing—had purchased 250,000 advance
              copies for distribution to doctors across the country.

              Tony Alamo, cofounder of the Alamo Christian Founda-
              tion (Music Square Church), is arrested on charges of
              child abuse.

1992   Church Universal and Triumphant's federal tax-exempt
              status is revoked. This status is restored two years later.

              The FBI arrests deprogrammer Galen Kelly in connec-
              tion with a conspiracy to abduct Lewis DuPont Smith,
              heir to the DuPont fortune. The arrest represents an im-
              portant reversal of the longstanding policy of law en-
              forcement officials to turn a blind eye to deprogramming
              as a "family matter."

1993   A force of 76 agents from the Bureau of Alcohol, Tobacco, and Firearms raid the Branch Davidian compound in Waco, Texas. The resulting standoff turns into a 51-day siege that ends when FBI agents launch a new attack on the Davidian complex. A fire ignites in the buildings and over 80 members die.

A new wave of intensive and negative media attention is focused on the Family (the Children of God) following raids on their homes in France and Argentina on charges of child abuse.

In a landmark decision, the IRS ceases all litigation and recognizes Scientology as a legitimate religious organization.

Margaret Singer and Richard Ofshe file a lawsuit in federal court against the American Psychological Association, the American Sociological Association, and a group of individual scholars for conspiring to discredit them as expert witnesses. Their suit is thrown out of court on August 9.

Reacting to the Supreme Court's decision in *Employment Division v. Smith*, a broad coalition of religious groups supports the Religious Freedom Restoration Act, a legislative measure explicitly intended to reestablish pre-*Smith* standards for the free exercise of religion.

1994   Fifty-three people, members of the Order of the Solar Temple, are murdered or commit suicide in Switzerland and Canada.

The Movement of Spiritual Inner Awareness (MSIA) attracts the attention of the media after it is discovered that the wife of Michael Huffington—who at the time was running for senator—had been active in MSIA. In the same year, Peter McWilliams drops out of the Movement and authors a bitter anti-MSIA book, *LIFE 102: What To Do When Your Guru Sues You.*

A longstanding libel case brought by Cynthia Kisser, at the time the leader of the Cult Awareness Network,

1994
(cont.)
against the Church of Scientology and its international president is dismissed in federal court. The case is similarly dismissed upon appeal in 1997. She simultaneously files a libel case in Illinois state court. The state case is dismissed with prejudice in 1995.

After failing to make their case in federal court, Margaret Singer and Richard Ofshe refile their lawsuit against the American Psychological Association et al. in California state court. The case is dismissed with prejudice.

1995
A poison gas attack occurs in a Tokyo subway, killing twelve people and injuring many others. Within a few days of the attack, AUM Shinrikyo, a controversial Japanese religious group, is considered the most likely suspect.

A small remnant of the Order of the Solar Temple commits suicide in France.

The Report of the Commission of Inquiry on Sects—usually referred to as the "French Report"—is issued.

1996
Following a declaration of bankruptcy in the wake of losing a deprogramming-related lawsuit, the Cult Awareness Network (CAN) name, mailing address, and phone number are purchased by the Church of Scientology.

The Liberal Democratic Party (LDP), the principal partner in Japan's ruling coalition, exploits fears generated by AUM Shinrikyo to attack its chief rival—the New Frontier Party that is associated with Soka Gakkai, Japan's largest new religion—and scores big in the national election.

1997
The bodies of 39 members of Heaven's Gate are found in a posh mansion outside San Diego, all victims of a mass suicide.

Responding to the Solar Temple murder/suicides that took place in Switzerland in 1994, the Swiss Report is released in February by the Canton of Geneva. Though more moderate in tone, its substantive proposals are more drastic than the French Report.

Additional members of the Order of the Solar Temple commit suicide in Quebec.

International ("Boston") Church of Christ wins an important case against a newspaper in Singapore, where it is illegal to refer to a religious group as a "cult."

The Belgian parliamentary commission on cults issues its official report. The "Belgium Report" is even more extreme than the French Report, naming five mainline Catholic groups, the YWCA, Quakerism, Hasidic Judaism, and almost all forms of Buddhism as dangerous cults.

Controversial Groups and Movements

3

Groups that have been labeled cults constitute a highly diverse set, both organizationally and doctrinally. The only feature that unites them is that they have in some way been controversial. In fact, many small and otherwise innocuous minority religions have been drawn into the controversy as the result of specific conflicts that have no intrinsic relationship with the wider anticult crusade.

For individuals or groups involved in certain kinds of struggles with members of minority religions, the cult stereotyping represents a potent ideological resource, which— if successful—marshals public opinion against their opponent, potentially tipping the balance of power in their favor. Situations in which this strategy can work are not restricted to the kinds of conflicts that are picked up by the news media. For example, the stigma of the cult label has been effectively deployed in child custody cases, in which one parent's membership in a minority religion is portrayed as indicative of her or his unworthiness as a parent.

Relevant social-psychological research also indicates that once a stereotype has been accepted, it structures our perceptions so that we tend to notice information that conforms to our image of the stereotyped group and to neglect or forget other kinds of information. What this means for any given confrontation is that as soon as the label has been successfully applied (i.e., accepted as appropriate by outsiders not directly involved in the conflict), the information that the public gathers is selectively appropriated so that almost every item of data conforms to the stereotype, thus effectively marshaling moral support for the person or group locked in conflict with a minority religion.

In ordinary language people talk as if there is an objective category of cult groups that can be distinguished from genuine religions. In this commonly accepted view, cults are by definition dangerous, false religions, led by cynical cult leaders who exploit followers for their own gain. This portrayal is, however, inaccurate, as has already been indicated in the introductory essay. While a handful of religious groups may fit the stereotype, "cult" is best understood as a socially negotiated label that frequently means little more than a religion one personally dislikes. For this reason, the inclusion of a particular religious organization in this reference book should not be taken as implying that it is thereby legitimate to refer to it as a cult, as this term is popularly understood.

The following pages contain information on forty-six controversial groups and movements. These run the gamut from tiny churches with less than a hundred members to organizations like the Soka Gakkai that number into the millions. Also included are entries on broader, less centrally organized phenomena such as Santeria and the Christian Identity movement.

Alamo Christian Foundation (Music Square Church)

The Alamo Christian Foundation, a Pentecostal church with doctrine similar to the Assemblies of God, was opened in 1969 in Hollywood, California, by Tony and Susan Alamo. It drew its early strength from the Jesus People movement. The foundation accepts the authority of the King James Version of the Bible and adheres to a strict moral code, condemning drugs, homosexuality, adultery, and abortions.

In the early 1970s the Alamo Christian Foundation became controversial and was heavily criticized because of what was viewed as heavy-handed proselytizing. Church members worked the streets of Hollywood, inviting potential converts to evening services. The mostly young recruits were taken by bus to the foundation's rural community in Saugus for an evangelistic meeting and meal. Many of those who converted remained in Saugus to be taught the Bible and become lay ministers.

In 1976, the church moved its headquarters to Alma, Arkansas, where Susan Alamo had grown up. There it developed a community of several hundred members and established printing facilities, a school, and a large tabernacle. As the organization expanded further, churches were opened in other cities. The church developed as an ordered community dedicated to evangelism. Converts who wish to receive the church's training and participate in its ministry take a vow of poverty, agreeing to turn over all real property to the church. In return, the church provides the necessities of life. Periodically members are sent out on evangelistic tours around the United States, frequently using the established church centers as bases of operation. Services are held daily at each of the church centers and free meals are generally served.

The church publishes a variety of evangelistic tracts which are passed out in the street and mailed. The church also distributes numerous tapes of sermons by Susan and Tony Alamo. Members include a number of talented musicians and the church has produced a set of records and tapes featuring Tony Alamo and other members. A national television ministry was begun in the 1970s but has been largely discontinued. In 1981 Music Square Church was incorporated. It superseded the foundation in 1982.

To support itself and as part of its rehabilitation program, the church developed several businesses in which members, many former drug addicts, could begin a process of reintegration into society. A number of former members who later aligned themselves with the anticult movement complained that they should have been paid at least minimum wage for their work hours while members. These complaints led to a series of lawsuits. In 1985 the IRS stripped the Music Square Church of its tax-exempt status. The church went to court to fight this decision.

In 1988 Tony Alamo was accused of beating the 11-year-old son of a member. Charges were filed and Alamo disappeared. During the next three years, Alamo became a fugitive from justice. During this time he moved about the country, frequently making calls to talk shows and even dropping into public offices for visits. Meanwhile, the church's property in Arkansas was seized to pay off court judgments against the organization. Tony Alamo was arrested in July of 1991.

Ananda Cooperative Community

The Ananda Cooperative Community, also known as the Ananda World Brotherhood Village, was founded in 1968 by Swami Kriyananda (J. Donald Walters) in Nevada City, California. Walters was born of American parents in Rumania in 1926. He was educated in Rumania, Switzerland, England, and the United States. At the age of 22 he became a disciple of Paramhansa Yogananda and received the monastic name Kriyananda. He lived with Yogananda until the master's death in 1952. Kriyananda served as a minister, director of center activities, and vice-president of the organization that Yogananda founded, the Self Realization Fellowship. In 1962, he separated from Self-Realization Fellowship to write, teach, and lecture on the implications of Yogananda's message for active yoga students and laypersons.

In 1968, Kriyananda founded Ananda Village near Nevada City, California, in response to Yogananda's directive to "cover the earth with world brotherhood colonies, demonstrating that simplicity of living plus high thinking lead to the greatest happiness." Ananda Village is situated at a 2,600-foot elevation on 750 acres of wood- and meadowland in the Sierra foothills of northern California. Members support themselves through a variety of businesses, some of which are privately owned and some of which are owned and operated by the community. The community includes 600 people from many cultural, ethnic, and racial backgrounds. About 25 nationalities are represented. A village council is elected annually by Ananda members.

Ananda operates a guest facility called the Expanding Light, which is open year-round for personal retreats, training courses, special events, and holiday programs. Ananda members practice regular daily meditation using the techniques of kriya yoga as taught by Paramhansa Yogananda. Resident members are all disciples of Yogananda. The group is directly involved in a worldwide outreach to those interested in the teachings of Paramhansa Yogananda and his line of gurus.

Ananda has five branch residential communities and 50 centers and meditation groups throughout the world. Ananda's church congregation was established in 1990 and has 1600 members. The church is open for membership to those who follow the teachings of Paramhansa Yogananda. The goal of the church is to provide fellowship and inspiration for those who want to find God through the practice of ancient raja yoga techniques, which were brought to the west by Paramhansa Yogananda. In recent years, Ananda's church has been engaged in an ongoing legal conflict with the Self-Realization Fellowship, the American organization founded by Yogananda and with which Kriyananda was formerly affiliated.

AUM Shinrikyo (AUM Supreme Truth)

On March 20, 1995, a poison gas attack occurred in a Tokyo subway that killed twelve people and injured many others. Within a few days of the attack, AUM Shinrikyo, a controversial Japanese religious group, became the most likely suspect. The leadership was eventually arrested and the organization disbanded.

AUM Shinrikyo was founded by Master Shoko Asahara in Tokyo in 1987. A form of Tantric Buddhism, AUM Shinrikyo's teachings emphasized yoga practices and spiritual experiences. Master Asahara, born in 1955, whose original name was Chizuo Matsumoto, had traveled to India seeking enlightenment. Before returning to Japan, he sought out the Dalai Lama and received what he believed was a commission to revive true Buddhism in the land of his birth. By the time of the subway incident, AUM Shinrikyo had acquired a large communal facility near Mt. Fuji and a following of approximately 10,000 members in Japan.

In addition to the teachings of traditional Buddhism, Master Asahara was also fascinated with the future. His preoccupation with divination may have grown out of the weakness of his physical senses, as he was born blind in one eye, with only partial use of the other. Before undertaking yoga and meditation practices, Asahara pursued the study of such divinatory practices as astrology. Like many other Japanese spiritualists, he was fascinated by Western biblical prophecies as well as by the prophecies of Nostradamus. Perhaps influenced by the apocalyptic flavor of these predictions, Asahara himself began preaching an apocalyptic message to his followers. In particular, he prophesied a confrontation between Japan and the United States before the end of the century that would destroy his home country.

Asahara was, in fact, so certain about an impending conflict between Japan and the United States that he began preparing to wage war. Unable to match the conventional military might of the United States, AUM scientists investigated unconventional weapons, from biological agents to poison gas. This research is reflected in Asahara's last book, *Disaster Approaches the Land of the Rising Sun*, which contains material reflecting a very un-Buddhist interest in various forms of poison gas, including sarin.

In retrospect, it is clear that certain highly placed AUM members carried out the subway attack. The attack was motivated by increased police scrutiny of the AUM Shinrikyo, with the aim of distracting police attention away from the movement. There had also been smaller-scale acts of violence carried out against the enemies of the group—in one case poison gas was released near their Mt. Fuji center in an attack on local critics. It was this latter assault that led the police to begin investigating AUM Shinrikyo in the first place.

In the end, it was Asahara's own pronouncements that drew police attention to AUM Shinrikyo. In particular, Master Asahara had predicted that gas attacks by terrorists would occur in the not-too-distant future. This made him an obvious target of suspicion. Hence the subway attack, far from diverting attention away from AUM Shinrikyo, actually had the opposite effect.

Black Judaism

Many African Americans have rejected Christianity in favor of religions with more distinctively black identities. For centuries a legend existed that black Jews, descendants of the Queen of Sheba, had lived in Ethiopia but had long ago disappeared. The rediscovery in the late nineteenth century of the Falashas, the black Jews of Ethiopia, by French explorer Joseph Halevy, spurred some black people to choose Judaism as an alternative to Christianity.

The first African American Jewish denomination was started by William Saunders Crowdy, who preached that Africans were the descendants of the lost tribes of Israel and thus the true surviving Jews. By 1899, Crowdy had founded churches in 29 Kansas towns. He called his denomination the Church of God and Saints of Christ, which, despite its Christian-sounding name, had from the start identified with Judaism. The Christ of the church's name refers to the awaited messiah. As it evolved, the doctrine of the Church of God and Saints of Christ became a mixture of Jewish, Christian, and black nationalist precepts.

In 1915, Prophet F. S. Cherry established the Church of God in Philadelphia, Pennsylvania. Cherry was influenced by both the Church of God and Saints of Christ and the Temple of the Gospel of the Kingdom (another early black Jewish group). Cherry taught that God is black and originally created black humans, who were the descendants of Jacob. The first white person, Gehazi, was the result of a curse. The church teaches that Jesus was a black.

Arnold Josiah Ford was a self-proclaimed Ethiopian Jew and the choirmaster for Marcus Garvey, founder of the Universal Negro Improvement Association. Ford later founded the Beth B'nai Abraham congregation, which suffered financial problems and collapsed in 1930. Ford then turned the membership over to Rabbi Wentworth Matthew and moved to Ethiopia. Arthur Wentworth Matthew had been a minister in the Church of the Living God, the Pillar and Ground of Truth, a black Pentecostal church that had endorsed the Universal Negro Improvement Association. In 1919 Matthew and eight other men organized the Commandment Keepers: Holy Church of the Living God. In Harlem, he had met white Jews for the first time and in the 1920s came to know Arnold Josiah Ford. Matthew began to study Orthodox Judaism, to learn Hebrew, and to acquire ritual materials from Ford. Ford and Matthew learned of the Falashas, the black Jews of Ethiopia, and began to identify with them.

The Original Hebrew Israelite Nation, or Black Israelites, emerged in Chicago in the 1960s around Ben Ammi Carter (born G. Parker) and Shaleah Ben-Israel. Carter and Ben-Israel were proponents of black Zionism whose purpose was a return to the Holy Land. Beginning in the late 1960s, they made attempts to migrate to Africa and then to Israel. Over 300 members of the group had migrated to Israel by 1971, when strict immigration restrictions were imposed. Other members of the group continued to arrive using tourist visas.

The House of Judah is a small black Israelite group founded in 1965 by Prophet William A. Lewis. Lewis was converted to his black Jewish beliefs by a street preacher in Chicago in the 1960s. Lewis opened a small storefront on the southside and in 1971 moved his group to a 22-acre tract of land near Grand Junction, Michigan. The group lived quietly until 1983 when a young boy in the group was beaten to death, which attracted national media attention. The mother of the boy was sentenced to prison for manslaughter. By 1985 the group had moved to Alabama. The group consists of about 80 people living communally.

The Nation of Yahweh, also called the Hebrew Israelites or the Followers of Yahweh, was founded in the 1970s by Yahweh ben Yahweh, who was born Hulon Mitchell, Jr. Yahweh ben Yahweh was the son of a Pentecostal minister and at one point joined the Nation of Islam. Yahweh ben Yahweh teaches that there is one God, whose name is Yahweh and who is black. Yahweh ben Yahweh calls himself the son of God, who has been sent to save and deliver the black people of America. Black people are considered to be the true lost tribe of Judah. In 1991, Yahweh ben Yahweh and 15 of his followers were arrested on a variety of charges, including racketeering and conspiracy to commit murder. At a trial in the spring of 1992, Yahweh ben Yahweh and seven of his codefendants were convicted of the conspiracy charges but were not convicted of racketeering.

Black Muslims

For many African Americans, Islam has provided an alternative to Christianity, which many argue failed to establish a truly racially inclusive society. The growth of Islam among African Americans is related to the idea that Islam is a religious faith that affirms their African heritage. Most nonimmigrant Muslims in America are African American converts.

The Black Muslim movement began when Timothy Drew, who became known as Noble Drew Ali, founded the Moorish Science Temple in Newark, New Jersey, in 1913. Ali was exposed to black nationalist leader Marcus Garvey's ideas after 1917, and these became central to the movement's ideology. The Moorish Science Temple came to prominence in Chicago in the 1920s. Temple members wore bright red fezzes and changed their slave names by adding the suffixes "el" or "bey" to them. After Garvey was deported in 1927, the Moorish American Science Temple wooed, and to a great extent won over, Garvey's followers.

The original Nation of Islam arose in Detroit in 1930. In that year Wali Farrad Muhammad (also called W. D. Fard) appeared and eventually established a temple in Detroit. Fard disappeared in 1934 and his top lieutenant, Elijah Muhammad, became leader of the movement.

Under the leadership of Elijah Muhammad, the Nation of Islam grew into a strong, cohesive unit. Muhammad moved the headquarters to Chicago and opened temples, mosques, schools, housing projects, stores, restaurants, and farms. Many themes taught in the Nation of Islam reflected traditional Islamic teachings: submission to Allah and repudiation of alcohol, sex outside of marriage, the eating of pork, and gambling. Other themes ran counter to traditional Islam: the white man as devil, the identification of W. D. Fard as Allah and Elijah Muhammad as a prophet, and the quasi-scientific theory of human history and purpose. Muhammad taught that blacks were the original humans, but a rebellious scientist produced and released genetically weakened pale stock.

In the mid 1950s a former nightclub singer named Louis Eugene Wolcott joined the Nation of Islam. He dropped his last name and became known as Minister Louis X. His oratorical and musical skills put him in charge of the Boston mosque. Malcolm X, the most famous member of the Nation of Islam, was the charismatic leader of the New York temple. He was eventually expelled and shortly thereafter killed by members of the Nation of Islam.

When Nation of Islam leader Elijah Muhammad died in 1975, many members thought that Louis X, who was by then known by the name of Abdul Haleem Farrakhan, would become the new leader of the Nation of Islam. However, Elijah Muhammad's son, Wallace, was chosen instead. During his first three years as leader of the Nation of Islam, Wallace Muhammad brought the organization into mainstream Islam and away from the racial and black national policies of his father. The organization went through a series of name changes and is now known as the American Muslim Mission.

The abandonment by Wallace Muhammad of his father's anti-white rhetoric and identification of Elijah Muhammad as prophet was not accepted by all members. At least four splinter groups left the American Muslim Mission and formed their own congregations that adhered to Elijah Muhammad's original doctrines. The best known of these is the splinter headed by Louis Farrakhan, who, with several thousand followers, left the American Muslim Mission in 1978 and reestablished the Nation of Islam as instituted by Elijah Muhammad.

Boston Church of Christ/ International Church of Christ

Boston Church of Christ began with a single congregation of the larger Church of Christ denomination. It has also been referred to as the Crossroads movement (actually a distinct movement from which the Boston movement developed), Multiplying Ministries, the Discipling movement, and the International Church of Christ.

The Crossroads movement was begun by Charles H. Lucas, who came to Gainesville, Florida, in 1967 to serve as campus minister. Campus Advance, as the new campus ministry was called, grew quickly. Two practices were characteristic of the ministry: "soul talks" and "prayer partners." Soul talks were evangelistic group Bible studies with prayer and sharing held in student residences. Prayer partners was the practice of pairing up a new Christian with a more mature Christian so that the new Christian could be given one-on-one direction. Both practices emphasized in-depth involvement of members in one another's lives.

In 1972, a freshman at the University of Florida, Kip McKean, was converted through Campus Advance. McKean trained at Lucas's new Crossroads Church of Christ while finishing his education. He left Crossroads and served as campus minister at other mainline Churches of Christ. In 1979, he accepted an invitation to take over the pulpit and campus ministry of a struggling 30-member church in a Boston suburb, the Lexington Church of Christ. The church was soon renamed the Boston Church of Christ. Within two years the 30-member church had grown to a membership of 300.

Kip McKean had a vision to establish churches in key metropolitan centers of the world that could in turn evangelize the cities around them. By 1993 the movement had grown to 42,855 members in 130 congregations worldwide. The church believes that it is unscriptural to have more than one congregation per city. Usually a church affiliated with the Boston movement will take the name of the city as its name, such as the Los Angeles Church of Christ or the Chicago Church of Christ.

Discipleship is very important to the Boston movement. In the movement, a disciple is one who is faithfully following Christ and has taken on the lifestyle and purpose of making disciples of all nations. The movement is very exclusivistic, meaning that a belief is that it is virtually impossible to be among the elect outside the ranks of the Boston movement.

While the Crossroads members chose their own prayer partners, in the Boston Church of Christ the leaders of the congregation arrange for older, stronger Christians to give direction to each of the younger, weaker ones. These partners are always of the same sex and are to have daily contact and weekly meetings. These partnerships are not considered optional. "Soul talks" as started in the Crossroads movement became "Bible talks" in the Boston movement. They are held weekly at regular times and places and are attended by an average of six to ten members. The Crossroads Church of Christ and the Boston Church of Christ have severed all ties with each other. The mainline Churches of Christ disavowed the Boston movement in the mid 1980s and are now ardent opponents of it.

The Boston Church of Christ has become the subject of considerable controversy, centering on the level of commitment expected of church members and the authority the church exercises in members' lives. Members are expected to put the church above all else, including job, friends, and family. Each week the average member attends at least four or five meetings for worship and/or Bible study. Numerous universities around the country either restrict or bar Boston movement activities on their campuses. The movement has experienced some cases of forcible deprogramming of members. A few ex-members have portrayed the movement in a negative light to the media, and two have produced books denouncing their former church. The leadership of the Boston movement has recognized that abuses of authority have occurred and retracted some of its earlier teachings on authority and submission. Despite the controversy, more people come into the movement than leave it.

Branch Davidians

In 1979, Vernon Howell, later David Koresh, began participating in study sessions at a Seventh-Day Adventist Church in Tyler, Texas, that his mother attended. There were a succession of incidents in which he preached his own theology to other church members and took over the pulpit to propound his own theological views. Howell learned of the Branch Davidians—a small group that had splintered from the SDA in the 1930s—and began working as a handyman at their Mt. Carmel center in 1981. He became a favorite of the leader, Lois Roden, who eventually named him as her successor.

Vernon Howell enunciated his controversial New Light doctrine in 1989. He asserted that as a messiah, he was the perfect mate of all the female adherents. Part of his mission was to create a new lineage of God's children from his own seed. These children would ultimately rule the world. The New Light doctrine made all female Branch Davidians spiritual wives to Koresh. The doctrine had the effect of annulling the spousal sexual exclusivity of all marriages within the church.

In 1990 Vernon Howell legally adopted the name David Koresh. "Koresh" is Hebrew for Cyrus, the Persian king who defeated the Babylonians 500 years before the birth of Jesus. In biblical language, Koresh is *a* (not *the*) messiah, one appointed to carry out a special mission for God. By taking the first name David, he asserted his spiritual descendency from the biblical King David. By 1992, Koresh had concluded that the apocalypse would occur in America rather than Israel, and the group began adopting a survivalist outlook, stockpiling large amounts of food, weapons, ammunition, and fuel. Koresh renamed the Mt. Carmel community Ranch Apocalypse.

The Branch Davidians retained a biblical base for teachings, but the Bible was supplemented, and in certain respects supplanted, by revelations of the living prophet. Members observed a Saturday sabbath and eschewed meat, alcohol, caffeine, and tobacco. They rejected ostentatious dress and grooming, birthday celebrations, and television viewing. In contrast to Christ, who was sinless and therefore an impossible role model, Koresh was a "sinful messiah." Koresh taught that human sinfulness does not prevent humans from attaining salvation. Koresh informed his followers that Armageddon would begin in the United States with an attack on the Branch Davidians.

Accusations of misbehavior on the part of Koresh and some other residents of the Branch Davidian headquarters began to circulate among anticultists and others. The accusations were those frequently used against many unconventional religions by their opponents. The most frequent accusations alleged child abuse and possession of firearms. Local authorities investigated the child abuse allegations and found them groundless. The federal Bureau of Alcohol, Tobacco, and Firearms (ATF) of the Department of the Treasury obtained search and arrest warrants on the weapons charges.

On February 28, 1993, a force of 76 agents of the ATF raided the Branch Davidian compound. The raid turned into a shoot-out between federal agents and Branch Davidians who chose to defend themselves. The resulting standoff turned into a 51-day siege that ended on April 19 when federal agents launched a new attack on the Davidian complex. Agents of the federal government used military equipment to batter holes in buildings through which they injected noxious gas in an attempt to force the Davidians outside. A fire ignited in the buildings and over 80 members died.

Christian Identity

The Christian Identity movement is an American offshoot of an older religious movement, British-Israelism (also known as Anglo-Israelism). In an 1840 set of lectures, John Wilson argued that the British peoples were actually the descendants of the migrating ten lost tribes who had forgotten their true identity. As developed by subsequent writers, British-Israelism posited a revisionist history of Britain and the ancient world and identified England as a divine instrument for the fulfillment of God's purposes.

By the late 1920s the American branch of British-Israelism had passed into the hands of a Massachusetts lawyer and organizer, Howard Rand. Rand brought American British-Israelites under the umbrella of a new organization, the Anglo-Saxon Federation of America. His colleague in this enterprise was Henry Ford's publicist, William J. Cameron. Together, they linked the Anglo-Saxon Federation with explicitly right-wing political agendas.

With the end of World War II, the stage was set for the emergence of Christian Identity doctrine in southern California. Southern California had absorbed a number of British-Israel influences during earlier decades. The key figures in the emergence of Christian Identity—Bertrand Comparet, William Potter Gale, and preeminently, Wesley Swift—were all associates of Gerald L. K. Smith. Based in Los Angeles, Smith was the most widely known anti-Semitic agitator of the 1940s and served as the center of an informal national network of those on the extreme right.

Christian Identity millennialist theology rejects the concept of a rapture, in which the saved will be lifted off the earth before the period of violence (the Tribulation) that climaxes in Armageddon. Instead, Identity followers believe they must survive a period of violence and persecution under the Antichrist, a time they often characterize in terms of race war.

Identity's most distinctive theological hallmark is its view of Jewish origins. Christian Identity asserts that Jews are the direct, biological descendants of Satan. They advance a myth of the Fall in which original sin consists of a sexual coupling between Eve and Satan or his humanoid instrument, begetting Cain, whom they call the first Jew. Hence in addition to more traditional anti-Semitic motifs, Christian Identity adds a link with primal evil.

By defining the world in racial terms, Identity creates a universe in which the chosen few battle against the evil world that surrounds them. In political terms, this vision of cosmic combat leads many Identity believers to identify state and national governments with the Jewish conspiracy and the forces of Antichrist. While the expression of this antipathy is most often limited to the written and spoken word, it has sometimes erupted into acts of open defiance.

In 1983, confrontations between law enforcement authorities and a North Dakota Posse Comitatus leader and Identity believer, Gordon Kahl, resulted in the deaths of two federal marshals. In 1985, federal law enforcement authorities besieged and captured the commune of a heavily armed paramilitary Identity group in Arkansas, the Covenant, Sword and Arm of the Lord, with no loss of life. In 1983/1984, an insurgent group of racial separatists known as the Order, or the Silent Brotherhood, engaged in a wave of crimes, mostly in the West, preparatory to the launching of attacks on the federal government. Half of its forty members were Identity believers. Between 1984 and 1986 the members of the Order were captured and tried (its leader, Robert Matthews, was killed in a shootout with the FBI), and with the organization's demise, the level of Identity-related violence dropped substantially. Nonetheless, because the movement is fragmented, the possibility of violent episodes in the future cannot be ruled out.

Christian Science (Church of Christ, Scientist)

Christian Science was founded in Lynn, Massachusetts, in 1879 by Mary Baker Eddy (1821–1919). Eddy had always been troubled with poor health, which worsened during the 1860s. She tried a number of different alternative treatments, until finally she placed herself under the care of Dr. Phineas Parkhurst Quimby, a mental healer in Portland, Maine. She soon experienced some relief and became his student. However, after his death in 1866, she was periodically disturbed by the return of her illness and the conflicts between his ideas and those she found in the Bible.

The "Biblical truth" was imparted while slowly and painfully recuperating from an injury that occurred when she slipped on icy pavement in 1866. Her health was immediately restored, marking the beginning of Christian Science. She claimed that there was no healing agent, either magnetic force or mind, other than God, and that God was the only life, the only reality of being. In the next few years she began teaching and writing her first book, *The Science of Man*, and the presentation of her teaching, entitled *Science and Health with Key to the Scriptures*.

Christian Science departs from orthodox Christianity in that it believes in what it terms the "allness of God" and hence the unreality of disease, sin, and death. Church doctrine states that Christ does not defeat evil but demonstrates its lack of reality beyond our belief in it. The impersonal aspect of God as Principle, Mind, Life, Truth, and Love is emphasized by Christian Science, which also distinguishes between the man Jesus and the eternal spiritual selfhood, Christ, Son of God, whom the church regards as having been expressed by men and women throughout the centuries.

Christian Science has been attacked since its beginnings. The major challenges to Christian Science came from a medical profession that, at the time of the founding of the church, was just consolidating its position as the normative authority in the treatment of illness in the United States. Numerous court cases were fought over the rights of Christian Scientists to refrain from the use of doctors and the rights of Christian Science practitioners to care for the sick.

During the 1980s, the issue of medical care for children was revived in a series of court cases across the United States, as Christian Science parents were accused of homicide, child abuse, and negligence. Cases of this kind forced judge and jury to consider as possibly criminal the behavior of loving parents who held deep religious beliefs against medical treatment. These cases had mixed results. For instance, a case from California led to the Supreme Court turning back a challenge to the prosecution of parents on the basis of religious freedom. In Florida, a couple was convicted of third-degree murder but after a long probation ordered to give their other children regular medical treatment. David and Ginger Twitchell were convicted of manslaughter in Massachusetts, another couple in California was convicted of child endangerment, while two other parents were acquitted in a similar case. Other cases filed against Christian Science were dismissed in Michigan and Minnesota and left inconclusive the status of parents who rely on Christian Science.

Church of the First Born of the Fullness of Times; Church of the First Born; Church of the Lamb of God

The Church of the First Born of the Fullness of Times was incorporated in 1955 by brothers Joel, Ross Wesley, and Floren LeBaron. The Church of the First Born was founded by Ross Wesley LeBaron after he left his brothers' church. The Church of the Lamb of God was founded by another LeBaron brother, Ervil, after he was dismissed from the Church of the First Born of the Fullness of Times.

The LeBaron family and its patriarch, Alma Dayer LeBaron, were members of the Church of Jesus Christ of Latter-Day Saints. In 1934, one of Alma's sons, Benjamin LeBaron, claimed to be the One Mighty and Strong, the prophetic figure mentioned in Mormon writings, and several family members substantiated his claims as a prophet. In 1944, the LeBaron family was excommunicated from the Church of Jesus Christ of Latter-Day Saints. The family then associated with the fundamentalist Mormon colony in Mexico directed by Rulon C. Allred, leader of the Apostolic United Brethren.

In 1955, the LeBarons left Allred's Mexican colony. Benjamin's brothers, Joel, Ross Wesley, and Floren established the Church of the First Born of the Fullness of Times. Joel claimed to have the Patriarchal Priesthood and had a revelation directing Rulon C. Allred to become his councilor. Both Allred and Joel's brother Benjamin rejected Joel's claims.

Also rejecting Joel LeBaron's claim to Patriarchal Priesthood was his brother and cofounder of the Church of the First Born of the Fullness of Times, Ross Wesley LeBaron. Ross Wesley left his brothers' church and formed the Church of the First Born. The doctrine of the Church of the First Born states that the church was first established by Adam and restored in Joseph. It believes in One Mighty and Strong to come as presented in the Doctrine and Covenants. Ross Wesley LeBaron disincorporated the church in the early 1980s. Joel's claim to the "patriarchal priesthood" followed a line of succession through his father, Alma, to Alma's grandfather, Benjamin F. Johnson, who was secretly ordained by founder Joseph Smith.

In 1970, the Church of the First Born of the Fullness of Times dismissed Ervil LeBaron, its second-highest ranking officer and the brother of its leader Joel LeBaron. Ervil formed the Church of the Lamb of God and claimed full authority over all of the polygamy-practicing groups, even going so far as to claim an authority to execute anyone who would refuse to accept him as the representative of God. Beginning with the establishment of the Church of the Lamb of God, a series of murders and assaults on polygamy-practicing Mormons began.

On August 20, 1972, Joel LeBaron, leader of the Church of the First Born of the Fullness of Times, was shot to death in Ensenada, Mexico. On June 16, 1975, Dean Vest, an associate of Joel LeBaron, was killed near San Diego, California. On May 10, 1977, Dr. Rulon C. Allred, leader of the Apostolic United Brethren, was murdered in his chiropractic office in Salt Lake City while attending patients. On May 14, 1977, an attempt was made on the life of Merlin Kingston, another polygamy leader. Thirteen other polygamy-practicing Mormons were killed before Ervil LeBaron was arrested for the murder of Rulon Allred. Ervil LeBaron was tried, convicted, and sentenced to prison in 1980. He died in prison of natural causes in 1981.

Joel LeBaron headed the Church of the First Born of the Fullness of Times from 1955 until he was murdered in 1972. He was succeeded by his brother Verlan, who led the church until his death in 1981. The current leader of the church is Siegfried Widmar. The Church of the First Born of the Fullness of Times has several hundred members, most of whom live in Mexico.

Church Universal and Triumphant

The Church Universal and Triumphant (CUT) is a Montana-based New Age church led by Elizabeth Clare Prophet. In terms of negative media coverage, by the late 1980s it had become the most controversial new religion in North America.

Mark L. Prophet, who had been active in two "I Am" splinter groups, eventually founded his own group, the Summit Lighthouse, in Washington, D.C., in 1958. The orientation of Prophet's new group was the publication and dissemination of the Masters' teachings. In the theosophical tradition, the spiritual evolution of the planet is conceived of as being in the hands of a group of divinely illumined beings (the Ascended Masters). In the tradition of earlier theosophical leaders, Mark Prophet viewed himself as serving as the mouthpiece for these Ascended Masters.

Elizabeth Clare Wulf joined the group in 1961, eventually marrying Mark Prophet. Over the course of their marriage, Elizabeth Prophet also became a Messenger. After Mark's death in 1973, Elizabeth took over his role as the primary mouthpiece for the Masters, as well as leadership of the organization.

The headquarters of Summit Lighthouse moved to Colorado Springs in 1966. In 1974, CUT was incorporated, taking over ministerial and liturgical activities, while Summit Lighthouse remained the publishing wing of the organization. After several moves within southern California, church headquarters was finally established in 1986 on the Royal Teton Ranch, in Montana, just north of Yellowstone Park.

When nontraditional religions became a public issue in the mid 1970s, Church Universal and Triumphant was not particularly prominent. While still in southern California, several members were kidnapped and deprogrammed. One major lawsuit, brought against the church by ex-member Gregory Mull, cost CUT several million dollars. Despite these struggles and some media attacks, the group remained a relatively minor player in the cult controversy until it moved its headquarters to Montana.

Much of the church's negative publicity derives from incidents focused on its extensive fallout shelters and its preparations for the possibility of a nuclear attack against the United States. At one point in the construction, for instance, fuel stored in several underground tanks (which were sold to the church in defective condition) ruptured and spilled gas and diesel oil into the water table. In 1990, members from around the world gathered in Montana because of the predicted possibility of an atomic holocaust—a gathering that would have gone all but unnoticed had not a local paper picked up the story and broadcast the news in a negative fashion through the AP wire service to the world.

Also, in 1989, two high-level church members attempted to acquire otherwise legal weapons in a nonpublic, illegal manner (to be stored in the underground shelters). The motivation was to avoid the negative media exposure that would have resulted if members had purchased guns in Montana. The plan backfired and resulted in a public relations disaster. This series of incidents, particularly the gun purchase fiasco, was the basis for subsequent accusations that Church Universal and Triumphant was a potential Waco.

ECKANKAR

A religious movement founded by Paul Twitchell in California in 1965, ECKANKAR is now an international organization headquartered in Minneapolis, Minnesota, with tens of thousands of members. Paul Twitchell asserted that in 1956 he experienced "God-realization" when he was initiated by a group of spiritual masters known as the Order of the Vairagi Masters who live and work on a spiritual plane linked to the mystic East. Twitchell claimed that he was assigned the role of 971st Living Eck Master by these higher spiritual beings.

Twitchell officially organized and incorporated ECKANKAR in 1965, soon afterwards moving its headquarters to Las Vegas, Nevada. For the next few years he wrote and published several key books of ECKANKAR theology. Paul Twitchell died unexpectedly in 1971. His wife, Gail, together with the board of ECKANKAR, chose his successor as 972nd Living Eck Master—Darwin Gross. Gross and Gail Twitchell married shortly afterwards. Under this leadership ECKANKAR grew and flourished. Its new headquarters was established at Menlo Park, California. Gross was succeeded as 973rd Living Eck Master by Harold Klemp.

A spiritual vision led Klemp and his right-hand man Peter Skelskey to move the headquarters of ECKANKAR to a suburb of Minneapolis, Minnesota, where a multimillion-dollar world Temple of Eck was built in the late 1980s. Under Klemp and Skelskey ECKANKAR has continued to grow and change.

ECKANKAR is "the ancient science of soul travel" and "the religion of the light and sound of God." Its basic cosmology is similar to that of the Radhasoami tradition of India that teaches initiates to hear divine sounds, see divine lights, and taste divine tastes. These basic techniques have been blended with Rosicrucian and Theosophical tendencies as well.

ECKANKAR teaches that God is Sugmad—an impersonal source of all being. Everything that exists is an emanation of this divine spirit. More attention is given to Eck than to God, however. Eck is "soul," a spiritual energy and life force in all things that emanates from Sugmad. It has various levels and on these levels takes different forms, including various intelligences. Eck can be sensed through chanting the mantra "hu," a special name for God in ECKANKAR. Chanting "hu" is ECKANKAR's central sacrament and it is alleged to bring one spiritual self-realization or God-realization and to burn off karmic debt.

ECKANKAR has studiously avoided controversy in the media. The only controversial time was during the initial phase of moving its headquarters and building its Temple of Eck in Minnesota. Some citizens of the city of Chanhassen attempted to prevent the city council from permitting it. Articles appeared in the Twin Cities press, the first time most people outside of California had heard of ECKANKAR.

Elan Vital (Divine Light Mission)

Elan Vital grew out of Sant Mat (literally, the way of the saints), a nineteenth-century spiritual tradition that developed in northern India. One of the goals of the movement was the instruction of the world in a type of yogic meditation technique that was said to connect the devotee to the universal primordial force that pervades everything through meditation on the Holy Name (Word) and on the Divine Light.

The Divine Light Mission was founded by Shri Hans Maharaj Ji. Upon his death in 1966, he was succeeded by his youngest son, Prem Pal Singh Rawat, who was initiated at the age of six and who, two years later, was recognized as the new "perfect master," an embodiment of God on earth and hence an object of worship and veneration, assuming the title of Maharaj Ji. When his father died, he was commissioned as the one to take the "knowledge" to the world. Although he became officially the autocratic leader of the mission, his whole family shared the authority because of his young age.

In 1971, Maharaj Ji made his first visit to the West, after having been invited by some Americans who became initiates while in India searching for spiritual guidance. Against his mother's wishes he went to Colorado, where a large crowd heard his first set of discourses given in America. A considerable number of people were initiated, and the American headquarters of the mission was established in Denver. By the end of 1973 several hundred centers as well as over twenty ashrams had emerged, and two periodicals, *And It Is Divine* and *Divine Times,* were begun. In November 1973, the mission suffered a major reverse because of the failure of

"Millennium '73," an event organized to celebrate the birthday of Maharaj Ji's father and the beginning of a thousand years of peace and prosperity. The event had been scheduled to take place at the Houston Astrodome, and all of the group's resources were poured into the event. When the anticipated large crowds of people failed to materialize, deep debt effectively crippled the group.

After the Millenium '73 fiasco, the mission gradually withdrew from the public scene. Many followers left the movement and many ashrams were discontinued. A number of ex-members became critics of the movement, attacking it with charges of brainwashing and mind control. Maharaj Ji himself was described by the anticultists as immature and unfit to be a religious leader, and his teachings were condemned as lacking in substance.

The movement also suffered from internal problems within Maharaj Ji's family. Mataji, Maharaj Ji's mother, disapproved of his lifestyle and of his marriage to his secretary Marolyn Johnson, whom he declared to be the incarnation of the goddess Durga. After accusing her son of breaking his spiritual disciplines, she took control of the mission in India by replacing him with his oldest brother. In 1975 Maharaj Ji took his family to court. He received control of the movement everywhere but in India, where his brother remained the leader. By the end of the 1970s, an estimated 80 percent of the followers had left the mission. In the early 1980s Maharaj Ji ordered all of the ashrams disbanded; he was no longer to be venerated as God. When the Divine Light Mission was disbanded, the organization Elan Vital was created in order to relate Maharaj Ji to his students on a one-to-one basis and to support his travels in 34 countries worldwide.

Erhard Seminars Training (est)/The Forum

Erhard Seminars Training, more commonly known as est, was begun in 1971 by Werner Erhard. While not a church or religion, est is included here because it has often been accused of being a cult.

In November 1970 Werner Erhard, born John Paul "Jack" Rosenberg, enrolled in a two-weekend course called Mind Dynamics. Mind Dynamics featured demonstrations and training in memory feats, enhancement of psychic powers, ESP, precognition, psychic diagnosis, and healing. Erhard was so impressed with Mind Dynamics that he immediately signed up to take instructor training. After a short time, he began to feel restricted by the confines of the Mind Dynamics program and set up a program of his own. Erhard Seminars Training (est) was incorporated as a profit-making educational corporation. The training was aimed at the broad public with the fee initially set at $150 for a two-weekend course. Within three years he had sold $3.4 million of est training sessions.

Est was known for its intensive, two-weekend workshops that promote communications skills and self-empowerment. The purpose of est was to transform one's ability to experience living so that the situations one had been trying to change or had been putting up with clear up in the process of life itself. The first two hours of est training were devoted to the rules: No one could move from his seat unless told to do so. No smoking, eating, or drinking were allowed in the room. One meal break was scheduled during the day. Students were commonly called "assholes" during the training.

Along with its success, est generated inevitable controversy. In 1977, two articles appeared in the *American Journal of Psychiatry* that described five patients who had developed psychotic symptoms, including paranoia, uncontrollable mood swings, and delusions, in the wake of taking the est training. Claiming psychological damage, several suits were filed against est by trainees and their families.

In 1978 Erhard vowed to end hunger in two decades and started the Hunger Project. The project was accused by *Mother Jones* magazine of collecting several million dollars and donating only a few thousand dollars to a San Francisco church that operated a soup kitchen at Christmas and to OXFAM, a prominent hunger organization. The author of the article concluded that Erhard was using the Hunger Project for self-aggrandizement and for promoting est, a profit-making corporation. In late 1990 Erhard formally broke all ties to the Hunger Project.

The name of the movement was changed to the Forum in 1985. The Forum runs self-awareness seminars, advanced courses, a program for those interested in becoming Forum leaders themselves, a Sales Course, and a More Time Workshop. In January 1991 Erhard sold the assets of Werner Erhard & Associates to his brother Harry Rosenberg and other employees.

On March 3, 1991, CBS aired a segment of "60 Minutes" that accused Erhard of beating his wife and children and raping his daughters. Subsequently, Erhard filed a lawsuit against CBS, claiming that the broadcast contained false, misleading, and defamatory statements. The lawsuit was dropped before a court decision was reached. Erhard left the United States in 1991, beginning a self-imposed exile. Meanwhile, the Forum has once again become one of the most successful programs of its kind.

The Family (Children of God)

The Family is the successor organization to the Children of God, a Christian group founded by David Brandt Berg (known to followers as Father David). Berg was a former minister in the Christian and Missionary Alliance Church, a conservative denomination, in which his mother was an evangelist. In 1967 Berg was informed by his mother about the increasing number of hippies in Huntington Beach, California. He moved there, taking over work previously begun by Teen Challenge, a youth Pentecostal ministry, which centered upon the Light Club Mission, a coffeehouse near the Huntington Beach pier.

Berg's critical attitudes toward many establishment structures, including the organized church, and his messages oriented to a total commitment to a Jesus revolution, attracted the attention of a number of street people, many of whom gave up drugs and began to live communally, calling themselves Teens for Christ. In 1969, after Berg received a revelation that the group should leave California because it was threatened by an earthquake, he and his followers moved to Tucson, Arizona.

Berg began to be referred to as Moses, after one of the members claimed to have had a revelation, and by February 1970 the members of the group started to call themselves "Moses and the Children of God." They moved to a ranch near Thurber, Texas. While there, William Rambur, a parent of a member of the group, organized Parents Committee to Free Our Sons and Daughters from the Children of God (FREECOG). Accusing the group of keeping members under drug-induced and hypnotic control, these parents, with the help of Theodore Patrick, initiated the practice of deprogramming—physically kidnapping members of the group and forcing them to renounce their fidelity to it.

By the middle of the decade, most of the Children had emigrated, spurred in part by Berg's warning of the destructive potential of Comet Kohoutek. Berg continued to exercise his leadership through a series of Mo Letters that guided the evolving organization and doctrine of the group, some sold on the street in order to spread the group's message and others internal documents.

Berg continued to exercise the role of a prophet, whose prophecies, which were increasingly seen as coming from spirit entities, assumed a fundamental role in supporting the ideas of the group. To the radical ideas about sexual freedom was added the most controversial practice of the group, "flirty fishing." This practice was introduced by Berg through a Mo Letter in the beginning of 1974, in which he ordered the women of the group to use their natural sexual appeal and talents to gain new members, to become Christ's fish bait—"hookers for Jesus." This practice was eventually abandoned but not before it had attracted extensive, negative media attention.

The image of the Children of God eventually became extremely negative. Berg decided to change the organization of the group and adopted the use of a family model, asking the followers to call him Dad and giving the Children the name Family of Love. World Services, which functions as a de facto headquarters, at least for the dispensing of literature, is located in Switzerland. Berg died in 1994.

The Family counts about 7,000 to 10,000 members widely dispersed around the world. For most of the past several decades, only a few hundred members have resided in the United States, where they were occasionally seen on the streets distributing literature. This situation began to change in the early 1990s, when members began returning to America in large numbers. They were subjected to a new wave of intensive negative media attention in the summer of 1993, following raids on their homes in France and Argentina on charges of child abuse. Although eventually exonerated of all charges, the sex cult image created by decades of negative media coverage remains largely unchallenged in the public consciousness.

Heaven's Gate

Marshall Herff Applewhite ("Bo," "Do") and Bonnie Lu Nettles ("Peep," "Ti") founded one of the most unusual flying-saucer religions ever to emerge out of the occult-metaphysical subculture. The Two, as they were sometimes called, met in 1972. In 1973, they had an experience that convinced them that they were the two witnesses mentioned in Revelation 11. Preaching an unusual synthesis of occult spirituality and UFO ideology, they began recruiting in New Age circles in the spring of 1975. Followers were required to abandon friends and family, detach themselves completely from human emotions as well as material possessions, and focus exclusively on perfecting themselves in preparation for a physical transition (i.e., beaming up) to the next kingdom (in the form of a flying saucer)—a metamorphosis that would be facilitated by ufonauts.

In the early phase of their movement, Applewhite and Nettles taught that the goal of the process they were teaching their followers was to prepare them to be physically taken aboard the spacecraft where they would enter a cocoonlike state, eventually being reborn in a transformed physical body. The notion of resurrection is central to Chapter 11 of the Book of Revelation, the biblical passage Applewhite and Nettles came to view as describing their particular ministry. In the early phase of their movement, Applewhite and Nettles prophesied that they would soon be assassinated. They further predicted that they would be resurrected three-and-a-half days later and taken up into a flying saucer. The Two asserted that this event would prove the truth of their teachings. They taught that heaven was the literal, physical heavens, and those few people chosen to depart with the Two would, after their physical transformation, become crew members aboard UFOs.

For followers of the Two, the focus of day-to-day existence was to follow a disciplined regime referred to as the overcoming process or, simply, the process. The goal of this process was to overcome human weaknesses—a goal not dissimilar to the goal of certain spiritual practices followed by more mainstream monastic communities. For Applewhite, however, it appears that stamping out one's sexuality was the core issue.

Details about how the group came to attach apocalyptic significance to the Hale-Bopp Comet are tantalizingly scanty. Someone outside the group had come to the conclusion that a giant UFO was coming to earth, "hidden" in the wake of Hale-Bopp. This individual then placed his opinion on the Internet. When Heaven's Gate retrieved this information, Applewhite took it as an indication that the long awaited pick-up of his group by aliens was finally about to take place. The decision that the time had come to make their final exit could not have been made more than a few weeks before the mass suicide.

The idea that the group might depart via suicide had emerged in Applewhite's thinking only within the last few years. The earlier idea—an idea that had set Heaven's Gate apart from everyone else—was that the group of individuals selected to move to the next level would bodily ascend to the saucers in a kind of technological rapture. Applewhite may have begun to rethink his theology after his partner died because, in order to be reunited with Nettles, her spirit would have to acquire a new body aboard the spacecraft. While the death of Nettles may or may not have been the decisive influence, he later adopted the view that Heaven's Gate members would ascend together spiritually rather than physically.

"I Am" Religious Activity

The "I Am" Religious Activity is a popularized form of Theosophy, reformulated to appeal to a broader audience than earlier theosophical organizations. The founder of the movement was Guy Ballard (1878–1939), who was born in Kansas. He had long been interested in occultism and had studied theosophical teachings. He married Edna Wheeler (1886–1971) in 1916; three years later their son Donald was born.

This group teaches that humanity began in America and that this is the seventh and last cycle of history, under the Lord of the Seventh Ray, Saint Germain. The history of this epoch will also end in America, which will be the vessel of light to bring the world into new and paradisal times.

These revelations were spread during the lectures of the three Ballards, who traveled in the 1930s as Accredited Messengers of the Masters. Further messages from the Ascended Masters, especially from Saint Germain and the Master Jesus, were sometimes produced in public or private. The main teaching is that the Mighty "I Am" Presence is God-in-action, which is immediately available. It is also said that one's individualized Presence is a pure reservoir of energy, from which power can be drawn at will.

Saint Germain and Jesus are considered the mediators between the "I Am" Presence and humans. The Ascended Masters were at one time all human beings who became able to transcend the physical world through purification of their lives. The goal of human life is represented by ascension.

The "I Am" Activity worked publicly from 1937 to 1940 to establish a group of devoted followers numbering over one million. With the death of Guy Ballard on December 29, 1939, the movement began to decline. Edna Ballard claimed that her husband had become an Ascended Master. However, the fact that Guy Ballard had experienced a physical death rather than bodily ascension threatened the movement's credibility. The following year a sensational trial of the leaders of the movement took place, after some members of Ballard's personal staff accused the Ballards of obtaining money under fraudulent pretenses. The indictment was voided in 1944 by the Supreme Court with a landmark decision on religious liberty. The case was finally dismissed after Justice Douglas, in the majority opinion, asserted, "Men may believe what they cannot prove. They may not be put to the proof of their religious doctrines or beliefs."

The "I Am" Activity experienced a new growth in the 1980s and is still active today in a number of cities, where it has temples, reading rooms, and radio programs. The "I Am" Activity was directed by Edna Ballard until her death in 1971. The current board of directors is formed by Gerald Craig and his wife, who are the

Appointed Messengers; Mt. Shasta is a major center. Every summer, in an amphitheater on the spotless grounds of the Saint Germain Foundation, the "I Am" Activity of the Saint Germain Foundation stages a pageant on the life of the "beloved master Jesus." In this version, the crucifixion is left out, whereas the ascension is what is believed to be important.

International Society for Krishna Consciousness (ISKCON; The Hare Krishna Movement)

The International Society for Krishna Consciousness (ISKCON), better known as the Hare Krishna movement, is a transplanted form of conservative Hinduism, representing one of the most conspicuous religious groups in America since the 1960s. It is characterized by a rigorous interpretation of the Krishna devotional tradition, and its followers, who practice ecstatic worship and close-knit communalism, are usually noticeable for wearing their orange or white robes.

Sri Srimad Bhakti Siddhanta Goswami was the guru of A. C. Bhaktivedanta Swami Prabhupada, born Abhay Charan De (1896–1977), the founder of the International Society for Krishna Consciousness. Asked by the Swami to write about Krishna Consciousness in English, he wrote a commentary on the *Bhagavad-Gita*. The Swami gave him a charge to carry Krishna consciousness to the West, a charge that he did not take seriously until after he retired in 1950.

In 1965, at the age of 70, he left for the United States. He began his missionary work in New York City on the Lower East Side, where he was chosen by a few hippies as their guru. Within a short time a center had been opened and the movement started to grow. Another center was opened in San Francisco in 1967.

Meanwhile, Swami Prabhupada continued to write and translate, working on the *Srimad-Bhagavatam* and on the *Caitanya-Caritamrta*. In 1968 a copy of his translation of the *Bhagavad-Gita, As It Is*, appeared. By 1972 over 60 400-page volumes of his work had been published by the Bhaktivedanta Book Trust. When Swami Prabhupada died in 1977, the 22-person Governing Board Commission, which included eleven people empowered to initiate new disciples, began to lead the international movement. Many senior disciples of Shrila Prabhupada were dissatisfied with the new leadership. By the mid 1980s, this internal dissatisfaction had evoked a reform movement that, eventually, overturned the guru system, resulting in the decentralization of spiritual authority within ISKCON.

Although the movement has maintained a high profile in American life, it has frequently been attacked for threatening common family patterns, with its ascetic, communal, and separatist lifestyle. Members of the movement were early the target of deprogramming, such as the one of Ed Shapiro by Ted Patrick in the early 1970s. Other anticult activities included arousing of public opinion against the group, imposing of some restrictions on the group's public soliciting at airports, and efforts to require building permits for the establishment of Krishna temples and parade permits.

Beginning in the mid 1970s, a number of Krishnas were arrested for soliciting without permit in Santa Claus outfits, although the Krishnas do not celebrate Christmas. In spite of their pacifist stance, they were reported to be stockpiling weapons. These accusations seemed to have substance when the local guru in the San Francisco Bay area was discovered to have a car trunk full of guns. He was severely disciplined by the society, who renounced him.

Despite attacks from anticult groups and the media, the society has received praise from religious scholars, such as J. Stillson Judah, Harvey Cox, Larry Shinn, and Thomas Hopkins, who praised Swami Prabhupada's translations and defended the group against distorted media images and anticult misrepresentations. The American Academy of Religion also welcomed various members of the society.

Jesus People USA

Jesus People USA (also known as JPUSA, pronounced Je-POO-sa) is an evangelical Christian communitarian group centered in Chicago. Originating within the Jesus movement of the early 1970s, the group has continued to play a dynamic role in Christian youth and alternative/underground cultures through its music, magazine, Jesus festivals, and lifestyle; the group also maintains a sizable inner city ministry.

Jesus People USA began as part of Jesus People Milwaukee, a communal Jesus People group founded by Jim Palosaari in 1971. The following year this original group temporarily divided into three ministries: Jesus People Europe, led by Palosaari, which traveled to Europe to do youth ministry abroad; Jesus People USA, led by John and Dawn Herrin, which traveled in the United States; and the original Milwaukee commune. The proposed reunion never occurred, however; the Milwaukee commune disbanded and Jesus People Europe returned to the United States to form the basis for the Highway Missionaries and, later, the Servant Community (both now disbanded).

The U.S. branch, after traveling to Florida and back, eventually settled in Chicago where members continued carrying out youth revivals, sponsoring a Christian rock group called the Rez Band, doing street theater and mime work, and publishing a well-produced street paper, *Cornerstone*. During the mid 1970s the community went through a number of changes. Several business ventures were started, including moving, painting, contracting, roofing, music recording, and graphics. Founder John Herrin was ejected from the group and plurality of leadership instituted in the form of a council of elders assisted by Dawn Herrin, the ex-wife of the former leader. In addition, the community merged with a communal African American Bible study group, resulting in an interracial presence often lacking in other Jesus People groups.

JPUSA affirms the existence and practice of the supernatural "gifts of the spirit," such as healing and speaking in tongues, though within the group these gifts tend to be employed privately rather than publicly. In spite of seemingly exclusivist theological beliefs, the group admits a certain latitude by affirming the spiritual unity of all true believers in Christ. Christian humanist strains are also present due to the community's encouragement of both individual and collective forms of musical, literary, and visual artistic expression.

Within the recent past, former members of the community have begun to hold annual reunions. Some individuals do not recall their time in the community and/or their departure with favor. Some have accused the group's leaders of excessive control of individuals, mismanagement, and nepotism. Others have complained that long-time members who choose to leave should be financially compensated for their time and effort spent on behalf of the community. Many of these complaints were publicized in *Recovering from Churches That Abuse*. The Jesus People USA community has responded by opening their community to even greater public scrutiny, including making public the correspondence dealing with the allegations. The community also published a double issue of its magazine examining the book's claims.

Kashi Church Foundation

The Kashi Church Foundation began in 1976 with the establishment of the Kashi Ashram, located near Sabastian, Florida, by a group of people that had emerged around a young spiritual teacher, Jaya Sati Bhagavati Ma. Ma, born Joyce Green, was formerly a housewife in Brooklyn, New York. Her life began to change radically, however, in December 1972, when she had a vision of someone she, though Jewish, recognized as Jesus Christ. He would reappear three more times. She turned for guidance to residents of a nearby Jesuit seminary who offered her both sympathy and understanding. Then in the spring of 1973 she had a second set of visions, this time of a person who called himself Nityananda. He appeared to her almost daily for a year to teach her.

At the time Nityananda appeared, she had no knowledge that such a person had actually lived in India, had begun a movement then headed by Swami Muktananda, and had a disciple named Swami Rudrananda who initially brought his teachings to America. Nityananda, as he appeared to her, taught her about what he termed *chidakash*, the state in which love and awareness are one. He gave her a new name, *Jaya* (Sanskrit for victory or glory), and mentioned a woman named Hilda. Green, who began to call herself Joya Santanya, soon found Swami Rudrananda and a short time later was led to Hilda Charlton, an independent spiritual teacher in Manhattan who encouraged her to become a teacher.

Through the mid 1970s, Joya Santanya's teaching activity led to the founding of thirteen small communities where people lived cooperatively and gathered for daily meditation. In July 1976 she moved to Florida where land was purchased and Kashi Ashram was established.

Kashi is an eclectic community tied together by the residents' acceptance of Ma as their guru. The dominant teaching is a form of Adavaita Vedanta, a worldview derived from the Vedas and the Upanishads, popular Hindu scriptures. Residents at Kashi come from very different backgrounds and have varying attachments to the religions in which they grew up. The individual's devotion to a particular religion is both recognized and nurtured at Kashi and shrines have been built to honor the major religions.

Through the 1990s Ma became best known for her ministry to HIV-positive people, especially those who had been unable to find basic support from their family or help from government and church-related facilities. Beginning with a small ministry in Los Angeles and southern Florida, the AIDS-related work has become a major aspect of ashram life.

The community is organized on a semicommunal basis. Each adult member is responsible for an equal share of the budget, which is adopted by community consensus. That money covers the residents' room and board, the operation of the school, and the upkeep of the ashram grounds. Thus all of the members, except for the few who work at the ashram, have outside jobs. The diet is vegetarian with small quantities of fish and milk. No narcotics, alcohol, or tobacco is to be consumed. Chastity is practiced except for married couples to conceive.

The Local Church

The Local Church, which is also known as the Little Flock or the Assembly Hall movement, was the target of one of the most intense battles in the cult controversy of the early 1980s. The controversy originated from differences of theological language and particular practices unique to the Local Church, although it claimed to be an orthodox evangelical Christian body of believers.

The Local Church was founded in the 1920s in China by Ni Shutsu (1903–1972), who is popularly known by the English translation of his name, Watchman Nee. Nee's movement, which had a modest beginning in Foochow, spread through China, with the foundation of congregations based upon the idea that there should be only one local church in each city as the basic expression of the unity of Christianity. He was the author of more than 50 books, which were mostly about Christian life and church life. The most important of them are *The Normal Christian Church Life* and *The Spiritual Man*, in which he explained his conception of the tripartite nature of human beings as body, soul, and spirit.

Nee was accused by the new People's Republic of China of being a spy for the Americans and the Nationalist government and was exiled from Shanghai and then imprisoned in 1952. He died in prison in 1972. During the 1930s, Nee was joined by Witness Lee, a former Protestant minister, who became within a few years one of Nee's most valuable assistants. He was sent by Nee to Taiwan, where the church was to flourish and spread around the Pacific basin.

The movement was brought to the West Coast by members migrating to the United States. Lee himself moved to the United States in 1962, where he founded Living Stream Ministry. Lee has been a source for innovation in the movement through his introduction of various theological emphases and his initiation of a number of practices such as "pray reading," a devotional practice that uses the words of Scripture as the words of prayer, and "calling upon the name of the Lord," an invocation of God by the repetition of phrases such as "O Lord Jesus." These practices have become the subject of controversy.

Much of the controversy between the Local Church and evangelical Christians who perceived Lee's theological innovations as departing from acceptable evangelical thought began in the early 1970s, when the church in Berkeley was housed in a building across the street from the World Christian Liberation Front, with which the church had several emotionally charged encounters. The controversy resulted in the split of the WCLF into two groups, each of which published a book charging Lee with heresy and suggesting that Lee denied the traditional doctrine of the Trinity. Both books also associated the Local Church with a variety of cultic practices, and one of them accused Lee of mismanagement of church funds and of being the source of psychological damage to members. Lee and many of the congregations filed lawsuits against the publishers of the two books, who apologized to the church. Since then, the Local Church has returned to a noncontroversial existence.

Maranatha Christian Churches

Maranatha Christian Churches began in 1972 as a campus ministry under the direction of Bob Weiner, formerly a youth pastor for the Assemblies of God, and his wife, Rose Weiner. Bob Weiner dropped out of the Evangelical Free Church's Trinity College at Deerfield, Illinois, and joined the U.S. Air Force. While in the Air Force he encountered Albie Pearson, a former baseball player turned evangelist-pastor, and received baptism. Following his discharge from the air force, Weiner joined with Bob Cording to form Sound Mind, Inc., to evangelize youth. In 1971 he began to tour college campuses as an evangelist. As a campus minister, Weiner sought to convert students and train them in the fundamentals of the Christian faith.

In 1972 he moved to Paducah, Kentucky, where his wife's father was minister in the United Methodist Church, and began a campus ministry at Murray State University. While focusing on Murray State, he continued to travel as an evangelist and develop other ministries. By 1980 Weiner had established 30 Maranatha Campus Ministries. As members graduated from college, Maranatha Campus Ministries became part of the larger work, which was named Maranatha Christian Churches. In Maranatha's early years, each center had a dorm in which converts could live while attending college. Maranatha's work is still focused in the campus ministry and all of the congregations are adjacent to a college or university.

During the early 1980s, a variety of accusations were made against Maranatha Campus Ministries concerning their intense program for training new members. Many of these accusations proved to be unfounded. In other cases program adjustments were made that have addressed many of the criticisms. A program of parent-student contact was broadly implemented that reduced the problems that had arisen because of lack of knowledge by parents of Maranatha and the life shared by its new student members.

General meetings of the fellowship are held weekly and most members also participate in small group fellowships. Maranatha Christian Churches are Pentecostal in doctrine. Prophecy is an important practice and is seen as ongoing confirmation of God's present activity in the church. Bob and Rose Weiner have written a series of books published by Maranatha Publications that are used as textbooks in the discipleship training work.

Maranatha Leadership Institute in Gainesville, Florida, offers more advanced training for people on a national basis. It often features a variety of charismatic leaders not otherwise associated with Maranatha. A world leadership conference is held every two years. In 1985, Maranatha began a satellite TV network show as a televised prayer meeting in which 60 churches tied together for the broadcast to pray for specific requests phoned in by viewers. There are 7,000 members worldwide and 150 churches in the United States.

Moksha Foundation

Andrew Cohen created this group in the late 1980s after a series of contacts with masters in oriental disciplines. When he was sixteen he began his search for an explanation of the expansion of consciousness he had undergone. His meeting with Swami Hariharananda Giri led him to the practice of martial arts and Zen meditation. More importantly for Cohen was his meeting in India with Harivansh Lal Poonja, who taught him the importance of realizing the spiritual freedom that everybody possesses. Poonja's message was an illumination for Cohen.

He began teaching in India and then in England, the Netherlands, and Israel. In 1988 he returned to the United States and established a group in Cambridge, Massachusetts. A year later he moved to Marin County, California, to join a communal group founded by some of his followers. During his teaching activity Cohen developed a different point of view from that of his original master, Poonja, and believed that individuals can express the Enlightenment in their lives. He concluded that his teachings had surpassed his master's and has since followed his own beliefs.

After years of quiet development, the Moksha Foundation was recently thrust into the public spotlight. For many years, Cohen has asserted that people in the spiritual subculture should not turn a blind eye to the moral and other failings of spiritual teachers, that a high state of spiritual development does not exempt them from ordinary morality. When Cohen's mother turned on her son and wrote a negative book accusing Cohen of being an egotistical guru who controlled his students, many other spiritual teachers affected by his critique were eager to accept these accusations as true. The Moksha Foundation has also been in the press as the result of actor Linus Roach joining the group.

Movement of Spiritual Inner Awareness

The Movement of Spiritual Inner Awareness (MSIA) is a contemporary religious movement that was founded by John-Roger Hinkins in 1971. While MSIA has often been characterized as New Age, and while it participates in the larger metaphysical subculture, MSIA's core spiritual practices lie squarely in the Sant Mat (Radhasoami) tradition. In 1963, while undergoing surgery for a kidney stone, Roger Hinkins fell into a nine-day coma. Upon awakening, he found himself aware of a new spiritual personality— "John"—who had superseded or merged with his old personality. After the operation, Hinkins began to refer to himself as John-Roger, in recognition of his transformed self.

In common with Sant Mat groups, MSIA pictures the cosmos as composed of many different levels or planes. At the point of creation, these levels sequentially emerged from God along a vibratory stream until creation reached its terminus in the physical plane. The Sant Mat tradition teaches that individuals can be linked to God's creative energy and that this stream of energy will carry their consciousness back to God. The Mystical Traveler Consciousness—which formerly manifested through John-Roger (it has since been anchored in John Morton, his spiritual successor)—accomplished this linkup during initiation, although the individual still had to appropriate and utilize the link through the practice of special meditation techniques (referred to as spiritual exercises), particularly meditation on the mantra Hu.

As a low-intensity group that does not make excessive demands upon either the time or the resources of most members, MSIA had largely escaped the attention of anticult movement until the late 1980s. In 1988, the *Los Angeles Times* published a highly critical article on MSIA. A similar article appeared in *People* magazine. Both pieces dwelt on charges by ex–staff members that Hinkins had sexually exploited them. Depending upon the testimony of disgruntled ex-members and drawing heavily on the cult stereotype, MSIA was portrayed as an organization that was created for no other purpose than to serve the financial, sexual, and ego needs of John-Roger Hinkins. After a brief moment in the spotlight, reporters turned their attention to other stories.

Two events occurred in 1994 that once again brought MSIA to the attention of the media. First was Michael Huffington's campaign to become a California senator. Arianna Huffington, Michael Huffington's wife, is a member of MSIA. When someone in the media discovered this fact, the link became a focus of a number of articles in which all of the earlier accusations against John-Roger and MSIA were uncritically repeated. In the same year as the campaign, Peter McWilliams, an MSIA minister who had coauthored a series of popular books with John-Roger, dropped out of the movement and authored a bitter anti-MSIA book, *LIFE 102: What To Do When Your Guru Sues You*, which attracted some media attention.

Northeast Kingdom Community/ Messianic Communities

The Messianic Communities, also known as the Northeast Kingdom Community Church, is a communal, utopian society that emerged from the Jesus People revival in 1972 under the leadership of Elbert Eugene ("Gene") Spriggs, whom community members consider an apostle, and his wife, Marsha, in Chattanooga, Tennessee. Members adopt Hebrew names and consider themselves as part of the Commonwealth of Israel forming in the last days, bound by the New Covenant in Messiah's Blood, as mentioned in Ephesians 2:12. The communities have evolved into a distinct culture emphasizing craftsmanship and handiwork; they have evolved their own devotional music and dance forms and unique, neoconservative patterns of marriage and childrearing. The group condemns abortion and homosexuality and upholds monogamy, premarital chastity, and home schooling.

The belief system is similar to evangelical Protestantism but contains certain theological differences in views on communal living, marriage, and eschatology. Ongoing collective revelations continue to reveal to the community its role in postmillenialist last days, its relationship to Yahshua, and levels of salvation after judgment. The communities define themselves as the lost and scattered tribes of the ancient Jews undergoing restoration in preparation for eternal life. They believe their community is undergoing a process of purification as the "pure and spotless bride awaiting her bridegroom" and that it will probably take three generations to be ready for the Second Coming. By increasing their ranks through conversions and childbearing, they are "raising up a people" in preparation for the Jubilee horn that heralds the return of Yahshua.

Church members have been the target of deprogrammers ever since the founding of communes in Chattanooga, but the most severe and widely publicized conflicts with secular authorities have involved child-beating allegations and child custody disputes. In 1984 the Vermont state police, armed with a court order and accompanied by 50 social services workers, raided the Island Pond Community homes and took 112 children into custody. District Judge Frank Mahady ruled that the search warrant issued by the state was unconstitutional, and all the children were returned to their parents without undergoing examinations. Child custody disputes and investigations by social services continue, partly due to the influence of the anticult movement and disillusioned apostates. The group's commitment to their biblically based disciplinary practices are the primary focus of concern. Parents are instructed to discipline children who do not obey upon "first command" with a thin, flexible "reed-like" rod (as mentioned in Proverbs 23:13) so as to inflict pain but not injury.

Since their "deliverance" from the raid the group has emphasized cooperation with state authorities and has reached out to neighbors in trying to foster a better understanding. In August 1993 the Island Pond members joined search parties to find the missing pilot whose plane had crashed in Essex County. On June 25, 1994, the church held a ten-year anniversary celebration "to commemorate [our] deliverance from the 1984 Island Pond Raid." Many of those 112 children, now in their teens and twenties, shared their traumatic memories of the raid, denied allegations of abuse, and declared their allegiance toward their parents and their community.

Osho (Rajneesh) Foundation International

Bhagwan Rajneesh (1931–1990), founder of the Rajneesh Foundation International and the Osho Commune International, was born Rajneesh Chandra Mohan in Kuchwada, India. On March 21, 1953, during his early college days, he announced an experience of *samadhi*, or enlightenment. He went on to receive his M.A. in philosophy in 1957 and took a professorship at Jabalpur University. Over the following years the tensions between his work as scholar and his position as unorthodox spiritual teacher became too great and he resigned from the university in 1966.

In 1970 he founded a congregation in Bombay and the next year adopted the title Bhagwan, or God. He intended this to signify his method of direct, soul-to-soul teaching, rather than an intellectualized experience. In 1974 his following had grown sufficiently to support the purchase of six acres in Poona, which became his headquarters. Drawing from sources as diverse as humanistic psychology and Sufism, he believed that releasing emotions and developing self-expression in freedom were key elements in the process toward enlightenment. He taught "dynamic meditation," which activated the body through various means, including regulated breathing, chanting, and screaming. He encouraged indulgence in sex as liberating and consciousness-raising. Initiates took vows, not to renounce life, but to embrace it with abandon.

His following became almost entirely European and American as Indians abandoned his teachings as immoral. Rajneesh moved to the United States in 1981 to a 64,000-acre ranch near Antelope, Oregon. As his unusual teachings and lavish lifestyle (93 Rolls-Royces) became known in the area, and particularly after he proposed building a communal village to be called Rajneeshpuram, opposition became as intense in Oregon as in India. In 1985 he was charged with immigration fraud and deported back to India, where he reactivated the Poona compound. In 1988 he dropped "Bhagwan" from his name in favor of "Osho," meaning "one upon whom the heavens shower flowers," and the organization was renamed Osho Commune International. On January 19, 1990, he died suddenly without having appointed a successor. The organization continues under the leadership of some of his close disciples.

Peoples Temple

Born in east-central Indiana on May 13, 1931, James Warren Jones married Marceline Baldwin in 1949, moved to Indianapolis in 1951, and soon became a self-taught preacher who promoted racial integration and a veiled communist philosophy within a Pentecostal framework that emphasized faith healing.

Organizationally, Peoples Temple began as a small church. Jones increasingly modeled the organization after the Peace Mission of America black preacher Father M. J. Divine. Combining the Pentecostal ethic of a caring community with the social gospel of liberal denominations, the temple established care homes for the elderly, ran a free restaurant to feed the hungry, and maintained a social service center for the down-and-out. In 1960, the unconventional congregation became affiliated with the Christian Church (Disciples of Christ), which long had been committed to a social ministry.

In 1964, tired of racial intolerance and citing fears of nuclear holocaust, the group moved to the quiet northern California town of Ukiah. By the early 1970s the temple was operating churches in

San Francisco and Los Angeles. In comparison to both conventional churches and retreatist countercultural communal groups of its day, Peoples Temple was an anomaly—a relatively disciplined, religiously and politically radical collective. By 1975 Peoples Temple was a formidable force in the left-liberal political surge in San Francisco, and the temple began to reap political rewards.

During 1972 and 1973 Jones used internal defections and small incidents of external persecution as the warrant to establish Peoples Temple's "Promised Land"—an "agricultural mission" eventually called Jonestown—in a remote corner of Guyana, an ethnically diverse, socialist-governed South American country bordering the Caribbean. In the summer of 1977 Jones finally ordered the collective migration for which the temple had begun preparing four years earlier. At the time, it was widely believed that they left California because of press criticism, in which opponents raised the key issue of custody over children in Peoples Temple.

In November 1978, Congressman Leo Ryan, a group of concerned relatives, and journalists flew to the capital of Guyana, Georgetown. At Jonestown, on the evening of November 17, 1978, Jonestown offered the visitors an orchestrated welcome. But during the festivities a note was passed to a reporter by community members who wanted to leave. The next day, at the Port Kaituma airstrip, as the travelers started loading two planes, a Jonestown man posing as a defector pulled out a pistol in the smaller plane and started shooting. Simultaneously, a tractor came up pulling a flatbed; from it the Jonestown sharpshooters shot toward the other plane. Left dead were Congressman Leo Ryan, three newsmen, and defector Patricia Parks.

At Jonestown, Jim Jones told the assembled community that they would no longer be able to survive as a community. With a tape recorder running, Jones argued, "If we can't live in peace, then let's die in peace." One woman spoke against the plan, but others argued in favor. Amidst low wails, sobbing, and the shrieks of children, people walked up to take the "potion" laced with cyanide, then moved out of the pavilion to huddle with their families and die.

Raelian Movement International

The Raelian movement was founded in 1973 by a French racing car driver and journalist, Claude Vorilhon (Rael to his followers), who was born in 1946 in Vichy, France. The movement began, according to Rael, with his encounter with extraterrestrials during a walking tour of the Clermont-Ferrand volcanic mountains in France. These beings, whom Rael describes in his book *Space Aliens Took Me to Their Planet*, entrusted him with a message for humanity. This message concerns the true identity of human beings: humans were "implanted" on earth by a team of extraterrestrial scientists, the "Elohim," who created humans from their own DNA in laboratories. Rael's mission is to warn humankind that since 1945 and Hiroshima, we have entered the "age of apocalypse" in which we have the choice of destroying ourselves with nuclear weapons or making the leap into planetary consciousness.

Denying the existence of God and the soul, Rael presents as the only hope of immortality a regeneration through science, and to this end members participate in four annual festivals so that the Elohim can fly overhead and register the Raelians' DNA codes on their machines. This initiation ritual, called "the transmission of the cellular plan," promises a kind of immortality through cloning. New initiates sign a contract that permits a mortician to cut out a piece of bone in their forehead (the "third eye") and mail it packed in ice to Rael, who in turn relays it to the Elohim.

The movement currently claims around 30,000 members worldwide, mainly in French-speaking Europe, Japan, and Quebec. Members are encouraged through summer courses to achieve worldly success in their careers, to have better health through avoiding all recreational drugs and stimulants, and to enlarge their capacity to experience pleasure, which, Rael claims, will strengthen their immune system and enhance their intelligence and telepathic abilities. Rael advises Raelians not to marry or exacerbate the planetary overpopulation problem, but to commune with the wonder of the universe by exploring their sexuality. To this end, Raelians participate annually in the Sensual Meditation Seminar in a rural setting, which features fasting, nudity and sensory deprivation/awareness exercises, and sexual experimentation, the ultimate goal being to experience "cosmic orgasm."

The Raelians have always captured the interest of journalists who have, until recently, tended to portray them as delightful, harmless nuts. The Raelians aroused some controversy in 1992 by distributing free condoms in the playground of the major high schools of Quebec in protest of the Catholic school board's decision not to have condom machines installed. Anticult organizations have portrayed Rael as a sexual libertine enjoying a luxurious life at the expense of his followers. Raelians have been portrayed in the media in France as satanists, child sex abusers, and anti-Semites. Lawsuits have been launched by relatives excluded from the wills of deceased Raelians.

Rama Seminars

Rama, born 1950, sometimes called Zen Master Rama, founder of the Rama Seminars, was born Frederick Lenz in San Diego, California. At age two the family moved to Stamford, Connecticut, where his father eventually became mayor. He received a B.A. from the University of Connecticut, then a Ph.D. in 1979 from the State University of New York. While working on his graduate degrees he was a lecturer in English at the New School for Social Research.

Meanwhile, beginning at age 18, he studied yoga under Sri Chinmoy, who gave him the name Atmananda. As Atmananda he taught yoga classes in New York. In 1979, after finishing his degree, he moved to San Diego, California, and opened a Chinmoy meditation center. The following year he closed the center, moved to Los Angeles, and founded Lakshmi, named after the Hindu goddess. He quickly gained a large following after students reported that during meditation sessions he could levitate, disappear, or exude beams of light.

At first teaching under his own name, he began to emphasize his previous incarnations as a Zen master. He taught what he called Tantric Zen. In 1983 he announced his new name of Rama, to indicate his status as the ninth incarnation of the Hindu god Vishnu. He teaches that humanity is at the end of a cycle, in this case a dark age immediately preceeding an incarnation of Vishnu. Rama is one of the names given a prior incarnation of Vishnu. While Lenz does not claim to be the same as that prior incarnation, he does claim to be an embodiment of a portion of that prior incarnation.

By 1985 he had about 800 full-time disciples in four centers—San Diego, Los Angeles, San Francisco, and Boston. To accommodate the new growth he dismantled Lakshmi and reincorporated as Rama Seminars. Rama Seminars then took up the task of enlightening those individuals who began with Lakshmi. The teachings are styled by Rama as Tantric Zen, a formless Zen that incorporates Chan, Vajrayana Buddhism, Taoism, and *jnana* yoga.

Rama has been the center of a series of controversies, many involving former women devotees who claim abuse and sexual exploitation. Some parents of current and former members formed an anticult group directed specifically at Rama, called Lenz Watch, and a number of followers have been kidnapped and assaulted by deprogrammers. Rama eventually concluded that at least some such followers were engaged in a prolonged revolt against their parents—a conflict they exacerbated by being his follower. As a consequence they were ejected from the organization, and the controversy around him died down.

In 1995 Rama closed down his teaching activities, dissolved his organization, and turned his full attention to the highly successful businesses in which he was engaged with some of his students. However, the recent success of his book, *Surfing the Himalayas*, has once again propelled him into public view and stirred up old controversies. Rama drowned near his home in 1998.

Ramtha's School of Enlightenment

Ramtha's School of Enlightenment is a gnostic esoteric organization founded and headed by JZ Knight, who channels Ramtha, a spiritual entity believed to have lived on earth approximately 35,000 years ago. Knight was born Judith Darlene Hampton in Roswell, New Mexico, on March 16, 1946. In Tacoma, Washington, in 1977, Knight had her first encounter with Ramtha one Sunday afternoon. She and her husband had been playing with pyramids, then a rage within the New Age community, when, without prior warning, Ramtha appeared to the startled housewife as she was alone working in her kitchen. Ramtha began to speak through her, and over the next few years she emerged as a channel. During her channeling, she is in a full trance and Ramtha operates as a second complete personality. Upon awakening, Knight has no memory of what has been said.

Knight first publicly operated as a channel in November 1978 to a small group in Tacoma and found an immediate public response. During 1979 she began to travel to gatherings in different parts of the country and allowed Ramtha to speak through her. The number of these events, termed Dialogues, increased dramatically in 1980, and through the early 1980s she expanded the amount of time she could stay in trance. By the mid 1980s she was regularly holding two-day weekend Dialogues drawing from 3,000 to 7,000 people.

Knight became the most prominent New Age channeler, and books, cassettes, and videotapes drawn from Ramtha's teachings could be found in metaphysical bookstores across North America. Several celebrities found their way to Ramtha's door, and the size of his audiences jumped after author Jess Stern included a chapter on him in his book *Soul Mates* (1984) and Shirley MacLaine spoke glowingly of Ramtha in her book *Dancing in the Light* (1985).

In 1988 Knight began withdrawing from public appearances and made a significant change in direction in the founding of Ramtha's School of Enlightenment. The school, formally opened in May 1988, was to become the place of the students' learning and practice of the spiritual disciplines required if they were to leave behind their limited existence and assume the essential godlike mastery which was their real goal and purpose in life.

During the late 1980s and early 1990s, Knight went through a period of intense criticism. Also in the 1980s, Knight's love of horses led her to begin a business of raising and selling Arabian horses. While the business prospered for several years, at one point in the mid 1980s when the bottom fell out of the Arabian horse market, her business went bankrupt and she was plunged into debt. A number of students who had invested in the business lost their money. Many had done so with an understanding that Ramtha had approved and sanctioned their investment.

As Knight recovered financially, she offered to pay back all of the students (as well as the other investors) any money they lost. While some refused her offer, she eventually returned the investment to all who accepted it. From 1988 to 1995, the Ramtha School issued no publications for circulation to the general public, but early in 1996 announced that a broad range of new books and tapes would be forthcoming.

Rastafarianism

The Rastafarian movement originated on the island of Jamaica. After the emancipation of the slaves in 1833, many former slaves joined the mission societies. However, when their material position did not improve, they founded or joined movements that had Afro-religious elements in their approach. Mayalism, which included aspects of the black Jamaican religions in its belief system, experienced a revival. Its followers, known as "angelic people," maintained that the world would come to an end and that Christ was coming, sent by Jah. Jah was their word for God—a word used later by the Rastafarians. The so-called mial people (from a belief system called Obeah-myal) were the first to envisage a transformed social cosmos.

Marcus Garvey came to the fore in the 1920s with his slogan "Africa for the Africans." It appealed to many blacks, both within and without Africa, and his message was nowhere as influential as on the island of Jamaica where he lived. He said in one of his speeches that blacks should look to Africa, that when a black king was born the time of their liberation would be near.

Africa represents a spiritual homeland for the Rastafarians. The first Rastafarians appeared in Jamaica in 1930 during the crowning of Haile Selassie as emperor of Ethiopia. Revelation 5:2–5 was seen by the group in a new light, especially the words, "And I saw a strong angel proclaiming with a loud voice, 'who is worthy to open the scroll and break its seals?'" "Then one of the elders said to me, 'Weep not lo, the Lion of the tribe of Judah, the Root of David, has conquered, so that he can open the scroll and its seven seals!'"

Since then the Rastafari movement has become an important subculture of Jamaica. It is a religion, an ideology, a cultural movement—but not a political innovation. Culturally, it has many African and Jamaican facets, with some Anglo-Spanish contents added. Politically, there was some connection with forces of the black liberation movement that rebelled against Jamaica's neocolonialism. The movement has much to do with deprived economic circumstances.

Leipold Howell was the most influential person in spreading the Rastafari doctrine. He stated that blacks were the true descendants of Israel but that they were enslaved by whites, the agents of Babylon. Ras Tafari, he believed, would soon end the rule of the white man and would send ships to return the children of Africa to Ethiopia. Between 1963 and 1978 the political issues were liberation and revolution. The movement moved out of the religious context into the political arena. With this politicizing stance, themes that emphasized the destruction of Babylon became central to their songs.

Conspicuous were their dreadlocks, long locks of hair that are in the Bible as an essential part of the real life (Leviticus 19:27; 21:5; Numbers 6:5). These dreadlocks are seen as symbols of their blackness, dignity, and honor. Because black people are like sheep, calm and unaggressive, they have wool on their heads, while whites have hair. Blacks who debase themselves by becoming like goats and using a comb, scissors, and a razor are responsible for the world's sin.

Many saw the Rastafarian or Rastaman type as a mentally retarded drug addict who would have a degrading effect on the moral order if not checked. In Jamaica the middle-class white and black Jamaican, as well as the Americans, generally avoided the Rastafarians since they considered the members to be mentally deranged and also criminals of the most dangerous type because some of their leaders concealed weapons and explosives. As indicated earlier, however, attitudes towards the Rastafarians changed in Jamaica during the latter part of the 1970s with growing appreciation of their cultural contributions.

Santeria

Santeria is a magical religion that had its origins among the Yoruba people of West Africa. In the early nineteenth century the Yoruba were enslaved in great numbers and taken to Cuba and Brazil, where they were able to form Yoruba-speaking communities. Yoruba priests and priestesses created new lineages of initiates dedicated to the Yoruba spirits called *orishas,* which was translated into Spanish as *santos* (saints). This led to the people calling the Yoruba traditions in Cuba "Santeria," the way of the saints. Since the Cuban revolution of 1959, over one million Cubans have come to the United States, some of them priests and priestesses of Santeria.

Santeria recognizes a remote and almighty supreme being who is best understood as a personification of fate or destiny. In Santeria God is invoked by the Yoruba title Olodumare, the Owner of all Destinies. Individuals are given their own destinies by Olodumare. In order to fulfill these destinies with grace and power an individual requires guidance from a variety of spirits called orishas. Trained priests and priestesses consult oracles to determine the sacrificial foods and actions necessary to secure the power and presence of an orisha. One particular orisha will begin to assert itself as an individual devotee's patron.

When Santeria first came to the United States with Cuban immigrants, the appeal of the religion was primarily to fellow immigrants. In the United States, the houses of the spirits offered services for cultural survival, mutual aid, and spiritual fulfillment. The houses have also offered spiritual opportunities to a variety of outsiders who have come in contact with the traditions for the first time in the United States. Teaching within Santeria has been done orally in the face-to-face context of initiation. The teachings are secret and available only to those who have been chosen by elders to receive them.

The most controversial element of Santeria in the eyes of outsiders is the slaughter of animals as part of feasts for the orishas. Most of the more important ceremonies require a feast to be prepared for the spirits and to be enjoyed by the assembled community. In order to fix the meal to the spirit's specifications, the foods must be prepared and cooked according to strict recipes and properly consecrated with certain prayers and rhythms. Animals for the feast must be slaughtered by a priest or priestess initiated specially to this task, in the presence of the community and to the accompaniment of the correct chants. This insistence on animal slaughter has caused a number of problems in the urban centers of the United States, particularly in the crowded neighborhoods of New York and Miami. Problems with the storage of the animals before the ceremony and the disposal of the remains afterward have caused concern on the part of municipal authorities.

In 1987, the city of Hialeah, Florida, enacted a ban against animal sacrifice directly aimed at the growing Santeria community of the city. One Santeria house decided to challenge the ban and brought the case before the Supreme Court in 1992. In June of 1993 the Supreme Court unanimously declared the Hialeah ordinances unconstitutional.

Satanism

Satanism, the worship of the Christian devil, has traditionally been associated with a number of practices that parody Roman Catholic Christianity. Among its rituals is the black mass, which usually includes the profaning of the central acts of worship, the repeating of the Lord's Prayer backwards, the use of a host that has been dyed black, and the slaughter of an animal, which is usually a cat or a dog, in order to parody the crucifixion. The worship usually culminates with the invocation of Satan for the working of malevolent magic.

Although Satanist groups were quite rare prior to the 1960s, Satanism has provided a variety of imaginative material for novels and horror movies. An examination of all evidence shows that no large organized Satanist movement or group exists. But an increase in the number of ritual remains found in graveyards, church break-ins and vandalism, and mutilated bodies of animals has been reported since the early 1970s, showing a rise of satanic activities. During the 1980s, the emphasis shifted to the New Satanism and the emergence of accounts by several hundred women who claimed to have been survivors of satanic ritual abuse.

The forms of Satanism characterizing the 1990s include a traditional Satanism consisting of ephemeral groups of teenagers and young adults; a new form of Satanism initiated by Anton LaVey and developed in various directions by the several groups that split off from his Church of Satan; and the New Satanism as defined by those who claim to be survivors of ritual abuse.

Many cases of small groups practicing a form of traditional Satanism were reported in the press during the 1970s and the 1980s. These were mainly teenage groups, who were usually into heavy drug use. In 1984 members of one of these groups in Long Island killed one of their own, and one of the youths arrested for the crime hung himself in his jail cell. The small group consisted of several classmates who had a history of drug use prior to the emergence of Satanism among them, which appeared as an expression of the youths' social alienation.

The social and psychological elements characterizing these traditionalist Satanist groups also underlie the widespread use of Satanist symbolism by many teenagers, most of whom are devotees of hard rock music. Satanic symbolism and content are used by several rock artists in their music and performances. However, only rarely has the use of satanic imagery by teenagers grown into the practice of full-scale devil worship.

The emergence of the serial killers who have adopted satanic trappings has represented the most tragic of all phenomena surrounding Satanism. These are the cases of individuals without any connections to a Satanist group, who utilize satanic symbolism as an additional expression of the rage leading them to become murderers.

Organized Satanism in the form of the Church of Satan originated from an attempt to reorganize modern occult and magical teachings around a satanic motif. The church preaches a philosophy of individual pragmatism and hedonism, rather than emphasizing the worship of Satan. It promotes the development of strong individuals who seek gratification out of life and practice the selfish virtues as long as they do not harm others.

All of the formal trappings of an organized religion were given to the movement by its founder Anton LaVey, who studied occult books as a teenager. He developed a deep fascination for magic, such as the practice of creating change in the world through the use of cosmic powers controlled by the individual's will. On April 30, 1966, he announced the formation of the Church of Satan.

In 1967 the church received the attention of the media, when LaVey performed the first satanic wedding and a funeral for a sailor. Membership grew rapidly, though the active membership was rarely over 1,000. In 1969 LaVey published the first of three books, *The Satanic Bible*, containing the perspective of the Church of Satan. It was followed by *The Compleat Witch* (1970), and *The Satanic Rituals* (1972). He also began to work as a consultant for the movie industry, becoming the occult adviser on several films, such as *Rosemary's Baby*, in which he appears briefly as the Devil.

Scientology, Church of

The Church of Scientology, one of the genuinely new religions to originate in the United States in the twentieth century, was founded by L. Ron Hubbard (1911–1986). Hubbard grew up mostly in Montana, but as a teenager traveled throughout Asia and the East. In 1929 he enrolled in George Washington University, studying mathematics, engineering, and nuclear physics. He subsequently took up a literary career, publishing numerous stories and screenplays in various genres, including adventure, mystery, and science fiction. Hubbard served in the United States Navy during World War II.

By 1950 Hubbard had completed enough of his research to write *Dianetics, the Modern Science of Mental Health.* This book described techniques designed to rid the mind of irrational fears and psychosomatic illnesses. *Dianetics* quickly became a bestseller, and groups were soon formed so that individuals could assist each other in the application of Hubbard's "auditing" techniques. He lectured extensively and wrote more books. In 1951 he announced that the "applied religous philosophy" of Scientology had been born. It was described as a subject separate from Dianetics, as it dealt not only with the mind of an individual, but with one's nature as a spiritual being.

In 1954, the first Church of Scientology was established in Los Angeles, California. In 1959 Hubbard moved to Saint Hill Manor in Sussex, England, and the worldwide headquarters of Scientology was relocated there. In 1966 Hubbard resigned his position as executive director of the church and formed the Sea Organization, a group of dedicated members of the church. In 1975 these activities outgrew the ships and were moved onto land in Clearwater, Florida. From this time until his death in 1986, Hubbard continuously wrote and published materials on the subjects of Dianetics and Scientology, as well as a number of works of science fiction.

The Church of Scientology has been involved in a considerable number of controversial episodes since 1958, such as battles concerning tax issues, a ten-year battle with the Food and Drug Administration regarding the electro-meters used to assist auditing, and conflict with the Australian government. The most notable series of events in the church began in July 1977, when the FBI conducted a raid on the Washington, D.C., and Los Angeles churches and seized many files of documents. The raid was declared illegal, but the documents remained in government possession and were open to public scrutiny. According to these documents, the church was keeping files on people it considered unfriendly, and there had been various attempts to infiltrate anticult organizations.

After the raid, the church sent a number of top officials incognito to selected government agencies that were collecting data on the church. However, several members were indicted and convicted for theft of government documents. The convicted members were released from their offices in the church, which began a reorganization and closing of the office responsible for initiating illegal activities.

Problems with the IRS continued through the 1980s and 1990s. L. Ron Hubbard was charged with criminal tax evasion, and the IRS often moved against the church in ways that questioned its tax-exempt status. These problems terminated in a landmark decision in 1993, when the IRS ceased all litigation and recognized Scientology as a legitimate religious organization. The church has also been extensively attacked in Europe, most recently in Germany.

Siddha Yoga Dham Associates

The Siddha Yoga Dham was founded in 1975 by the *siddha* master Swami Muktananda Paramahansa (1908–1982), also known as Baba. He left home at the age of 15 and began wandering throughout India, studying philosophy and practicing the various branches of yoga. In 1947, he received *shaktipat* initiation from Bhagwan Nityananda. After nine years of intense spiritual practice he attained full self-realization. He succeeded Nityananda in the siddha lineage and established an ashram, Gurudev Siddha Peeth, near the town of Ganeshpuri, where the first American seekers began to arrive in the 1960s.

In 1970, Baba was invited to undertake his first world tour, which lasted three months, and included stops in Europe, New York, Dallas, Los Angeles, and Australia. Shortly after his visit, the first centers were established in America. Large centers were established in South Fallsburg, New York, and Oakland, California, and several hundred smaller centers were founded throughout the world.

Among the visitors of Ganeshpuri was Werner Erhart, founder of Erhart Training Seminars, who invited Baba to return to the West for two years. His final journey, lasting three years, was made in 1978. He spent the last years of his life in Ganeshpuri. Swami Chidvilasananda, known as Gurumayi, succeeded Baba at his death. She is now the head of the siddha lineage and travels the world, giving initiation and teaching.

Siddha yoga is based on the shaktipat initiation, the awakening of the spiritual energy known as kundalini, through the grace of the guru. This practice includes meditation, chanting, service, and devotion to the guru. The Siddha Yoga Dham was involved in two major scandals during the 1980s. After Baba's death, he was accused by some of his associates of taking sexual liberties with female disciples. In addition, in 1986 the *Illustrated Weekly of India* published two stories concerning charges made by Swami

Nityananda against his sister Swami Chidvilasananda. However, a defamation case was filed against the magazine, which in 1987 published a full retraction and apology.

Sikh Dharma (Healthy, Happy, Holy Organization)

Yogi Bhajan (born 1929), a well-educated Sikh from Delhi, India, moved to Toronto in 1968. From Toronto he moved to Los Angeles in December 1968, and in 1969 he founded an ashram and the Healthy, Happy, Holy Organization (3HO) to teach kundalini yoga. Corporately, 3HO was later supplanted by Sikh Dharma, and 3HO retained as Sikh Dharma's educational wing.

The Sikh religion was founded by Guru Nanak (1439–1538), the first of ten gurus to be recognized by Sikhs. Nanak asserted that there was one God, the Creator, and that he transcended the barriers of race, caste, and creed. His followers were taught to earn an honest living through hard work and to share their possessions with those in need. His writings and those of his successors, compiled into the *Siri Guru Granth Sahib*, became the guru for the movement following the death of the tenth guru, Guru Gobind Singh.

Individuals associated with Bhajan's Sikh Dharma are usually Westerners rather than Indians. They are encouraged to seek formal initiation and join the Khalsa, the Brotherhood of the Pure Ones, a fellowship begun by Guru Gobind Singh. Members of the Khalsa are required to keep the traditional practices introduced by Guru Gobind Singh that became the distinguishing marks of the Sikh community: 3HO Sikhs are vegetarian, usually preferring natural foods; fish, meat, alcohol, and drugs are prohibited; several members have opened vegetarian restaurants and groceries. They also prefer natural methods of healing. The traditional holidays of Sikhism are observed by 3HO Sikhs, such as Balsakhi Day, the birthday of Khalsa in April; the martyrdom days of Guru Tegh Bahadur in November and Guru Arjun Dev in May; and the birthdays of the ten gurus.

The first controversy involving the Sikh Dharma concerned its relationship to the older Punjabi Sikh community. American Sikhs criticized Punjabi Sikhs for becoming lax in their discipline, especially in their adherence to "the five k's." An attack followed on Yogi Bhajan by Narinder Singh Kapany, editor of the *Sikh Sangar*, the magazine of the Sikh Foundation, who condemned Bhajan's emphasis on yoga and diet. Other Sikh leaders echoed Kapany's criticisms in the United States, as well as in India. Although these issues were never resolved, Bhajan's emphasis on orthodoxy was supported by the headquarters of Sikh authority in Amritsar.

Sikh Dharma has received relatively little attention from the anticult movement. Few deprogramming attempts have taken place. In the early 1980s militant Sikhs announced a policy of actively opposing any attempts by deprogrammers to attack their organization. No further attempts were reported.

Yogi Bhajan was accused by one ex-member of sexual involvement with several of his staff members, but there was no verification of the charges. In 1984 a number of high-ranking leaders in the Sikh Dharma left the organization, complaining of the intense discipline and being cut off from the Sikh community as a whole and from American culture.

Controversy has also focused on other issues, such as members' dress, especially the turban, as in the case of Thomas Costello who, in 1971, faced a military court-martial for refusing to either cut his hair or remove his turban.

Although this case led to a change in army regulations granting permission for Sikhs to wear turbans, in 1983 Gurusant Singh Khalsa was not allowed to enlist in the army because he was a Sikh. In 1984 Karta Kaur Khalsa was threatened with losing her teaching certificate because she refused to take off her turban during classes, but in 1985 the Oregon Court of Appeals declared the law under which she was suspended to be unconstitutional.

Soka Gakkai International

Soka Gakkai International (SGI) is a Japanese Buddhist group with a comparatively large following in the United States and other Western countries. Founded in the 1930s, Soka Gakkai has grown to become Japan's largest and most controversial new religion. Although classified as a new religion, SGI's roots lie in thirteenth-century Japan.

Like most other Japanese Buddhist groups, SGI belongs to the Mahayana school. One characteristic of many Mahayana Buddhist texts is that they extol the merit gained by reading, copying, and otherwise propagating that particular scripture. Reading these claims, later generations of Buddhists were led to ask the question, Which text is the most potent? This question was the subject of debate in thirteenth-century Japan, when the Buddhist reformer Nichiren concluded that the *Saddharmapundarika* (the *Lotus of the True Law*), better known simply as the Lotus Sutra, was the most important of all Buddhist sutras. Nichiren felt that the message contained in the Lotus Sutra was so profound that all one had to do was chant Nam-myoho-renge-kyo (which can be translated in various ways, including "I dedicate myself to the Lotus Sutra") to develop wisdom and attain enlightenment as described in its pages.

Nichiren and his teachings gave rise to a monastic movement that eventually splintered into different sects. Soka Gakkai began as a movement of lay practitioners attached to the Nichiren Shoshu (Orthodox Nichiren Sect). The founder, Tsunesaburo Makiguchi (1871–1944), was an educator who was arrested as a "thought criminal" in the prewar period for rejecting the compulsory worship of the emperor and State Shinto as well as criticizing the Japanese militarist regime. He died in 1944, in prison, having refused to compromise his ideals. After the war, Josei Toda (1900–1958) took over as president and built Soka Gakkai into a major religion. This period of rapid growth was accompanied by negative media attention. The group matured under the presidency of Daisaku Ikeda, who became the third president of Soka Gakkai after the passing of Toda.

Soka Gakkai also spread to the United States, where it attracted attention as a consequence of the intensive proselytizing activities that characterized the organization's early years. Although never as controversial as groups like the Hare Krishna movement or the Unification church, Soka Gakkai (which in the United States went under the name Nichiren Shoshu of America until recently) was not infrequently stereotyped as a brainwashing cult, particularly by anticult authors.

In recent years Soka Gakkai has been attacked in Japan because of its support of political activity that challenges the ruling coalition. Exploiting the negative public reaction to AUM Shinrikyo—the Japanese religious group responsible for the 1995 poison gas attack in the Tokyo subway system—the LDP (the Liberal Democratic party, which is the dominant party in the ruling coalition) has attempted to weaken its principal political rival, the New Frontier party, which Soka Gakkai supported. The LDP has engaged in a campaign to portray religion in general, and Soka Gakkai in particular, as being incompatible with the principles of democracy.

Solar Temple

The founder/leader of the Solar Temple, Luc Jouret (1947–1994), trained as a medical doctor and became an accomplished practitioner of homeopathy. He also lectured on naturopathy and ecological topics and was active in the wider circuit of the French-speaking New Age movement. About 1981 he established the Amenta Club, an organization managing his conferences. He spoke in New Age bookstores (in France, Switzerland, Belgium, and Canada) and in eclectic esoteric groups such as the Golden Way Foundation of Geneva.

Amenta was the outer shell of an esoteric organization. Those who most faithfully attended Jouret's homeopathic practices and conferences were given the invitation to join a more confidential, although not entirely secret, inner circle: the Archédia Clubs, established in 1984, in which one could already find a definite ritual and an actual initiation ceremony, with a set of symbols taken from Masonic and Templar teachings. The Archédia Clubs were not yet the truly inner part of Jouret's organization. These most trusted members were invited to join an even more inner circle, this one truly a secret organization: the International Order of Chivalry Solar Tradition (OICST), Solar Tradition for short, later to be called Order of the Solar Temple.

Luc Jouret's teachings stressed occult-apocalyptic themes, bringing together three traditions concerning the end of the world: (1) the idea found in some (but by no means all) New Age groups of an impending ecological catastrophe; (2) some neo-templar movements' theory of a cosmic "renovation" revealed by the Ascended Masters of the Grand Lodge of Agartha; (3) the political ideas of a final international conflict propagated by survivalist groups both on the extreme right and on the extreme left of the political spectrum, with which Jouret had contacts in different countries. It seems that, in the years 1986 to 1993, Luc Jouret kept receiving revelations, until it was revealed to him that between the end of 1993 and the beginning of 1994 the earth was to have been forsaken by its last "guardians."

On March 8, 1993, a crucial episode in the history of the Solar Temple occurred in Canada. Two Temple members, Jean Pierre Vinet, 54, engineer and project manager for Hydro-Quebéc, and Herman Delorme, 45, insurance broker, were arrested as they were attempting to buy three semiautomatic guns with silencers, illegal weapons in Canada. Daniel Tougas, a police officer of Cowansville and a Temple member, was temporarily suspended from office on charges of having helped the two. On March 9, Judge François Doyon of Montreal committed them to trial, freeing them on parole. Luc Jouret—who according to police reports asked the two to buy the weapons—was also committed to trial, and an arrest warrant was issued against him, but the temple leader could not be found, as he was in Europe at the time. The event drew the attention of the Canadian press on what newspapers called "the cult of the end of the world."

On October 4, a fire destroyed Joseph Di Mambro's villa in Morin Heights, Canada. Among the ruins, the police found five charred bodies, one of which was a child's. At least three of these people seemed to have been stabbed to death before the fire. On October 5, at 1:00 in the morning, a fire started in one of the centers of the Solar Temple in Switzerland, the Ferme des Rochettes, near Cheiry, in the canton of Fribourg. The police found 23 bodies, one of which was a child's, in a room converted into a temple. Some of the victims were killed by gunshots, while many others were found with their heads inside plastic bags. The same day, at 3:00 A.M., three chalets, inhabited by members of the Solar Temple, caught fire almost simultaneously at Les Granges sur Salvan in the Valais Canton. In the charred remains were found 25 bodies, along with remainders of devices programmed to start the fires, and the pistol that shot the 52 bullets destined for the people found dead in Cheiry.

Sukyo Mahikari

Mahikari is the Japanese word for Divine True Light, believed to be a spiritual and purifying energy. Mahikari began in 1959 when Kotama Okada (1901–1974) received a revelation from God concerning how the use of the Divine Light of the Creator could produce health, harmony, and prosperity. Mahikari is viewed as a cleansing energy sent by SUSHIN, the Creator of Heaven and Earth, that both spiritually awakens and tunes the soul to its divine purpose. In 1963, he organized what became known as the Sekai Mahikari Bunmei Kyodan (Church of World True Light Civilization). Okada soon became known as Sukuinushisama (Master of Salvation).

God also revealed to Okada the existence of a Divine Plan. According to his teachings, all of the phenomena of the universe have been controlled by the Plan of the Creator. Under this plan, human souls are dispatched to the earth for the specific purpose of learning to utilize its material resources, in order to establish a highly evolved civilization governed by spiritual wisdom. These revelations and teachings are to be found in *Goseigen (The Holy Words)*, the Mahikari scriptures, an English-language edition of which was published in 1982.

Okada dedicated his life to teaching the art of the Divine Light to anyone desiring to be of service to the Creator. Today it is taught in a three-day session at which attendees may learn to radiate the Light through the palm of the hand, a process known as *Mahikari no Waza*. At the time of initiation, new members receive an *Omitama*, a pendant used to focus the light.

In 1974, following a divine revelation just prior to his death, Okada passed the mission to his daughter, Seishu Okada, the present leader. In 1978, subsequent to another revelation, Seishu Okada changed the name of the organization to Sukyo Mahikari (*Sukyo* means universal laws). Under her guidance, a new international headquarters was established in Takayama, Japan. In 1984, she completed the mission to construct a World Main Shrine (Suza) in Takayama.

It is said that there are approximately 800,000 members worldwide and 5,000 members in North America (United States, Puerto Rico, and Canada). There are 16 centers in the United States, two centers in Puerto Rico, and two centers in Canada. There are associated centers in over 75 countries. As with any large organization, Mahikari has experienced some problems in Japan. Despite a comparatively modest presence in Europe, the group is beginning to be attacked as a dangerous sect. In Belgium, for instance, there have been moves by authorities to force Mahikari to disband.

Synanon Church

The Synanon Church was begun in 1958 by Charles E. Dederich in Ocean Park, California, as Synanon Foundation, Inc., a therapeutic group for alcoholics and drug addicts. The group, which within a year grew and moved to Santa Monica, gained a considerable reputation for rehabilitating drug addicts. During the 1960s, Synanon communities began to appear along the West Coast, as well as in the East and Midwest and in Puerto Rico. In 1968, Dederich settled in Marin County, where three rural Synanon communities were established near the town of Marshall.

Although its religious nature had been tacitly recognized since the beginning of its existence, Synanon was never formally called a religion because many of the people assisted by it had rejected organized religion, while many others outside Synanon regarded it as a therapeutic community. However, as its community life developed, Synanon's religious nature could no longer be denied. The Articles of Incorporation signed in January 1975 designated the Synanon Foundation as the organization through which the Synanon religion and church is manifest, and in November 1980 the name Synanon Church was formally adopted.

Synanon's theological perspective derives from Buddhism and Taoism, as well as from such Western mystics as Ralph Waldo Emerson and Aldous Huxley. Members of the Synanon community seek to manifest the basic principles of oneness in themselves and in their relations with each other. The "Synanon game" represents the group's central sacrament and the principal means for the search for unity. It is "played" by a small group of members who meet together as equals in a circle to share in an intense and emotionally expressive context. The outcome of a successful game consists of mutual confession, repentance, and absolution, while offering complete pastoral care.

Synanon members follow the golden rule and help each other, believing that the most effective way to redeem humanity from alienation is to form religious communities based upon the beliefs and practices of the Synanon religion and church.

Synanon has been the subject of controversy since its inception, and during the last several years over forty people associated with it have been indicted by grand juries. In December 1961, Dederich went to jail on a zoning code violation. Synanon's practices and techniques have been attacked by the *San Francisco Examiner*, against which Synanon filed a libel suit that ended with a large settlement. However, the most controversial event occurred in 1978 when an attorney suing Synanon was bitten by a rattlesnake that had been placed in his mailbox by Synanon members. In the following year, Dederich suffered three strokes, and as the trial date approached, he found himself unable to pursue the defense of the case. Thus, those charged settled the case by pleading no contest.

Transcendental Meditation and the World Plan Executive Council

The Transcendental Meditation (TM) movement, at one time a widespread fad, is now institutionalized into the World Plan Executive Council, founded by Maharishi Mehesh Yogi. TM consists primarily of a simple system of daily meditation through the use of a mantra, a word that is repeated as one sits in silence.

This type of meditation derives from an old and honored Hindu technique. Maharishi advocated the use of a single mantra, given to each student at the time of his or her taking the basic TM course. Each mantra is supposed to suit the nature and way of life of the particular individual. These mantras are given out only at *puja* ceremonies, simple Hindu devotional services venerating the lineage of gurus. Maharishi claimed his authority from these gurus.

The World Plan Executive Council has asserted that the practice of TM has extraordinary effects, the validity of which has been tested by scientists who took the basic TM course. The council claims that the regular practice of TM can produce changes in the body, leading to increased intelligence, improved academic performance, higher job productivity, improved resistance to disease, and better psychological health. TM is generally claimed to transform a person's life.

In 1967 the Beatles became followers of Maharishi. George Harrison, who was later connected with the Hare Krishna movement, took lessons from Indian musician Ravi Shankar and, having learned of Maharishi's presence in London, persuaded the other Beatles to attend his meetings. In January 1968, the Beatles went to Maharishi's center in India with actress Mia Farrow, becoming the first of a number of celebrities to learn meditation, which helped make Maharishi a celebrity among older teens and young adults.

During the early 1970s, the movement experienced considerable growth in Europe and the United States and, by the end of the decade, almost a million people had taken the basic TM course. However, the World Plan suffered several major reverses in the mid 1970s, and around 1976 the number of new people taking the basic TM course in North America dropped drastically. As a response to the decline, the council announced an advanced siddha program, which included the teaching of levitation to meditators.

Maharishi and the World Plan have often been the target of criticism and controversy, centering on three issues. TM's claims to scientific verification have often been challenged, particularly those related to the physical effects of TM, which, according to the psychologists studying yoga and meditation, can be produced from a wide variety of practices. Also, scientists have pointed out that these positive results can only be obtained from certain samples of meditators.

Critics interested in the separation of church and state, supported by evangelical Christians who oppose TM, challenged the use of state funds to spread the practice, arguing that the World Plan Executive Council was in fact a Hindu religious organization and TM a practice essentially religious in nature. TM critics have also charged the movement with an element of deception, claiming that Maharishi, in his effort to bring TM to America, attempted to create a new and scientific image that denied religious elements and that argued that the practice of TM led to reduced dependence on drugs. In 1978 a federal ruling ruled that TM is a religious practice and denied public funds to support teachers.

During the 1970s, TM was attacked by Bob Kropinski, who took the organization to court, charging fraud and psychological damage from the practice of the siddha program. According to Kropinski, the advertisements promised to teach students the ability to levitate, but in fact only a form of hopping while sitting in a cross-legged position was taught. The organization has yet to produce generally verifiable evidence of the siddha program involving the ability to levitate, walk through walls, or become invisible.

Unification Church

The Unification church (UC), formally the Holy Spirit Association for the Unification of World Christianity (HSA-UWC), refers to an international messianic religious movement led by the Reverend Sun Myung Moon (born 1920). It also is a complex network of media, industrial, commercial, cultural, and educational enterprises worldwide. Derided in the West as "the Moonies," the UC's emergence has been accompanied by intense and sustained global reaction, rendering it quite possibly the most controversial new religious movement of the latter twentieth century.

Core beliefs of the Unification church are contained in its primary doctrinal and theological text, *Divine Principle* (1973), itself derived from two earlier Korean texts, *Woli Kang-ron* (1966) and *Woli Hae-sul* (1955). These texts express aspects of the "new truth" or "principle" revealed through Sun Myung Moon. Utilizing familiar categories of Christian theology, key chapters include Creation, the Fall, Resurrection, Predestination, Christology, and History. While polemical opponents have identified departures from orthodoxy, the major novelty is the explicitness with which the text identifies the present as the time of the Christ's Second Advent.

An oral tradition consisting mainly of Rev. Moon's speeches exists alongside the official doctrinal texts. Many of these speeches deal with the topic of the Second Advent arriving in the persons of Rev. and Mrs. Moon. UC members believe them to be the True Parents of humankind, ushering in the Completed Testament Age. Since 1992, when this age is regarded as having begun, pronouncements of this nature have become increasingly public. Widespread and enhanced spiritual sensibility, the liberation of oppressed peoples, the emergence of global culture, and advanced technological development are all associated by the movement with the Second Advent and Completed Testament Age. Ever greater numbers of couples are participating in the joint weddings or Blessings presided over by the True Parents.

The UC has not been subject to the apocalyptic conflagrations associated with such movements as the People's Temple, Branch Davidians, and AUM Shinrikyo. Nevertheless, the scope and duration of reactions accompanying its emergence have rendered it quite possibly the most controversial new religious movement of the latter twentieth century.

Negative reaction is apparent from the UC's mid 1950s Korean origins. There was an intense negative reaction to UC proselytization efforts on Seoul university campuses, especially Ehwa Women's University, which led to Rev. Moon's imprisonment and to allegations that the UC was a cult. Although the UC gained a degree of credibility with the Korean military government after 1961, relations were tenuous; successive regimes have been embarrassed by UC activities, the most recent being Rev. Moon's unauthorized visit to North Korea and Kim Il Sung in late 1991, which was repudiated by Seoul. Korea's Christian population has consistently rejected the UC as heretical.

In the United States, the UC has faced widespread suspicion, hostility, and a negative press. Kidnapping and deprogrammings were common in the mid 1970s, and a 1977 Gallup survey found that Sun Myung Moon "elicited one of the most overwhelmingly negative responses ever reported by a major poll." During the 1980s, the UC found some favor under conservative Republican administrations. However, during this period, Rev. Moon was convicted and jailed on tax evasion charges. Similar patterns of response have been prevalent elsewhere in the world, notably Europe, the Commonwealth of Independent States, Southeast Asia, and Latin America.

Vajradhatu (Tibetan Buddhism)

The Vajradhatu movement has been responsible for stimulating the growth of Tibetan Buddhism in the United States. It was founded by Chogyam Trungpa Rinpoche (1939–1987), who taught Buddhism as a practice to awaken the mind in three ways: (1) meditation, the state of being in the present moment, which consists of training the mind to exist in the here and now; (2) study, which sharpens the understanding of the experience of meditation and the communication of the experience to others; and (3) work, which allows the meditator to share what has been learned with others.

Trungpa was born in the village of Geje in northeast Tibet and was identified as the tenth incarnation of Trungpa Tulku by the monks of the Buddhist sect Karmapa Kargyupa. He was trained at

Dudtsi-til Monastery and received his degrees when he was a teenager. He became a monk and, after the invasion of Tibet by China in 1959, went to India where he learned English. He was then allowed to go to the West, and in 1963 he went to Oxford, where he studied art, psychology, and comparative religion.

During his stay in Oxford, he discovered the Buddhist contemplative center Johnstone House in Scotland. After a severe injury in 1969 he decided to become a layman in order to better communicate to Western people the complicated and sophisticated Tibetan tradition. *Cutting through Spiritual Materialism* is one of Trungpa's early books, as well as a major theme of his teaching, according to which the primary mistake of Western followers of a spiritual discipline was their conversion of what they had learned to egotistical uses.

After marrying Diana Judith Pybus in 1970, he immigrated to the United States. In Vermont, some of his followers built Tail of the Tiger Monastery. He gave several lectures around the country and established many centers, such as the Rocky Mountain Dharma Center at Ft. Collins, a small facility used primarily for meditative retreats and other short-term programs. In 1973 he established Vajradhatu.

In 1974, he held the first seminar. This led to the formation of Naropa Institute, which has received the support of Buddhist leaders and scholars throughout North America. During the same year he received the visit of Gyalwa Karmapa, the international leader of the Kargyupa Buddhists, who performed the famous black hat ceremony and recognized Trungpa as a Vajracarya, that is, a spiritual master.

In 1976, Trungpa named Thomas Rich, an American disciple, as his Dharma successor. Rich, who took the name Osel Tendzin, assumed administrative leadership of the community when Trungpa died. In 1989 the *Los Angeles Times* broke the story that Tendzin had AIDS. It was also reported that for three years he had known of his infection and had continued to have sexual relations with others without telling them of the risk. He was then asked by Vajradhatu's board to take a permanent leave of absence. Tendzin died in 1990. Trungpa's son, Sawang Osel Rangdrol Mukpo, succeeded him, returning some stability to the organization.

Since its formation, Vajradhatu has grown consistently, although it was early the center of controversy because of Trungpa's unmonklike personal habits, such as eating meat and using both alcohol and tobacco. One controversial episode occurred in fall 1975, when a pacifist student attending the classes for advanced students at Naropa Institute was disturbed by the bloody images in some of the Tibetan material used during the sessions. The student, an outstanding poet, was stripped of his clothes after being ordered by Trungpa to return to a Halloween party at Naropa that he had left earlier in the evening with a friend.

Voodoo

Voodoo is a magical religion that originated in Haiti in the late 1700s. The precursor of voodoo was the religion of the Fon people of West Africa who were brought as slaves to Haiti. Voodoo (or vodou) means "spirit" in the Fon language. In Haiti, the Fon systems of veneration of the spirits came into contact with other African religious traditions and French Catholicism to produce what we call voodoo. It has spread via emigration to New Orleans and other major cities in the United States.

The central religious activity of voodoo involves possession of devotees by a number of African deities. In ceremonies led by a priest, each possessed individual enacts a highly specific ritual performance involving dance, song, and speech appropriate to the particular possessing deity. Possession is directed toward healing, warding off evil, and bringing good or evil fortune.

Voodoo recognizes a remote and almighty Supreme Being who is a personification of fate or destiny. In voodoo this God is called Bondye. Individuals are given their own destinies by Bondye. In order to fulfill these destinies with grace and power, an individual requires guidance from a variety of spirits called *lwa*. The religion of voodoo is a system of actions toward the development of closer relationships with the lwa. Human beings and spirits interact through divination and sacrifice. Trained priests and priestesses consult oracles to determine the sacrificial foods and actions necessary to secure the power and presence of lwa. One particular lwa will begin to assert itself as an individual devotee's patron. When the spirit wills it, the individual will undergo an initiation into the mysteries of his or her patron spirit. This initiation will mark the member's entry into the priesthood of voodoo and give him or her the authority to found his or her own house and consecrate other priests and priestesses. The spirit will identify with the devotee's inner self, and this intimate relationship will offer the devotee health, success, and wisdom. Voodoo first came to the United States with Haitian immigrants. In more recent years, white as well as black Americans have been going to voodoo houses.

The most controversial element of voodoo is the slaughter of animals as part of feasts for the lwa. Most of the important ceremonies require a feast to be prepared for the spirits and to be enjoyed by the assembled community. In order to fix the meal to the spirit's specifications, the foods must not only be prepared and cooked according to strict recipes, but they must be properly consecrated with certain prayers and rhythms. Animals for the feast (fowl, goats, and sheep) must be slaughtered by a priest or priestess initiated specially to this task, in the presence of the community and to the accompaniment of the correct chants. Particularly in the crowded neighborhoods of New York and Miami, animal slaughter as part of voodoo ceremonies has caused some problems, including storage of the animals before the ceremony and the disposal of the remains afterward.

Healing is a high priority of voodoo and includes psychic and psychological counseling and the dispensing of folk remedies such as rattlesnake oil. Worship is held on the evening of the new moon and consists of ecstatic dance accompanied by flute and drum and led by the priest and priestess. As they dance, members enter trances and are said to receive revelations and messages from the spirits. Spirituals are also sung. Voodoo teaches faith, love, and joy.

The Way International, Inc.

The Way International, a conservative Pentecostal Christian group, was founded in 1942 by Victor Paul Wierwille (1916–1985), a minister in the Evangelical and Reformed church, as a radio ministry under the name of Vesper Chimes. It assumed its present name in 1974, after being named the Chimes Hour in 1944 and the Chimes Hour Youth Caravan in 1947. Wierwille earned his B.D. at Mission House Seminary in Minnesota and did graduate work at the University of Chicago and Princeton Theological Seminary, earning a M.Th. in 1941. In 1948, he was awarded a Ph.D. by the Pikes Peak Bible College and Seminary, in Manitou Spring, Colorado.

The first Power for Abundant Living (PFAL) class, given in 1953, contained the initial results of his research on biblical truth. After one year, he began to study Aramaic, under the guidance of Dr. George M. Lamsa, translator of the Lamsa Bible, and began to accept a view of biblical doctrine that was more and more distinct from that of his church. In 1957 he resigned his ministry from the Evangelical and Reformed church in order to devote himself full time to his work. He led his ministry, which was chartered as The Way, Inc., in 1955, and then changed to The Way International in 1975, until 1983, when he retired. The headquarters is at the family farm outside New Knoxville, Ohio.

The Way grew steadily during the 1950s through the initiation of the PFAL classes and *The Way Magazine* (1954). After experiencing a slow growth in the 1960s, The Way underwent a period of rapid growth in the 1970s, as the ministry suddenly burgeoned at the time of the national Jesus People revival across the United States. The Way expanded its facilities at New Knoxville, which hosted the first national Rock of Ages Festival, an annual gathering of Way members, in 1971.

An eleven-point statement summarizes the beliefs of The Way. The Way rejects the Trinitarian orthodoxy of most Western Christianity and denies the divinity of Jesus, as it is emphasized in Wierwille's *Jesus Christ Is Not God* (1975). The Way believes that Jesus is the Son of God but not God the Son.

The Way International is one of the largest groups to be labeled a cult. It has also been the target of many deprogrammings, particularly in the early 1980s. It has often been accused by anticult groups of brainwashing and mind control. Additionally, there have been two serious charges that have often been repeated in anti-Way literature: The first charge, in the 1970s, was that The Way was training members in the use of deadly weapons for possible future use against enemies of the organization. These accusations originated from the adoption at The Way's College at Emporia of a State of Kansas program in gun safety, which was primarily directed to hunters. The second charge came to the fore in the 1980s, as Christian anticultists attacked The Way for its radical departure from orthodox Christianity, its adoption of Arianism, and the denial of the divinity of Jesus and the Trinity.

The Way experienced a period of turmoil after Wierwille's death. Charges of improprieties by Wierwille and many of his close friends resulted in the defection of several leaders, a few of whom established rival groups. As a result, The Way lost support, although it recovered by 1990, when the attendance at the annual Rock of Ages festival began to return to its former level. The Internal Revenue Service questioned The Way's alleged partisan political involvement and its business activities at New Knoxville. Although its tax-exempt status was revoked in 1985, that ruling was reversed by the Supreme Court in 1990.

Witchcraft (Wicca)

Also referred to as the Craft, Wicca has the following characteristics:

1. Worship is polytheistic and always includes an exalted concept of a Goddess as being close to the ultimate level of divinity.

2. Worship occurs in the small group known as a coven (which may consist of anywhere from three to around twenty members), according to the phases of the Moon. These monthly meetings for worship (and the working of practical magic) are referred to as esbats. Worship also occurs in larger groups, which may be two covens meeting together or several hundred people, some coming from long distances, for the sabbats, of which there are eight in each year.

3. In addition to worship, coven activity focuses on the working of magic, which is highly psychologized, eclectic, and variegated, since the magical training procedures used in any one coven will depend on what training in magic, psychic abilities, psychology, or other disciplines the coven's leaders have had in academia, New Age groups, or other occult groups.

Despite the anarchism of neopagan witches, they are just as clear as members of other religions are about which individuals and groups belong to their religion and which do not.

The publication of Margaret Murray's *The Witch-Cult in Western Europe* (Oxford University Press, 1921) set off a burst of interest in paganism, since Murray proposed that the witch hunters of medieval and early modern times were actually finding the remnants of the pagan religions of northern Europe. The idea of recreating the kind of witch cult described by Murray was discussed by English occultists during the 1920s and 1930s. However, the first successful attempt to recreate Murray's witch cult was apparently actually carried out by Gerald B. Gardner, a retired British civil servant, and his colleagues among the New Forest occultists, under the leadership of Dorothy Clutterbuck, a locally prominent homeowner and socialite, during World War II.

In 1953 Gardner initiated Doreen Valiente, who soon became the High Priestess of the central coven and who rewrote the coven's "Book of Shadows" (liturgical manual) into the form that is still used in the movement. The "Book of Shadows" contains rituals for the coven's full moon esbats, for the eight sabbats at the solstices, equinoxes, and cross-quarter days, and for various rites of passage, as well as some basic magic techniques. The central coven divided in 1957, with Gardner and Valiente each taking a half; but Gardner soon went off on his own again, initiating new priestesses and founding new covens at a fairly rapid pace until his death in 1964, and these have enthusiastically carried on the Craft.

Raymond Buckland, after a long correspondence with Gardner, was initiated in 1963 in Perth, Scotland, by Lady Olwen. Buckland then brought the Craft back to the United States, and, with his wife Rosemary as High Priestess, founded the New York coven in Bayside, Long Island, which became the center of the Gardnerian movement and the neopagan movement in America for the next twenty years.

Court Decisions, Legislation, and Governmental Actions

4

In addition to the struggle that has taken place around deprogramming, the cult controversy has been fought in the courts and the media (and, by extension, popular opinion). Perhaps paradoxically, the anticult movement has, in general, suffered defeat in the courts but been victorious in the media. One of the principal reasons why minority religions have had success in the legal arena is that the courts have been compelled to treat such groups as religions and thus as being entitled to all of the rights and privileges normally accorded mainstream denominations. Critics of new religious movements would like to draw a sharp line between religions and cults and treat cults as pseudoreligious organizations. The courts, however, are unable to approach such groups differently as long as group members manifest sincerity in their religious beliefs.

This situation explains why none of the legislative efforts to regulate new religious movements have been successful. For example, the New York state legislature tried to enact a law (Bill AB9566-A, introduced 10/5/77) that would have made starting a pseudoreligion a felony, but it failed to pass because—among other factors—it lacked an objective criterion for distinguishing false from true religions. Without a truly neutral standard, any such law violates the establishment clause of the First Amendment. It is, in fact, the separation of church and state mandated by the First Amendment that has discouraged legislation in this area. This has left the courts to bear the burden of adjudicating the controversy, making an overview of the relevant legal activity far more lengthy and involved than with most other public issues.

Because cases involving contemporary minority religions are often argued in terms of religious liberty issues, earlier religious liberty decisions are directly relevant to the present controversy. Anticultists have accused minority religions of hiding behind the First Amendment but have been largely unsuccessful at persuading the legal system to set aside First Amendment concerns when dealing with controversial minority religions. The necessity of taking these alternative religions seriously as "real" religions explains why it is necessary to refer back to earlier legal decisions involving Mormons, Jehovah's Witnesses, and others.

The following discussion begins with an overview of court cases and legislation not dealing explicitly with contemporary groups but nevertheless relevant to the controversy because of issues of religious liberty. An examination of the first important "new religion" cases prior to the emergence of the cult controversy as an important public issue follows. In addition to the initial efforts of governmental bodies to regulate minority religions by passing new laws, deprogrammers and their clients began using conservatorship laws to legitimize their kidnapping activities. While initially experiencing some limited success, in the long run this strategy was defeated in the courts.

Following the demise of the conservatorship tactic, torts by ex-members claiming damage at the hands of their former religious groups became the chief strategy by which to weaken controversial minority religions. Once again this tactic initially had a few notable successes, only to be ultimately frustrated by the defeat of coercive persuasion/brainwashing arguments in the courts. Of the other legal arenas in which the cult controversy has been fought, perhaps the most important has been the issue of child abuse/child custody. Other areas have been zoning, solicitation, and taxation issues.

For a time, it seemed that the new religions and their enemies were more or less evenly matched in the courts, although the balance of power would periodically swing one way or the other. This situation changed dramatically in the mid to late 1990s with the decisive defeat of the brainwashing notion in the courts and with the declaration of bankruptcy by the largest anticult organization in the United States.

Relevant Court Decisions Not Directly Involving Contemporary New Religions

Mormon Polygamy Cases

Religious beliefs are fully protected under the First Amendment to the Constitution. However, it has become a well-recognized principle of constitutional law that religious conduct may be circumscribed. In *Cantwell* v. *Connecticut,* for instance, the U.S. Supreme Court ruled that religious conduct "remains subject to regulation for the protection of society."

According to the Court, religious practices may be regulated even at the expense of religious freedom. This view dates back to the time of Thomas Jefferson, who proposed legislation in the Virginia House of Delegates recognizing that government may "interfere when [religious] principles break out into overt acts against peace and good order" (quoted in *Reynolds* v. *United States*). This governmental interference includes allowing for recovery to those who suffer harm as a result of conduct by another. Religious organizations are not exempt from liability for tortious conduct.

Because of the First Amendment, religious liberty cases are almost by definition Supreme Court cases. The first Supreme Court decision having a direct bearing on the contemporary debate over alternative religions was the 1878 case, *Reynolds* v. *United States.* Stories about the plural wife practices of the Church of Jesus Christ of Latter-Day Saints had circulated for over three decades—stories implying that Mormon polygamy was a thinly veiled excuse for sexual indulgence. Congress legislated against plural marriage as a form of bigamy in the *Revised Statutes of the United States,* sect. 5352: "Every person having a husband or wife living, who marries another, whether married or single, in a Territory, or other place over which the United States have exclusive jurisdiction, is guilty of bigamy, and shall be punished by a fine of not more than $500, and by imprisonment for a term of not more than five years." George Reynolds was a member of the Mormon church convicted under this statute. Reynolds asserted that, because plural marriage was prescribed by his religion, his constitutional rights of the free exercise of religion of the First Amendment were violated.

In 1878 this case was considered by the Supreme Court. When Chief Justice Morrison Waite wrote the Court's majority decision, he was aware that history was being made: This was the first judicial effort to interpret the meaning of the "free exercise of religion."

Justice Waite's decision cited, among other things, scholarly opinion of the time that polygamy was detrimental to a free society and concluded that in the First Amendment "Congress was deprived of all legislative power over mere opinion, but was left free to reach actions which were in violation of social duties or subversive of good order." In other words, while Congress cannot prescribe laws against what one may *believe* (opinion), it may legislate against *actions* harmful to society—which the plural wife system was judged to be.

This decision was amplified in a second Mormon case, *Davis* v. *Beason*, decided by the Supreme Court in 1889. Samuel D. Davis, a member of the Mormon church, had had his voter registration in Idaho rescinded on the grounds that the church advocated polygamy. Davis argued his case, like Reynolds, on the free-exercise provision of the First Amendment. Associate Justice Stephen Field wrote the Court's majority decision, asserting, like Waite had before him, that not every action prescribed by a religion can be protected by the First Amendment:

> History discloses the fact that the necessity of human sacrifices, upon special occasions, had been a tenet of many sects. Should a sect of [this kind] ever find its way into this country, swift punishment would follow the carrying into effect of its doctrines, and no heed would be given to the pretence that, as religious beliefs, their supporters could be protected in their exercise by the Constitution of the United States.

Finally, in the decision in two other Mormon church cases, Justice Joseph Bradley responded to the free exercise of religion argument by stating that "no doubt the Thugs of India imagined that their belief in the right of assassination was a religious belief." (Bradley wrote a joint decision for the Supreme Court in *Mormon Church* v. *United States* and *Romney* v. *United States*.)

Following *Reynolds* and the other Mormon church decisions, the standards for measuring the harmfulness of religious conduct have been based on socially accepted, traditional notions of religious practice. Because the practice of polygamy was offensive to the notions of traditional religious institutions and because the Court in *Reynolds* assumed that there were innocent victims who suffered harm from such conduct, the religious practice was not allowed to continue.

In *Reynolds*, the Court relied on various excerpts from writings by Thomas Jefferson, one of the proponents of the free exercise clause. Jefferson believed that "religion is a matter which lies solely between man and his God; . . . that the legislative powers of the government reach actions only, and not opinions" and that government may not judge the validity of a religion but may only regulate actions that are in violation of social duties or subversive of good order.

The Court in *Reynolds* deferred to contemporary social norms and opinions concerning polygamy and ruled that it was a harmful practice and void under the common law. The Supreme Court upheld the trial court's jury instructions, which reminded the jury of the harmful consequences that followed from plural marriages. Those "evil consequences" were the subject of numerous books and articles published by anti-Mormons during the second half of the nineteenth century as well as congressional testimony. Thus, the *Reynolds* decision reflected the willingness of the highest court at the time to adopt a standard consistent with majoritarian social norms to the detriment of minority religious practices.

Together, *Reynolds, Davis,* and other examples involving the new religion of the day all asserted the absolute right of the government to regulate religious activity. In hindsight, these specific decisions may appear contrary to the spirit of the free exercise clause. In the context of the contemporary cult controversy, anticult spokespersons have sometimes referred back to the belief-action dichotomy laid out in *Reynolds* v. *United States.*

Jehovah's Witnesses Cases

The Jehovah's Witnesses were the most controversial new religion of the mid-twentieth century. Like the Mormon church, the Witnesses remain the focus of much contemporary Christian anticultism because of perceived doctrinal deviations from the evangelical mainstream. The group's aggressive proselytizing in combination with members' refusal to participate in such patriotic activities as saluting the flag led to persecution and arrests. In response, the Witnesses formed a legal wing for the express purpose of challenging these arrests on First Amendment grounds.

The first important Supreme Court victory for the Jehovah's Witnesses was the 1938 case *Lovell* v. *City of Griffin.* The Supreme Court's decision in this case overturned the conviction of a Witness for distributing literature without a permit. The permit ordinance left too much discretion for the relevant city official, making it unconstitutional on the basis of the free speech (as opposed to the freedom of religion) of the First Amendment.

The freedom of religion clause was brought into play two years later in another significant Supreme Court victory for the Witnesses, *Cantwell* v. *Connecticut*, a case that extended the freedom of religion provision of the federal constitution to the states and that served to call into question the 1887 *Reynolds* decision giving government the power to regulate religious actions. *Cantwell*'s departure from the Mormon cases is reflected in the decision composed by Associate Justice Owen Roberts: "The Amendment embraces two concepts—freedom to believe and freedom to act. The first is absolute but, in the nature of things, the second cannot be. Conduct remains subject to regulation for the protection of society. The freedom to act must have appropriate definition to preserve the enforcement of that protection. In every case the power to regulate must be so exercised as not, in attaining a permissible end, unduly to infringe the protected freedom."

The *Cantwell* decision was reinforced by further cases decided three years later. In 1943, four cases involving the right of Jehovah's Witnesses to canvass door-to-door reached the Supreme Court. Three were decided in favor of the Witnesses (*Jones* v. *Oplika*, *Murdock* v. *Pennsylvania*, and *Martin* v. *Struthers*). The fourth case (*Douglas* v. *Jeannette*) was decided against the Witnesses, but on technical grounds. Associate Justice William O. Douglas wrote the Court's decision in *Jones* and *Murdock*, referring to the tradition of itinerant evangelism as support for the argument that the solicitation activity of Witnesses was a religious activity and thus protected by the First Amendment.

Another case involving the refusal of Witnesses to salute the flag, *West Virginia State Board of Education* v. *Barnette*, was decided the same year. *Barnette* was decided in favor of the Jehovah's Witnesses, overturning a related Supreme Court decision, *Minersville School District* v. *Gobitis*, made against the Witnesses in 1940. The decision in *Barnette* was made on free exercise of religion rather than free speech grounds.

The Sherbert-Yoder Test

In 1963, the Supreme Court decided *Sherbert* v. *Verner*, a key case for what would become known as the Sherbert-Yoder test for deciding free exercise of religion cases. In this case, the Supreme Court decided in favor of a Seventh-Day Adventist who had been denied unemployment benefits because she had not been able to accept employment requiring work on Saturday. *Wisconsin* v. *Yoder*, decided six years later, concluded that a state law mandating high school education was an excessive burden on the Amish religion.

The resulting Sherbert-Yoder test sets forth criteria for adjudicating conflicts between the interest of the state and the dictates of a religion. These criteria have been summarized by William C. Shepherd as follows

1. Are the religious beliefs in question sincerely held?
2. Are the religious practices under review germane to the religious belief system?
3. Would carrying out the state's wishes constitute a substantial infringement on the religious practice?
4. Is the interest of the state compelling? Does the religious practice perpetuate some grave abuse of a statutory provision or obligation?
5. Are there alternative means of regulation by which the state's interest is served but the free exercise of religion is less burdened? (Shepherd 1985, 13)

The Sherbert-Yoder test has become the definitive standard for deciding cases involving the free exercise of religion. It would be the crucial criterion for determining the outcome of later cases involving new religious movements.

To get a sense of the importance of the Sherbert-Yoder test, we might look briefly at a few decisions made prior to and after *Sherbert*. In 1949 in *Bunn* v. *North Carolina*, for example, a lower court ruled that public safety outweighed the concern for the free exercise of religion involving the handling of poisonous snakes. The U.S. Supreme Court dismissed the appeal without comment. Only two years before *Sherbert*, in *Braunfeld* v. *Brown*, the Supreme Court had decided against Orthodox Jewish merchants protesting Pennsylvania laws requiring them to close their stores on Sunday.

In 1981, the Supreme Court ruled in *Thomas* v. *Review Board*. In this case, a Witness had quit his job rather than work in an armaments factory and had been denied unemployment benefits. The Court decided in favor of the Jehovah's Witnesses, echoing the decision in *Sherbert*. This case is important as the first major case after *Yoder* to be decided according to the Sherbert-Yoder test. In 1993 the Court overturned a Hialeah, Florida, ban against animal sacrifice aimed at the growing Santeria community of the city as unconstitutional in *Church of Lukumi Bablu Aye* v. *City of Hialeah*.

The Sherbert-Yoder test was the standard until the 1990 case of *Employment Division* v. *Smith*. In this decision, the Supreme Court ruled against the right of Native American Church members to use peyote. The case evoked outrage from church-state scholars and others, who characterized the decision as supplanting religious sincerity with the values of the majority as the standard for determining which religious acts merit the protection of the free exercise clause of the First Amendment.

Reacting to the Supreme Court's decision in *Employment Division* v. *Smith,* a broad coalition of religious groups supported and pushed through the Religious Freedom Restoration Act (RFRA), a legislative measure intended to reestablish Sherbert-Yoder standards for the free exercise of religion. In 1993 the RFRA was overwhelmingly endorsed by both houses of Congress.

Earliest Cases Involving Contemporary New Religions

The *Ballard* Decision

Prior to the emergence of the modern cult controversy and even prior to the formulation of *Sherbert* v. *Verner,* there was one extremely important Supreme Court case involving a contemporary new religion. This 1944 case, *United States* v. *Ballard,* focused on the belief system of "I Am" Activity, a neo-Theosophical group from which a whole family of other groups—including Church Universal and Triumphant—traces its roots. The case was built around the charge of mail fraud, based on the "ridiculous" nature of the group's beliefs. In the words of Justice Jackson who wrote the dissenting opinion in *United States* v. *Ballard:*

> Scores of sects flourish in this country by teaching what to me are queer notions. It is plain that there is wide variety in American religious taste. The Ballards are not alone in catering to it with a pretty dubious product.
>
> The chief wrong which false prophets do to their following is not financial. The collections aggregate a tempting total, but individual payments are not ruinous. I doubt if the vigilance of the law is equal to making money stick by over-credulous people. But the real harm is on the mental and spiritual plane. There are those who hunger and thirst after higher values which they feel wanting in their humdrum lives. They live in mental confusion or moral anarchy and seek vaguely for truth and beauty and moral support. When they are deluded and then disillusioned, cynicism and confusion follow. The wrong of these things, as I see it, is not in the money the victims part with half so much as in the mental and spiritual poison they get.

The founder of the movement, Guy Ballard, had long been interested in occultism and Theosophy. He married Edna Wheeler in 1916, and together they founded the "I Am" Activity in the 1930s. Ballard's revelations from Saint Germain were spread during the lectures of the Ballards, who traveled in the 1930s as Accredited Messengers of the Masters. Further messages from the Ascended Masters, especially from Saint Germain and the Master Jesus, were sometimes produced in public or private.

Saint Germain and Jesus were considered the mediators between the "I Am Presence" and humans. The Ascended Masters were at one time all human beings who were able to transcend the physical world through the purification of their lives. The goal of human life is represented by ascension. In 1938, the "I Am" Activity was said to have been given a dispensation according to which persons who had devoted themselves so much to the movement that they had not given all they might to personal purification could upon normal death ascend from the after-earth state without reembodiment.

The "I Am" Activity worked publicly from 1937 to 1940 to establish a group of devoted followers numbering over one million. With the death of Guy Ballard on December 29, 1939, the movement began to decline. Edna Ballard claimed that her husband had become an Ascended Master. However, the fact that Guy Ballard had experienced a physical death rather than bodily ascension threatened the movement's credibility. The following year a sensational trial of the leaders of the movement took place, after some members of the Ballards' personal staff accused the Ballards of obtaining money under fraudulent pretenses.

The indictment was voided in 1944 by the Supreme Court with a landmark decision on religious liberty. The case was finally dismissed. Justice Douglas, in stating the prevailing opinion, wrote:

> Heresy trials are foreign to our Constitution. Men may believe what they cannot prove. They may not be put to the proof of their religious doctrines or beliefs. Religious experiences which are as real as life to some may be incomprehensible to others. Yet the fact that they may be beyond the ken of mortals does not mean that they can be made suspect before the law. . . . If one could be sent to jail because a jury in a hostile environment found one's teachings false, little indeed would be left of religious freedom. . . . The religious views espoused by respondents might seem incredible, if not preposterous, to most people. But if those doctrines are subject to trial before a jury

charged with finding their truth or falsity, then the same can be done with the religious beliefs of any sect. When the triers of fact undertake that task, they enter a forbidden domain.

Founding Church of Scientology v. United States

What the Jehovah's Witnesses were to the mid–twentieth century, the Church of Scientology became to the latter part of the century. Like the Witnesses, Scientology early set up a strong legal wing that litigated for religious rights as well as for human rights more generally. One of the first new religions to be embroiled in controversy, Scientology would prevail in most of its legal suits and would eventually play a major role in bringing down the Cult Awareness Network, the most important anticult group in the United States.

The Church of Scientology was one of the genuinely new religions to originate in the United States in the twentieth century. The church was founded by L. Ron Hubbard, a talented writer and adventurer with a consuming interest in the human mind. By 1950 Hubbard had completed enough of his research to write *Dianetics, the Modern Science of Mental Health*, which quickly became a bestseller. In 1951 he announced that the "applied religious philosophy" of Scientology had been born.

Auditing, Scientology's core technique, consists of guiding someone through various mental processes in order to first free the individual of the effects of the "reactive mind," and then to fully realize the spiritual nature of the person. Electrical devices called E-Meters, which rely upon the same basic technology as lie detectors, are used to help the auditor discover emotionally loaded memories. When the individual is freed from the effects of the reactive mind, she or he is said to have achieved the state of "clear."

Somewhat naively, Hubbard contacted the medical and the psychiatric associations, explaining the significance of his discoveries for mental and physical health and asking that the American Medical Association and the American Psychological Association investigate his new technique. Instead of taking this offer seriously, these associations responded by attacking him. The subsequent popular success of Dianetics did nothing to improve the image of Hubbard in the minds of the medical-psychiatric establishment and was likely instrumental in prompting the Food and Drug Administration raid against the church.

On January 4, 1963, the Founding Church of Scientology in Washington, D.C., was raided by U.S. marshals and deputized longshoremen with drawn guns, acting in behalf of the Food and Drug Administration. Five thousand volumes of church scriptures, 20,000 booklets, and 100 E-Meters were seized. It took eight years of litigation to finally obtain the return of the materials. In 1971, the U.S. District Court for the District of Columbia issued the *Founding Church of Scientology* v. *United States* decision. The Food and Drug Administration was ordered to return the books and E-Meters that had been taken in the 1963 raid. In its decision, the court recognized the church's constitutional right to protection from the government's excessive entanglement with religion.

Deprogramming in Court

The cult controversy proper did not get under way until after the collapse of the 1960s counterculture. Rather than reengaging with mainstream society, many former counterculture members continued their quest for an alternative lifestyle in a wide variety of religions. Hence the membership of many unusual religious groups that had existed quietly on the margins of American society suddenly increased dramatically.

In many cases, friends and family of cult members found it difficult to believe that, without coercion and brainwashing, loved ones could choose to embrace something that they found offensive. They sought deprogramming as the natural antidote to this mental programming or brainwashing. By attempting to deprogram the church member, friends and family believed they were helping the member recognize the wrongfulness of his or her choices.

When a person is targeted for deprogramming, he or she is enticed away from the organization or is actually kidnapped and taken to a remote place. While at the remote location, the person is subjected to intensive discussions in which he or she is presented with the "truth" about the religious organization, its tenets, and leaders. Numerous anticult organizations promoted kidnapping and deprogramming of alternative church members.

Family members are often the initiators of the kidnapping and deprogramming, and the deprogrammers are the facilitators. In addition to deprogrammers, bodyguards are sometimes hired to prevent the member from escaping. The fact that family members are often involved makes prosecution of the perpetrators difficult. The state has been reluctant to prosecute a family member for kidnapping. If family members are not prosecuted, judges and juries appear reluctant to convict others who become involved at the request of the family members. Further, family members often refuse to testify against the perpetrators, making it virtually impossible to convict.

In deprogramming cases, there is generally testimony by former members. This testimony is filled with a high level of hostility, which increases the prejudice of the judge and jury. The testimony of former members also tends to confuse the legal issues with religious questions. This entanglement of legal and religious issues often confuses the judge and jury and results in placing the religious practices of the church on trial.

In the case of LaVerne Collins (now LaVerne Macchio), a member of Church Universal and Triumphant, LaVerne's mother and sister decided to "rescue" LaVerne from the church because they believed it was seriously damaging LaVerne and her family. Family members hired deprogrammers and bodyguards to kidnap and deprogram Collins. At the time of her abduction, LaVerne was thirty-nine years old and the mother and primary caretaker of four children ranging in age from three to fourteen. She was a part-time schoolteacher and had resided in the same house in Ada County, Idaho, for fifteen years. Collins was missing for several days, and there was concern in the community for her safety.

After LaVerne's escape from the deprogrammers, charges were filed against LaVerne's mother and sister, the deprogrammers, and the bodyguards for kidnapping and false imprisonment. Later, at Collins's request, all charges against family members were dropped. As a result, the deprogrammers were acquitted. The bodyguards, who were to be tried separately, reached an unusual plea bargain with prosecutors: They would enter guilty pleas on either a felony kidnapping charge or a misdemeanor false imprisonment charge, depending on the outcome of an appeal challenging the judge's ruling to allow the deprogrammers the use of the "necessity defense" at their trial.

When authorities have attempted to resist efforts to kidnap and deprogram members of religious groups by prosecuting those involved, defendants have often been able to assert successfully the defenses of necessity and "choice of evils." The necessity defense has been a major factor in the acquittal of the deprogrammers. The jury appeared to accept the contention that the illegal actions of the defendants were necessary to protect the victim from her own choices and that the church was the greater evil—a view reflecting traditional prejudices.

One element that must be proved under the necessity defense is that there was imminent danger requiring the kidnapping. The courts have had difficulty establishing an objective standard by which to measure the danger or threat to the deprogramee. When the "choice of evils" defense is raised, courts have often allowed the jury to consider evidence concerning the supposed evils associated with the church's religious practices.

There is a long line of cases in the area of deprogramming. *People v. Brandyberry*, for example, involved a member of the Unification church who was kidnapped and held in captivity for several days in an attempt to deprogram her. The trial court balanced the "method of cult indoctrination" and of "coercive persuasion" against the evils of abduction and of forced deprogramming to justify kidnapping; however, the court of appeals evaluated only the imminence of grave injury to the victim. The court of appeals acknowledged that to proceed in the manner permitted by the trial court would invite the jury to "consider the morality and desirability of church doctrine and practices rather than whether in fact the victim was threatened by the prospect of a grave or imminent injury."

The trial judge in *Brandyberry* relied on a decision from the Minnesota Supreme Court, *Peterson v. Sorlien*, 299 N.W. 2d 123 (Minn. 1980), *cert. denied*, 450 U.S. 1031 (1981). The *Sorlien* court allowed parents to deprogram their child without fear of civil liability when the parents reasonably believed that the child was being unduly influenced by the religion and that the child had lost his or her capacity to reason.

Another common issue raised in deprogramming cases is that of involuntary treatment. Deprogrammers have sought orders requiring involuntary treatment for those who have been deprived of their free will and coercively persuaded to join a new religion. They argue that these individuals must be subject to involuntary treatment because they have lost their capacity to reason by virtue of the controlled environment and brainwashing to which they have been subjected. The control of the environment includes control over eating, sleeping, and other basics of life. Most courts have been reluctant to order such involuntary treatment. However, when courts permit the necessity or "choice of evils" defense, an individual's rights under the free exercise clause and right to be free from compulsory medical treatment are often abused.

Those who have experienced deprogramming have also brought civil actions against kidnappers and deprogrammers. These actions have included claims for violations of civil rights, intentional infliction of emotional distress, conspiracy, and false imprisonment. These actions have had mixed results, but generally the cause of action has been allowed. In fact, one appeals court recognized that deprogrammers practice patterns of coercion similar to those alleged against the church. However, in most cases, when civil claims are brought against deprogrammers or family members, the defendants try to make the religious practices of the church the focus of the trial. The defenses of necessity and "choice of evils" allows the trier of fact to review the religious organization's practices, and the degree to which those practices comport with the trier of fact's values may affect the outcome of the case.

Legislative Efforts and Conservatorship Cases

Attempting to Legislate against Cults

In the early years of the cult controversy, parents concerned about the religious choices of their adult children lobbied various legislatures. A number of states established committees and hearings to investigate. Some resolutions were passed, but legislative bodies were ultimately unwilling to act against minority religions because of the church/state separation issue. The strongest effort ever made by a U.S. legislature was New York state assembly bill AB9566-A, which would have made "promoting a pseudo-religious cult" a felony, introduced by Robert C. Wertz on October 5, 1977:

> A person is guilty of promoting a pseudo-religious cult when he knowingly organizes or maintains an organization into which other persons are induced to join or participate in through the use of mind control methods, hypnosis, brainwashing techniques or other systematic forms of indoctrination in which the members or participants of such organization engage in soliciting funds primarily for the benefit of such organization or its leaders and are not permitted to travel or communicate with anyone outside such organization unless another member or participant of such organization is present.

A number of different groups, including the American Civil Liberties Union, lobbied heavily against the bill, and it was ultimately defeated.

Efforts to Amend Conservatorship Laws

Failing to win the support of legislatures, some parents of cult members turned to deprogrammers. To protect themselves legally, it was sometimes possible to use existing conservatorship laws to legitimize their kidnapping activities. Conservatorships were originally designed to protect very elderly or very disturbed people from being unfairly taken advantage of. Such individuals are reduced to the legal status of children, unable to do such things as independently enter into contracts.

In some early cult conservatorship cases, psychiatrists sympathetic to the plight of concerned parents signed conservatorship orders without ever meeting the adult child—feeling that mere membership in a group like the Hare Krishna movement or the Unification church was sufficient evidence for declaring her or him incompetent. After this practice was challenged, anticultists pushed for amended conservatorship laws that would de facto legitimate deprogramming. Once again, such an amendment almost succeeded in the state of New York, where it was defeated only because the governor vetoed it. This measure was introduced on March 25, 1980, as 11122-A. The flavor of this proposed amendment is captured in its first section, "Persons for whom a temporary conservator may be appointed":

> The supreme court and the county courts outside the city of New York, shall have the power to appoint one or more temporary conservators of the persons and the property of any person over fifteen years of age, upon showing that such person for whom the temporary conservator is to be appointed have become closely and regularly associated with a group which practices the use of deception in the recruitment of members and which engages in systematic food or sleep deprivation or isolation from family or unusually long work schedules and that such person for whom the temporary conservator is to be appointed has undergone a sudden and radical change in behavior, lifestyle, habits and attitudes, and has become unable to care for his welfare and that his judgment has become impaired to the extent that he is unable to understand the need for such care.

The Faithful Five/Faithless Four Case

The primary conservatorship decision involving a stigmatized minority religion was *Katz* v. *Superior Court* (73 Cal. App. 3d 952,

141 Cal. Rptr. 234, 1977), also referred to as the Faithful Five/Faithless Four case. *Katz* was initially decided in favor of parents seeking conservatorships for their five adult offspring who were members of the Unification church—only to have the appeals court overturn the decision almost immediately. Four out of five of these individuals left the church anyway, hence the unusual nickname for this case.

Katz was set in motion when the parents asked a California superior court to grant 30-day conservatorships for their adult children. The goal was to forcibly incarcerate the five members in the Freedom Ranch Rehabilitation Center, a deprogramming facility run by the Freedom of Thought Foundation of Tucson, Arizona. The parents contended that conservatorships were necessary because of their offsprings' "mental illness or weakness and unsound mind" and propensity "to be deceived by artful and designing persons." The parents' counsel further argued that the five had been victims of "psychological kidnapping."

One expert witness in the case, psychiatrist Samuel Benson, described the five as suffering from a wide variety of pathological symptoms, including "memory impairment," "short attention spans and a decreased ability to concentrate," "limited ability towards abstractions," "defensive attitudes toward id urges," and "various degrees of regression and childlike attitudes." Benson further contended that these symptoms were the direct result of "coercive persuasion"—brainwashing—techniques, as reflected in literature on former Korean War and Vietnam War POWs.

Despite countertestimony by the five Unificationists and their own psychological/psychiatric consultants, and despite the obvious constitutional issues that were relevant, the judge decided for the parents, declaring that "we're talking about the very essence of life here, mother, father and children. There's nothing closer in our civilization. This is the essence of civilization." When some of the conservatees petitioned the order, a California appellate court heard their appeal. The court of appeals found the conservatorship statute unconstitutionally vague: "In the field of beliefs, and particularly religious tenets, it is difficult, if not impossible to establish a universal truth against which deceit and imposition can be measured." The appellate court also pointed out that there had been no demonstrated emergency that the conservatorship law required. In the absence of demonstrable physical deprivation, the equal protection and due process of law forbade involuntary confinement: "If there is coercive persuasion or brainwashing which requires treatment, the existence of such a mental disability and the necessity of legal control over the mentally disabled person for the purpose of treatment should be ascertained after compliance with the protection of civil liberties provided by the Welfare and Institutions Code. To do less is to license kidnapping for the purpose of thought control."

Finally and perhaps most importantly, the court of appeals held that the conservatorship orders had violated the Unificationists' rights to freedom of association and freedom of religion. The beliefs and behaviors used as criteria to determine the pathological state of the alleged victims (and to become the targets of the "treatment" to be administered at the Freedom Ranch Rehabilitation Center) were those that stemmed from religious conviction—precisely the arena into which the court system was forbidden to inquire. Hence, "in the absence of such actions as render the adult believer himself gravely disabled," state processes "cannot be used to deprive the believer of his freedom of action and to subject him to involuntary treatment."

The *Katz* decision did not immediately deter other parents from applying for temporary conservatorships for their adult children. There were also ongoing efforts to amend conservatorship laws so as to target members of minority religions. Retrospectively, however, it is evident that *Katz* marked an important watershed, after which the conservatorship tactic went into a gradual decline and eventually died out.

Ex-Member Lawsuits against Minority Religions

The issue of conservatorships for members of controversial religions was eventually completely eclipsed by tort cases brought by ex-members against their former religious groups. Because the Constitution does not protect all religiously motivated conduct, courts have come to award damages to individuals who claim to have incurred personal injury because of their religious affiliation. Underlying the rationale for such decisions is the traditional notion that religion should benefit and improve one's life and well-being. When religious beliefs and practices do not fulfill these expectations but instead are viewed as subjecting a person to personal harm, those beliefs and practices become suspect and generally open to scrutiny by the courts.

Unfortunately, the courts have tended to examine nontraditional religious practices in light of mainstream traditions. Since the emergence of the cult controversy, many minority religious groups have been accused of brainwashing or coercive persuasion. It is claimed that these religious practices subject the individual to a controlled environment in which individuals lose their capacity to reason and think for themselves.

In the early 1990s a judge considered religious practices when sentencing an individual who had pled guilty to charges of murder for hire and conspiracy to tamper with a federal witness. The court sentenced Richard LeBaron to five years for killing a man and his daughter at point-blank range because he had been "brainwashed" by a church to which he had belonged since he was a child. The court believed that because of this brainwashing, LeBaron had lost his capacity to reason and think for himself while committing the crimes, that his thoughts were coerced and not his own, and that he was not totally responsible for his choices and actions.

Religious practices that are seen as diminishing the individual's capacity to reason and to give consent foster suspicion and leave the religious organization open to harassment and liability. The courts may, and often do, consider the religious beliefs and practices of nontraditional churches in the context of civil and criminal litigation. Since religious freedom is not absolute, as long as the courts are convinced that certain religious practices cause harm to society or to individual church members, all religions will be subject to scrutiny and regulation by the courts and government. When children are involved, the scrutiny is even more exacting. Although the First Amendment was meant to protect individual rights, the courts' willingness to delve into religious beliefs and practices affecting a variety of areas has at times resulted in biasing juries against nontraditional religious practices. This has been the case especially in civil suits.

Religious groups, both traditional and nontraditional, have been named in suits for intentional infliction of emotional distress and liability for "outrageous conduct" through spiritual counseling. When counseling by clergy goes awry, the minister or pastor becomes subject to litigation for intentional infliction of emotional distress. The emotional distress arises from beratement for sinful conduct and the member's perception that the pastor's counseling is malicious and intended to demean. A variety of different minority religions have been besieged with lawsuits by ex-members for personal injury claims ranging from fraud to intentional infliction of emotional distress.

In his 1995 book, *Understanding New Religious Movements,* John Saliba points out that contemporary minority religions have been taken to court for a wide variety of reasons:

1. The mental distress and psychological damage they have caused
2. Kidnapping and brainwashing young adults, thus forcing them to become members
3. The corruption of minors
4. Sexual servitude
5. Defamation
6. Alienation of affections
7. Wanton misconduct and outrageous acts
8. Harassment
9. Wrongful death

Decisions in such cases have varied so widely that general conclusions are difficult to draw. All of the better known and many of the lesser known new religions have been involved in such cases. The *Molko-Leal* case will be examined because of its significance for later developments in the cult controversy. The *Mull* case will be examined, partially because of its influence on a later tax case.

The *Mull* Case

In this prominent case, Gregory Mull, a San Francisco building designer, became a member of Church Universal and Triumphant in 1974 at the age of 57. He relocated to the Los Angeles area in 1979 and became employed at the church's Malibu headquarters doing design work.

The church loaned Mull a total of $37,000 during the time he was relocating, for which Mull signed two promissory notes. His tenure on church staff lasted about eight months; then he resigned from the organization over a dispute involving repayment of the notes. The church filed an action against Mull in 1981 for repayment of the $37,000; Mull counterclaimed for fraud, duress, undue influence, involuntary servitude, assault, extortion, and intentional infliction of emotional distress seeking total damages of $253 million. The case was tried in 1986 in Los Angeles superior court.

Mull claimed at the trial that he was a victim of church mind control and that when he signed the notes he lacked the legal capacity to do so. He also claimed that church officials unduly pressured him through psychological and emotional manipulation to sign the notes.

Mull asserted that while he was on staff he was physically debilitated by decreeing (a form of church prayer) and from a vegetarian diet and various health practices, such as fasting and enemas. Mull also claimed that, subsequent to his resignation, he had been assaulted at a church event and that church officials had publicly disclosed private facts causing him personal suffering. Finally, he claimed that for his design services while he served on staff, he should be compensated $2 million.

At the four-week jury trial, the judge allocated one day to evidence involving the promissory notes and the remainder to testimony on a variety of church practices and beliefs. The testimony by numerous expert witnesses, appearing for both sides, and by both present and ex-members covered reincarnation, the Ascended Masters, and the church founder's role as a prophet of God, with each side alternately supporting and ridiculing same. The claims of involuntary servitude and extortion were dismissed before trial. The jury gave a general verdict on all of the remaining claims, finding against the church and its leader, Elizabeth Clare Prophet, for $1.5 million in compensatory and punitive damages.

The results in *Mull* are not particularly surprising given the plaintiff's emotionally charged claims and the willingness of the court to allow evidence that was not relevant to his claims but which the appeals court also ruled was not prejudicial. The case has probably made the church more willing to compromise on subsequent claims.

Not all such cases have been decided in favor of plaintiffs. William Purcell, another ex-member of Church Universal and Triumphant, also brought an action against the church and its leaders, claiming fraud, clerical malpractice, psychological malpractice, cancellation of written instruments, involuntary servitude, intentional infliction of emotional distress, and seeking the imposition of a constructive trust. When Purcell filed his suit in 1984, he sought the return of contributions that he had made, claiming that he had made the contributions based on false representations by the defendants. The action was dismissed in 1986 on summary judgment in favor of the church and its leaders.

Molko & Leal v. Unification Church

David Molko and Tracey Leal had been members of the Unification church for approximately six months when they were kidnapped and deprogrammed. Not long after leaving, they sued the church for fraud, intentional infliction of emotional distress, and false imprisonment. They also sought the return of $6,000 worth of donations and payment for the work they did while members. The Unification church countercharged that the psychological harm Molko and Leal had experienced was caused by deprogramming procedures rather than by church-related activities.

This case dragged on for years. In the first round, charges against the Unification church were dismissed in 1986. Then, three years later after a number of appeals, the case was finally cleared for trial by the California supreme court. For a number of different reasons, this case was finally settled out of court in November 1989.

This case is particularly important because of an amicus brief (a brief filed by an outside party interested in the outcome of the case) initially filed on behalf of the Unification church by the American Psychological Association and a number of individual scholars. Margaret Singer, one of the expert witnesses in this case, and Richard Ofshe would later sue the APA, citing this amicus brief as the basis for an accusation of a conspiracy against them.

Child Abuse and Governmental Intervention in Nontraditional Religions

Child Abuse

On the morning of Sunday, July 26, 1953, a force of 120 Arizona peace officers, together with 100 news reporters, drove across unpaved roads to the Mormon fundamentalist community of Short Creek, Arizona, to arrest 36 men, 86 women, and pick up 263 children. It was a surprise attack and was compared by one Associated Press reporter to "a military assault on an enemy position." Sect members were clearly outnumbered as there were two officers for every home in the community. Although the element of surprise was not completely successful, the officers arrested most of the targeted men and women, and the Arizona governor announced on the radio that the purpose of the raid was "to protect the lives and futures of 263 children" and that the religious community was "the foulest conspiracy you could imagine," which was "dedicated to the production of white slaves." Apparently, some officials in the Mormon church (which had only abandoned polygamy itself fifty years earlier) not only applauded the raid but may also have provided relevant information to the police and other civil authorities.

Shortly after the raid, the mothers and children were bused to Phoenix where they were initially kept in crowded conditions and were told they would remain there for up to a month before being placed in permanent foster homes. Eventually, juvenile hearings were held in Arizona state courts that resulted in the placement of most of the children in foster homes around Arizona, often accompanied by their mothers. Then in March 1955, an Arizona superior court judge ordered that all of the children be restored to their families, which brought an end to Arizona's efforts to segregate children from fundamentalist parents.

The Short Creek raid bears certain strong parallels with the Northeast Kingdom raid described in the opening sections of this book. In both cases, governmental authorities intervened directly in the affairs of religious communities with the aim of protecting children from abuse, only to discover that no such abuse was occurring.

Much the same thing happened in Waco, but with far more tragic consequences. Although child abuse is technically the jurisdiction of the state rather than the federal government, concern that the Davidian children were being abused was one of the principal reasons cited by authorities as justification for both the initial ATF attack and for the concluding FBI assault. On April 21, White House spokesperson George Stephanopoulos, defending the actions, asserted that there "is absolutely no question that there's overwhelming evidence of child abuse in the Waco compound" (Ellison and Bartkowski, 112). Others criticize this line of defense, arguing that even if the Davidians practiced such abuse, the government's actions were unjustified.

However, on the very day of Stephanopoulos' remarks, the Justice Department publicly acknowledged that they had no solid evidence of child abuse—only speculation by mental health professionals who had been studying Koresh from a distance. Also on the same day, 1,100 pages of unsealed documents relevant to the case were released. These included only two allegations of child abuse by disgruntled former members.

Certainly during the siege itself, the FBI showed little regard for the children when it cut off electricity and water to the compound and used psychological warfare. The weird light and sound show, which included recordings of dentists' drills and dying rabbits, would hardly have promoted any child's sense of well-being. Deteriorating sanitary conditions, caused by decaying bodies and the buildup of sewage, were also given as a justification for attacking Mt. Carmel on April 19. The attorney general told Larry King on national television that she feared that "if I delayed, without sanitation or toilets there . . . I could go in there in two months and find children dead from any number of things."

The Texas Department of Human Services had investigated Mt. Carmel on child abuse allegations on at least three different occasions. No credible evidence for such accusations was found.

The same can be said for the twenty-one children released from Mt. Carmel between the ATF raid and the FBI assault—no hard evidence of child abuse. On March 5, Janice Caldwell, director of the Texas Department of Protective and Regulatory Services, stated that "they're in remarkably good shape considering what they have been through. No signs of physical abuse have been found." The March 6 edition of the *Houston Post* noted that "all the youths appear to be in good condition psychologically and physically." In the same article, a social worker asserted that "the children are remarkably well-educated."

The lack of any solid evidence for Davidian child abuse probably explains the reason that the attorney general and the FBI dropped this explanation as soon as reporters began to raise questions about specific evidence for abuse. Child abuse is one of those issues like AIDS and the plight of the homeless that has been uppermost in the public consciousness during the last decade or so. As a consequence, accusations of child abuse are more effective at attracting attention than other kinds of charges. What this means for nontraditional religions accused of child abuse is that such groups sometimes lose their chance for a fair hearing.

One of the earliest cases involving children in a religious setting was *Prince* v. *Massachusetts* (1944). Prince, a Jehovah's Witness, was the custodian of her nine-year-old niece. She was convicted of violating state child-labor laws for taking her niece with her to sell religious literature. The U.S. Supreme Court upheld her conviction. It stated that "the family itself is not beyond regulation in the public interest, as against a claim of religious liberty. . . . [N]either rights of religion nor rights of parenthood are beyond limitation" (*Prince* v. *Massachusetts*, 321 U.S. 158, p. 166).

The state has an interest in protecting juveniles under its traditional role as *parens patriae* (literally, "parent of the country," referring to the state's sovereign role as guardian of persons under legal disability). The state's interest is in restricting any conduct that is harmful to the child. "The state has a wide range of power for limiting parental freedom and authority in things affecting the child's welfare; . . . this includes, to some extent, matters of conscience and religious conviction" (*Prince* v. *Massachusetts*, 321 U.S. 158, p. 167). The Court indicated that parents could become martyrs if they wanted to, but they did not have the right to make martyrs of their children and subject them to emotional, psychological, or physical injury. The Court left no doubt that if a judge perceives that a religious practice or religious belief may be harmful to a child, the Court can and will restrict the religious conduct.

There are other situations of child endangerment where the concern of the state to protect children is more legitimate. Courts have even, at times, restricted the religious practices and beliefs of parents when it is believed that those practices and beliefs harm the child.

In a California case, *Walker* v. *Superior Court*, a court allowed the prosecution of a mother on charges of involuntary manslaughter and felony child endangerment because the mother had not sought medical treatment for her daughter when the daughter was dying of acute meningitis. Although certain statutes allowed parents to seek spiritual treatment of children, when the life of the child was seriously threatened, "the right of a parent to rely exclusively on prayer must yield" (*Walker* v. *Superior Court*, 763 P. 2d 892 [Cal. 118, p. 866]). The court had little tolerance for religious practices and beliefs when the parent endangered the child's life by pursuing his or her own religious interests and not putting the general welfare of the child paramount. Prayer treatment was accommodated only as long as there was no serious risk of harm or danger to the child's life. When a child's life is threatened, religious beliefs take a second seat. The California court quoted the U.S. Supreme Court in *Prince* v. *Massachusetts:* "The right to practice religion freely does not include liberty to expose the community or child to communicable disease or the latter to ill health or death" (*Prince* v. *Massachusetts*, 321 U.S. pp. 166–167). When the religious beliefs and practices of parents interfere with the general welfare of a child, the courts show no reluctance to interfere.

In another example of this pattern, a jury in Minneapolis recently reviewed the religious practices of the Christian Scientists. An eleven-year-old boy with diabetes died because his mother would not seek treatment because of her religious beliefs. After the child died, the father brought suit and obtained a $14.2 million jury verdict against the church and his ex-wife.

Child Custody Cases

Religious practices and beliefs have also become the subject of child custody cases where nonmembers attempt to challenge nontraditional aspects of a spouse's or ex-spouse's religion to obtain custody of a minor child, sometimes arguing that the church's influence is mentally, physically, or emotionally detrimental to the child's well-being. Nonmembers have been successful when the court determines that the practices harm the child.

In a Kentucky custody case, Melanie Pleasant-Topel was allowed to retain custody of her minor son, Sean Pleasant, but was given strict guidelines by the court as to the religious practices of the Church Universal and Triumphant to which she could expose her son. For example, she was required to follow what American society dictates as a normal and appropriate diet, rather than a vegetarian or nontraditional diet (which the church does not require in any event). She was also required to send him to the school he had been attending rather than to a church school. However, to the extent the custodial member parent raised the child within the framework the court deemed normal, the court did not interfere with the custody.

In another case in which a member of Church Universal and Triumphant was involved, the church and its practices were central to the action. The mother, Charlene Viau, had been a member of Church Universal and Triumphant for approximately eleven years. The father contended that the church was an "armed camp" and raised serious concerns that the church environment would be harmful to the child, but the court awarded custody of the minor child to the mother, finding that there was no reasonable likelihood of future impairment to the minor child.

Another child custody action involving this church occurred in Indiana. The court found that the influence of Church Universal and Triumphant would be harmful and detrimental to the children and that the mother's association with the church demonstrated her poor judgment and inability to properly raise the children. Custody of the children was given to the father.

While these results seem contradictory, individual facts and circumstances often dictate results. Unfortunately, all the relevant circumstances are not always apparent from court records. In other cases, decisions are often result-oriented, and their stated rationale may be misleading. Nevertheless, certain basic principles are almost universally recognized in these types of cases.

In New Mexico, a father who was a devout Sikh in Yogi Bhajan's Sikh Dharma organization sought to change the custody of his children. Until their divorce, both parents had actively practiced the Sikh religion as brought to this country by Yogi Bhajan and involved their children in the religion. Following her remarriage, the custodial mother withdrew from the Sikh religion and discouraged her children from participating in it. The father wanted his children raised in the Sikh religion and sought to modify the custody order to give him custody of the children so that he could guide their religious upbringing. The court noted that the paramount concern was the general welfare of the children. The court also recognized that religious restrictions on visitation "have been upheld where evidence of physical or emotional harm to the child has been substantial." The courts have not hesitated to interfere when it is shown that the child suffers anxiety and other emotional distress because of the religious differences of his parents.

In an action in Tennessee to modify visitation, the court noted that the general trend in custody cases is to not allow religious beliefs to be controlling. "The law tolerates and even encourages, up to a point, the child's exposure to the religious influences of both parents even if they are divided in their faiths." Courts will generally not interfere with the religious training a noncustodial parent gives his or her children absent "a clear and affirmative showing that these activities and expressions of belief are harmful to the child." However, courts will not allow conflicting beliefs of parents to cause the children emotional harm; the paramount interest of the court is the general welfare of the child.

Many child custody cases exemplify how the cult stereotype may be used as an ideological resource in specific social conflicts. There is enough ambiguity in the cult label to make its application in particular cases a matter of negotiation. Occasions for such negotiation arise in the context of social conflicts. For individuals or groups locked in certain kinds of struggles with members of minority religions, the stereotype represents a potent ideological resource that—if they are successful in making the label stick—marshals public opinion against their opponent, potentially tipping the balance of power in their favor.

The stigma of the "cult" stereotype has been particularly effective in more than a few child custody cases, in which one parent's membership in a minority religion is portrayed as indicative of her or his unworthiness as a parent. For such legal conflicts, it is difficult to deploy the stereotype unless there is some larger, earlier conflict that led to press coverage in which the particular minority religion in question was labeled as a cult. Lacking earlier bad press, the cult label can still sometimes be made to stick on the basis of testimony by disgruntled former members.

For the most part, individuals involved in such relatively limited conflicts do not become full-time anticult crusaders. While they may enter into a relationship with the anticult movement, they normally drift away from this involvement within a short time after the termination of their particular struggle. Also, if anticult rhetoric fails to accomplish their end but some other tool works in their particular conflict, they are usually quite ready to dispose of the cult stereotype and adopt an entirely different angle of attack.

One case in which the employment of the cult stereotype was clearly opportunistic involved the mother's association with the Movement of Spiritual Inner Awareness (MSIA). Her affiliation was effectively used against her by her ex-husband in a dispute involving their mutual offspring. In this particular case, a divorced mother petitioned the court to permit her to relocate in order to take a position in an MSIA-inspired organization offering human potentials seminars. The ex-husband argued that he did not want his son involved in a cult and brought up old rumors about MSIA and MSIA's founder in an effort to prevent his ex-wife from leaving the state. Perceiving that not only would she have a difficult time winning her case but also that her husband might undertake further actions that could result in her son being taken from her, she dropped the case.

What is especially ironic about this case is that for several decades this particular father had been deeply involved in est—a human potentials group that had very frequently (far more frequently than MSIA) been labeled a "cult." As someone whose participation in est has likely sensitized him to the cult controversy, the ex-husband's utilization of the stereotype is clearly opportunistic.

Tax Cases

Churches act as fiduciaries, enter into contracts, purchase property, and otherwise conduct business within the communities where they are located. Churches expose themselves to tax liability when their conduct is not purely religious. Scrutiny becomes particularly focused on churches when they are the recipients of gifts, devises, or other transfers of property, or are otherwise benefited. There have been a number of IRS cases involving minority religions in which the Internal Revenue Service has revoked the tax-exempt status of controversial new religions, often at the prompting of enemies of the particular religion involved.

In 1985, for example, The Way International's tax-exempt status was revoked following allegations of partisan political involvement and certain business activities at its New Knoxville headquarters. The ruling was reversed by the Supreme Court in 1990. Most recently, in 1993, the IRS ceased all litigation and recognized Scientology as a legitimate religious organization. This followed years of contentious litigation between the agency and the Church of Scientology.

Church Universal and Triumphant

Church Universal and Triumphant is a Montana-based New Age church led by Elizabeth Clare Prophet. An indirect spin-off of the

"I Am" Religious Activity that grew quietly in its early years, by the late 1980s it had become the most controversial new religion in North America in terms of negative media coverage. Founded as the Summit Lighthouse by Mark L. Prophet in 1958, Elizabeth Prophet took over his role as the primary mouthpiece for the Masters after her husband's death in 1973. The group moved to Montana in 1986. Much of the church's negative media derived from incidents clustered around its extensive fallout shelters and its preparations for the possibility of a nuclear attack against the United States. In 1990, members from around the world gathered in Montana because of the predicted possibility of an atomic holocaust—a story picked up by the AP wire service.

On the heels of this extensive publicity, Church Universal and Triumphant had its tax-exempt status revoked in October 1992. The revocation followed an inquiry that began in 1989 under the Church Audit Procedures Act. Three reasons were given for the revocation: the church was alleged to be involved to an excessive degree in nonexempt commercial activities; it had made an allegedly improper payment on behalf of a church official as part of a court judgment (the *Mull* case); and it had allegedly been involved at an official level in a scheme by two church employees to illegally purchase weapons. The IRS claimed Church Universal and Triumphant owed back taxes on business income, employment taxes, and excise taxes.

The church strongly disputed all three reasons given for the revocation, filing a declaratory judgment action to reverse the IRS decision. The church and the IRS entered into extensive settlement negotiations, and the court extended various pretrial hearing dates to accommodate the negotiations. In taking its action against the group, the IRS was clearly influenced by negative publicity, including coverage from the Gregory Mull case, investigative articles in the *Bozeman Daily Chronicle* discussing Church Universal and Triumphant operations, an ex-member's claim that the Church Universal and Triumphant supported international rebel groups, the appearance of Elizabeth Clare Prophet's daughter on the *Oprah Winfrey Show*, a Montana newspaper article about gun ownership by Church Universal and Triumphant members, and the guilty pleas of church members Vernon Hamilton and Edward Francis to charges that they had illegally purchased weapons.

Initially, the focus of the IRS investigation appeared to be the church's potential liability for unrelated business income tax; the church's tax-exempt status was secondary. However, the information gleaned from newspapers, particularly the illegal gun purchases by Hamilton and Francis, changed the focus to the tax-exempt status of the organization. There were, however, irregularities in the agency's investigation that led to a compromise agreement in mid 1994—a compromise that included restoring the church's status as a charitable organization.

Rev. Sun Myung Moon's Income Tax Evasion Case

The Unification church, formally the Holy Spirit Association for the Unification of World Christianity, has been one of the most controversial new religions in late-twentieth-century North America. We have already noted a number of cases above in which the Unification church has been involved. Derided in the West as "the Moonies," the Unification church is an international messianic religious movement led by the Reverend Sun Myung Moon, a Korean national. While polemical opponents have identified any number of departures from Christian orthodoxy, the major novelty is the explicitness with which the present is identified as the time of the Christ's Second Advent.

After the departure of the Children of God (later known as The Family) from the United States in the mid 1970s, the Unification church became the most controversial religion on the American scene. This was in part due to the activities of the group itself, which attracted attention by staging major rallies across the nation in 1976. The California branch of the organization was also involved in a deceptive recruiting operation. Perhaps most importantly, however, the leadership of the anticult movement made a conscious choice to focus attention on the Unification church. The strategy was that, if the government could be moved to act against the Unification church, this would establish a precedent that could then be turned against other minority religions. However, as we have noted, the anticultists were largely unsuccessful in evoking governmental action.

One of the few areas in which the assault on this religion was successful was in a tax case involving the founder, Rev. Sun Myung Moon. In 1982, Rev. Moon was convicted and jailed on tax evasion charges for failure to pay a purported tax liability of $7,300 over a three-year period. This liability came about as a result of a church checking account that had been opened in Rev. Moon's name by early missionaries in New York rather than as a result of an intentional action on his part. It should also be noted that having a church account in the name of the pastor is a common practice in such denominations as the Baptist church. This case was regarded by most jurists, civil libertarians, and religious leaders as biased and an intrusion on essential religious freedoms, and the Unification church decried the case as religious persecution.

The case briefly made headlines, and the anticult movement congratulated itself on finally having achieved a victory in the area of invoking a governmental response. In the long run, however, the results of the case were mixed. Clergymen from a wide variety of different congregations, liberal and conservative, came to Rev. Moon's defense, including such national figures as Jerry Falwell. The Unification church thus acquired contacts and allies it could never have hoped to have made without the case.

Like many other Christian denominations, the Unification church embraced a theology of redemptive suffering that could speak directly to the conviction and incarceration of the church's founder. Accepting this turn of events as divinely ordained, Rev. Moon also stood up well under the conditions of his imprisonment. In the end, the Unification church probably emerged stronger than it had been prior to the case.

Zoning and Solicitation

Minority religions have also encountered problems with local ordinances governing zoning and solicitation. These cases have had varied results. A few solicitation cases that made it all the way to the Supreme Court will be discussed. In 1981 in *Heffron* v. *International Society for Krishna Consciousness,* the Supreme Court supported the state's right to require solicitors—including members of the Hare Krishna movement—to be confined to booths at the state fair. However, the very next year in *Larson* v. *Valente,* the Supreme Court decided in favor of the Unification church against a solicitation law that, it was clear, targeted new religious groups.

Zoning has also often been an area of conflict. Residents often resent any intrusion into their neighborhood that disturbs the status quo. People purchase homes in certain neighborhoods specifically relying on the zoning codes and the general tenor of the neighborhood and are suspicious of new groups using property in the neighborhood for other, nontraditional purposes.

Church Universal and Triumphant

The Church Universal and Triumphant has encountered several zoning problems over the years. One high-profile case involved its purchase of a large mansion in Minneapolis in an area zoned for single-family residential dwellings but that also allowed for usage by churches and religious organizations. The property and building purchased by the church had previously been used as a duplex. Church Universal and Triumphant proposed to use the building for worship services and as a religious community residence and teaching center.

As soon as the church purchase was completed, the local homeowners expressed concern about the group being located in the area. The residents did not understand the religion, particularly since its tenets did not fit into the traditional religious mold. The residents encouraged and then joined a suit by the city of Minneapolis to stop the church from using the property, claiming that it offered insufficient parking and that the religious community and center did not constitute a valid accessory use. In Minnesota, a church sanctuary as well as a monastery and rectory can be situated in a single-family residential zoning area. The court found that the teaching center qualified as a church monastery or rectory and that the group was in "substantial compliance" with the zoning code's parking requirements. The Minnesota supreme court upheld this decision.

The hostility encountered by Church Universal and Triumphant in Minneapolis is not unique. When the Church of Jesus Christ of Latter-Day Saints tried to purchase property in Seattle and Portland to construct temples for worship by its members, strong sentiments were expressed in opposition. A comparable situation has generated a long-running conflict with respect to a retreat facility established by the Movement of Spiritual Inner Awareness.

The Movement of Spiritual Inner Awareness

In the mountains overlooking Santa Barbara, California, the Institute for Individual and World Peace (an organization founded by John-Roger, founder-leader of the Movement of Spiritual Inner Awareness) purchased some property—later named Windermere—for the purpose of building a peace retreat facility. Bordered on one side by a national forest, the property is also directly adjacent to a semirural neighborhood populated by individuals who purposely moved away from the city. Some of these people viewed their new neighbors with concern. When they heard about plans to build a facility that might attract large numbers of outsiders from the Los Angeles area who might disturb their peaceful rural setting, some were upset. Eventually some neighbors organized the

Cielo Preservation Organization (named after the main road in the area) to oppose the construction of the retreat—construction that could not proceed without approval from the county.

Not long after a negative article about MSIA appeared in the *Los Angeles Times*, almost everyone in the neighborhood received a copy when an anonymous person placed it in all the mailboxes. This article immediately became a centerpiece in some of the neighbors' opposition to IIWP's retreat plans. By 1994, the *Times* report had been superseded by the considerable publicity Arianna Huffington's MSIA connections were generating in the southern California media. Thus in a December 1994 article in the local Santa Barbara paper on the conflict between Windermere and the neighborhood, Huffington and her connections were brought up and discussed near the beginning of the article: John-Roger's "teachings drew national attention during this year's California Senate race between incumbent Diane Feinstein and Rep. Michael Huffington because the Montecito congressman's wife, Arianna, had ties to the John-Roger organization, which some critics claim is a cult. Arianna Huffington has said it is not a cult, and described her past connection with MSIA as a casual one." Despite the cautious wording of this passage, the net effect of mentioning such accusations is that otherwise uninformed readers may conclude that the "cult" label is probably appropriate for MSIA, thus influencing them to side with the retreat's opponents.

This labeling has been highly successful in generating anti-IIWP/anti-MSIA sentiment in Santa Barbara County. The point here, however, is that the Cielo Preservation Organization is less concerned about the ranch owners' religious persuasion than about preventing, in the words of a local organizer, hordes of "L.A. cowboys" from invading the area, thus spoiling their rural privacy. The claim that the Windermere Ranch is populated by "weird cultists" is simply one among many accusations hurled at IIWP that represent an all-out effort to short-circuit their retreat plans rather than representing a deep commitment to the anticult position.

Libel Cases

Considering the often highly charged debate in this controversy, it is surprising that there have been so few libel cases. These few cases have, however, been significant. Overseas, there was a long-running libel case in England that the Unification church had brought against the *Daily Mail*. This case was eventually decided in favor of the newspaper. Perhaps the most significant libel case concerning nontraditional religions in the United States was the 1985 Local Church libel case won against authors who had accused the church of being a "destructive cult."

The Local Church Libel Case

The Local Church, also known as the Little Flock, was founded in the 1920s in China by Ni Shutsu, popularly known as Watchman Nee. Accused by China of being a spy for the Americans and the Nationalist government, he was sent to prison in 1952, where he died twenty years later. Among Nee's followers was Witness Lee, founder and elder of the church at Chefoo. The movement spread around the Pacific basin and was brought to the West Coast of the United States by migrating members. Lee himself moved to the United States, where he founded Living Stream Ministry and led the spread of the Local Church.

While highly orthodox in doctrine, Lee brought innovation to the church by introducing a number of theological emphases as well as new practices, such as "pray reading" and "calling upon the name of the Lord." "Pray reading" is a devotional practice using the words of Scripture as the words of prayer. During this practice, which is supposed to allow the Scripture to impart an experience of the presence of God in the person praying, people repeat words and phrases from the Scripture over and over, often interjecting words of praise and thanksgiving. "Calling upon the name of the Lord," on the other hand, represents an invocation of God by the repetition of phrases such as "O Lord Jesus." Both these practices have been subjects of controversy.

A controversy emerged in the 1970s between the Local Church and some members of the larger evangelical Christian community who regarded the innovations of Lee as departing from acceptable evangelical thought. This controversy culminated in a series of legal actions in the mid 1980s. A number of anticult writers accused the Local Church of heresy and attacked its unique forms of Christian piety. The lawsuits instituted by the Local Church brought retractions and apologies from all organizations except the Spiritual Counterfeits Project, a Christian anticult group that had published the book *The God-Men*, attacking the church. This case went to trial, and in 1985 a financial settlement was ordered against the Spiritual Counterfeits Project, which was driven to bankruptcy in the face of an $11 million judgment.

The Local Church case was important to people who regularly wrote on the cult controversy. Subsequently, writers moved away from referring to many minority religions by name and instead shifted to writing about "cults" in general. The only groups named were religions that had been decimated or eliminated by violence, such as the People's Temple.

Cynthia Kisser v. the Church of Scientology

In 1990, Michael Rokos, then president of the Cult Awareness Network (CAN), resigned when it was discovered that he had been arrested several years earlier for propositioning a young policeman who had been posing as a teenager. After Cynthia Kisser, CAN's executive director, took over the day-to-day running of the organization, members of some of the groups attacked by CAN began investigating her background in hopes of finding a similar skeleton in the closet. Eventually they discovered that Kisser had worked briefly as a topless dancer in the 1970s. Critics—including Heber Jentzsch, president of the Church of Scientology, International—seized upon this information and attempted to discredit the organization. Kisser responded by suing Jentzsch and the Church of Scientology for defamation of character in 1992. She filed two suits, one in federal court and one in state court. Both were dismissed, the first in 1994 and the second in 1995. Kisser's appeal met a similar fate.

In dismissing her federal case, U.S. District Judge James B. Zagel remarked:

> Statements charging Kisser with exposing her breasts in public for remuneration could affect the public's assessment of her as a critic of religious cults. Some might regard such activity as the symptom of a character so deeply flawed that they could expect other symptoms, such as untruthfulness. Some who regard topless dancing as base, immoral or sinful . . . might consider a former topless dancer less likely to understand, appreciate or fairly judge the motives and practices of organizations claiming spiritual inspiration and purpose, or their members' lifestyles.

Zagel further noted that Kisser did not "offer any clear and convincing evidence showing a reckless disregard for the truth," as required by law. Not long after the federal case had been decided, her state case was dismissed with prejudice. Kisser's appeal of the federal decision was finally dismissed in 1997. These defeats took place around the same time that the Cult Awareness Network itself was being dismantled in the courts, in what must stand as the worst losing streak in the anticult movement's short history.

The Defeat of Anticultism in the Courts

For many years the legal struggle between minority religions and their critics went back and forth in the courts, so that, throughout the 1980s, it appeared to longtime observers as though the conflict had reached a kind of stasis. It was thus somewhat surprising when, in the 1990s, the scale tipped decisively in favor of the new religious movements. The defeat of anticultism in the courts took place in two distinct arenas: In the first place, mind control/coercive persuasion/brainwashing was rejected as a theory that could have a bearing on the outcome of any legal case. In the second place, the Cult Awareness Network was sued out of existence in the wake of a deprogramming-related lawsuit. Subsequently, the Cult Awareness Network (CAN) name, mailing address, and phone number were purchased by the Church of Scientology.

The *Fishman* Decision

For many years, Dr. Margaret Singer, a clinical psychologist, had been the most weighty expert witness in court cases involving the notion of coercive persuasion, popularly known as brainwashing. Part of her legitimacy as an expert derived from her association with other psychological researchers who had examined American soldiers released from POW camps following the Korean War. Singer had testified in such prominent cases as *Katz*, *Mull*, and *Molko-Leal*, to name just a few.

Her demise as an expert witness began, ironically, with an effort of Singer and some of her colleagues to legitimize the anticult position on mind control within the psychological profession. This group had formed a task force on "deceptive and indirect methods of persuasion and control" within the American Psychological Association (APA). This task force submitted its report to the Board of Social and Ethical Responsibility for Psychology of the APA. The report was rejected by the board in May 1987, with the statement that, "in general, the report lacks the scientific rigor and evenhanded critical approach needed for APA imprimatur." Task force members were explicitly warned not to imply that the APA in any way supported the position the report put forward.

The other document that would be brought forward to discredit Singer was an amicus brief filed by the APA and 23 scholars in support of the Unification church in the *Molko-Leal* case. Singer had already testified in this case, and the foreword to the amicus brief was harshly critical of Singer: "APA believes that this commitment to advancing the appropriate use of psychological testimony in the courts carries with it a concomitant duty to be vigilant against those who would use purportedly expert testimony lacking scientific and methodological rigor." The wording at the end of this statement clearly reinforced the decision of the APA board to reject the task force report, although this brief had been filed before the report was rejected.

These two events subsequently led to the rejection of Singer as an expert witness in a series of cases, culminating in *U.S.* v. *Fishman* in 1990. Stephen Fishman had argued that his criminal behavior, mail fraud, had been caused by the Church of Scientology's mind control/thought reform techniques to which he had been subjected. U.S. District Court Judge D. Lowell Jensen reviewed the scientific status of Singer's theories—as well as the related ideas of sociologist Richard Ofshe, whom the defense had also called as an expert witness—in some detail. Ofshe was rejected out of hand as an expert witness. Singer could testify as a mental health professional, on the condition that she not "support her opinion with testimony that involves thought reform, because the Court finds that her views on thought reform, like Dr. Ofshe's, are not generally accepted within the scientific community." This turned out to be a landmark decision, which was subsequently used to disqualify Singer and Ofshe from testifying in other cult cases.

Singer and Ofshe then sued the APA and the ASA, alleging that these two organizations had conspired with twelve scholars to discredit them. On August 9, 1993, a federal judge threw their suit out of court. They refiled an almost identical suit in state court in California, but this new suit was thrown out in June 1994. Upon appeal, the case was dismissed with prejudice. With this last dismissal, "cultic mind control" was finally finished in the courts.

The *Scott* Case and the Demise of the Cult Awareness Network

For many years, the Church of Scientology had invested its legal resources in fighting various governmental agencies—most recently, a host of cases involving the Internal Revenue Service. In 1993, the IRS halted all Scientology-related litigation and extended unqualified recognition to the church and its various affiliated organizations. This action had many different spin-off effects, including the freeing of Scientology's legal resources. It was thus almost inevitable that the church would turn its attention to the Cult Awareness Network.

Despite public statements to the contrary, the CAN regularly referred worried parents to vigilante deprogrammers. It was in this practice that Scientology found the weak point that would eventually bring the organization down. In a criminal case in the state of Washington, deprogrammer Rick Ross and his associates had been referred to the mother of Jason Scott by the Cult Awareness Network. Scott, a member of a Pentecostal church, had been handcuffed, silenced with duct tape across his mouth, abducted, and forcibly held against his will for days in a failed attempt to destroy his beliefs. The Church of Scientology supported this case in a number of ways, such as by supplying witnesses against Ross and CAN.

When the criminal case failed to convict Ross, the church helped Scott file a civil suit against his kidnappers and the Cult Awareness Network. The jury in this new case found the conduct of some of the defendants "so outrageous in character and so extreme in degree as to go beyond all possible bounds of decency... atrocious and utterly intolerable in a civilized community," and approved a $4.875 million verdict against Ross and CAN. When the defendants moved to have the verdict set aside as "unreasonable," U.S. District Judge John Coughenour denied the motion, stating, "The court notes each of the defendants' seeming incapability of appreciating the maliciousness of their conduct towards Mr. Scott. . . . Thus, the large award given by the jury against both CAN and Mr. Ross seems reasonably necessary to enforce the jury's determination on the oppressiveness of the defendants' actions and deter similar conduct in the future."

The Cult Awareness Network initially filed for bankruptcy under Chapter 11, hoping to continue its operations. However, the organization was finally forced to file Chapter 7 bankruptcy in June 1996. When CAN's resources were auctioned to raise money for the settlement, the Church of Scientology purchased the Cult Awareness Network name, phone number, and post office box address. Thus, if the former CAN eventually reestablishes itself, it will have to be under a new name.

References

Ellison, Christopher G., and John P. Bartkowski. "Babies Were Being Beaten: Exploring Child Abuse Allegations at Ranch Apocalypse." In Stuart A. Wright, ed., *Armageddon in Waco*. Chicago: University of Chicago Press, 1995.

Homer, Michael W. "New Religions and Child Custody Cases: Comparisons between the American and European Experience." In James

R. Lewis and J. Gordon Melton, eds. *Sex, Slander and Salvation: Investigating The Family/Children of God.* Stanford, CA: Center for Academic Publishing, 1994.

————. "Protection of Religion under the First Amendment: Church Universal and Triumphant." In James R. Lewis and J. Gordon Melton, eds. *Church Universal and Triumphant in Scholarly Perspective.* Stanford, CA: Center for Academic Publishing, 1994.

Lewis, James R. *Seeking the Light.* Los Angeles: Mandeville Press, 1997.

Morgan, Richard E. *The Supreme Court and Religion.* New York: Free Press, 1972.

Saliba, John A. *Understanding New Religions.* Grand Rapids, MI: Wm. B. Eerdmans, 1995.

Shepherd, William C. *To Secure the Blessings of Liberty.* Chico, CA: Scholars Press, 1985.

Facts and Data 5

Documents

Beyond the court decisions that have already been reviewed, there are few definitive documents in this controversy. The four documents reproduced in this chapter are intended to give the reader a more concrete sense of the controversy through contact with primary materials. All of these documents are from the mid to late 1970s and embody some of the passion with which this controversy was waged in that decade.

The National Council of Churches took an early interest in the cult controversy. While expressing some mixed feelings about the controversy more generally, the statement reproduced below takes a very strong stand against deprogramming. The "Resolution on Deprogramming" was adopted by the National Council of Churches in 1974.

University scholars have understandably tended to analyze rather than to take a stand on the cult controversy. Public school teachers, however, showed no such reticence. The resolution on cults was passed at the National Parent Teacher Association's national convention in Atlanta, Georgia, in 1978.

Before governmental bodies came to realize that constitutional prohibitions would effectively prevent them from legislating against controversial religious groups, there was a period in the 1970s when a number of hearings and investigating committees were established to investigate the dangers posed by new religious movements. The third document reproduced in this section is the statement of Rev. Barry W. Lynn from the Legislative Counsel of the Office for Church in Society, United Church of Christ, delivered at the second Dole hearing in 1979.

The final document is from hearings held by the Vermont Senate in 1976. John G. Clark, Jr., assistant professor of psychiatry at Harvard Medical School was one of the earliest professional advocates of interpreting participation in new religions in terms of psychiatric abnormality. His testimony to the Vermont Senate was widely reprinted and circulated among anticult groups as well as mainline denominations. He later published an expanded version in the *Journal of the American Medical Association* (1979).

Resolution on Deprogramming: "Religious Liberty for Young People Too"

Adopted by the Governing Board of the National Council of Churches, February 28, 1974

In this country, kidnapping a young person for ransom is a federal crime of utmost seriousness, but kidnapping such a person in order to change his or her religious beliefs and commitments has not thus far actuated federal authorities to invoke the statute. Grand juries have refused to indict and petit juries to convict persons charged with such acts, apparently because done at the behest of parents or other relatives and ostensibly for the good of the victim.

Sometimes the victim is unarguably a minor, subject to the authority of his or her parents. In other instances, the victim is over 25 or 30, clearly an adult competent to make his or her own commitments in religion as in other matters. The rest are between 18 and 21 years of age, and their claims to adulthood are clouded by the vagaries and variety of federal, state and local laws.

The Governing Board of the NCC believes that religious liberty is one of the most precious rights of humankind, which is grossly violated by forcible abduction and protracted efforts to change a person's religious commitments by duress. Kidnapping for ransom is heinous indeed, but kidnapping to compel religious deconversion is equally criminal. It violates not only the letter and spirit of state and federal statutes, but the world standard of the Universal Declaration of Human Rights, which states: "Everyone has the right to freedom of thought, conscience and religion; this right includes freedom to change his religion or belief, and freedom, either alone or in community with others and in public or private, to manifest his religion or belief in teaching, practice, worship and observance."

The Governing Board is mindful of the intense anguish which can motivate parents at the defection of their offspring from the family faith, but in our view this does not justify forcible abduction. We are aware that religious groups are accused of "capturing" young people by force, drugs, hypnotism, "brainwashing," etc. If true, such actions should be prosecuted under the law, but thus far the evidence all runs the other way: it is the would-be rescuers who are admittedly using force.

The Governing Board recognizes that parents have the ultimate responsibility for the religious nurture of their children until they become adults in their own right, and parents are morally and legally justified in using reasonable force to carry out their responsibility (even if in matters of religion it may be unwise, ineffective or counterproductive). Nevertheless, at some point, young people are entitled to make their own decisions in religion as in other matters. What that point should be may vary from family to family, since emancipation is surely in most cases virtually complete by 18.

The Governing Board has previously urged the right to vote for 18 year-olds and welcomes the action of those states which are making all rights of citizenship effective at 18 rather than 21. The right to choose and follow one's own religion without forcible interference should likewise be guaranteed at least by that age.

Resolution on Pseudo-Religious Cults

National PTA Convention, June 1978

Whereas, the PTA Objects include: "To promote the welfare of children and youth . . . to raise the standards of home life . . . to secure adequate laws for the care and protection of children and youth . . . to secure the highest advantages in physical, mental, social and spiritual education for all children and youth": and

Whereas, the statements of PTA Principles include that: (1) We believe that the home is the basic unit in the structure of our society and should be the most constructive influence in building character, a sense of values, and a concept of the world for children and youth; (2) We believe that the concept of health as physical, mental, emotional, and social well-being is vital to the welfare of the individual citizen, the community, and the nation; and (3) We believe that individual freedom, individual rights, individual responsibility, and individual dignity are indispensable components of a democracy; and

Whereas, the National PTA has had a long-standing disapproval of any project that involves children in the collecting of money; and

Whereas, certain of the new and destructive pseudo-religious cults (i.e., Unification Church, Hare Krishna and Children of God) alienate our youth from their families, churches, schools and work; and

Whereas, the techniques used by these cults include intensive use of (1) separation from families; (2) intense group pressures; (3) isolation from familiar places, people and ideas; (4) sleep deprivation; (5) severe dietary restrictions; (6) continuous chanting and bizarre rituals; (7) frequent coercion and terror; (8) ultra-strict rules of chastity, poverty and obedience; (9) other means designed to maintain a totalistic society; and

Whereas, these cults are more political in their ambitions than religious; and

Whereas, there is available testimony showing that youths are exploited by these cults by working an 18 hour day and turning all their money over to cult leaders; and

Whereas, these cults eliminate an individual's freedom of choice through the use of mind control, and that the cults require an individual to give up all of his material possessions to a human master, and the recruit is subsequently a slave to that human master; and

Whereas, tens of thousands of our youth are being manipulated by leaders of cults for personal power and wealth through mind controlling techniques; be it therefore

Resolved, that the National PTA/PTSA sponsor workshops and develop means to disseminate information that will inform and educate parents and youth of the true facts concerning these pseudo-religious cults and how they use mind control to accomplish their goals;

Resolved, that the National PTA/PTSA take appropriate steps to keep these pseudo-religious cults from infiltrating our public schools; and be it further

Resolved, that the National PTA/PTSA urge the federal government to pursue further their investigation of the activities of these groups.

Testimony of Rev. Barry W. Lynn

Congressional Hearing on Religious "Cults," 1979

Senator Dole and Members of the Committee:

My name is Barry W. Lynn. I am an ordained minister in the United Church of Christ, and a member of the District of Columbia Bar. Much of my theological training was in the area of the psychology of religion. I am speaking today on behalf of the Office for Church in Society of the United Church of Christ. I do not claim to speak for all of the 1.8 million members of our denomination.

The United Church of Christ and its predecessor denominations, however, have maintained a clear commitment to the protection of the guarantees of the First Amendment to the Constitution. In June of 1973, the Ninth General Synod, our most representative body, called upon our agency to offer legislative testimony in behalf of the preservation and protection of First Amendment rights, including those of speech, press, and religion.

The Eleventh General Synod in 1977, faced with the growth of many new forms of religious activity, affirmed as well that we should work to extend the precious heritage of religious freedom to new groups with which we are not in theological agreement.

This morning, I would like to discuss the restraints under which the Congress must act in the attempted regulation or even investigation of activities which are labelled by their participants to be religious in nature.

Regulation of Religious Activity   The First Amendment guarantees both that the Congress shall not establish religion and that it shall not abridge the free exercise thereof. Proponents of regulation of religious activity frequently allege that the Congress cannot limit beliefs, but may limit acts which are labelled "religious." This simplistic view does not reflect Constitutional standards. It is now clear that only the gravest abuses endangering paramount state interests give occasion for Constitutionally permissible limitations of religious activity.

Even such a worthy goal as compulsory high school education has been held to be insufficient to counterbalance the claim of religious freedom. Subsequently, courts have upheld the refusal of jury duty, use of certain otherwise illegal drugs, and rejection of life-saving therapy on "free exercise" grounds. Certainly legitimate state interests were involved in these cases, but they were not seen as sufficiently compelling to override the sincere practice of one's religious faith.

Congress must resist efforts to restrict the non-criminal acts of new religious groups or so-called "cults," although this is urged by many of the witnesses today. Professor Richard Delgado, for example, in his widely read article on this subject, suggests that the government has an "interest in regulating the recruiting and indoctrinating practices of extremist religious groups" when they prove "harmful." These bases for demonstrating harm, however, do not rise to a compelling state interest which warrants restrictions.

Mr. Delgado and others allege harm through the precipitation of psychological problems in some members of such groups. To arrive at this conclusion they engage in an unsystematic chronicling of terrifying anecdotes and quasi-scientific reports which lead them to belief in a theory of "mind control" at least as dubious and incomprehensible as the theologies of the religious groups they attack.

There is no question that some members of such groups develop psychological problems. That, however, does not rise to the level of a compelling state interest to regulate religion. We do not even know if those psychological difficulties are solely or primarily related to their religious experience, or to earlier developmental problems. Furthermore, we are not a nation which legislates on the basis of possible damage to the most susceptible, gullible, or weak-willed persons. We do not restrict free speech merely because some sensitive persons are emotionally distressed by the words of Nazis or Communists. We should not attempt through law to infringe upon the proselytizing, instructing, praying, chanting or preaching of any religious group because some persons who hear it might become unreasonably influenced. Although I too find some of their educational methods distasteful, they are not as a legal matter different in quality than the tactics used by virtually every religious faith and secular institution in our society.

Mr. Delgado and others posit regulation on alleged social harms caused by "cults" as well. Most documented incidents, such as the rape of new converts, the physical abuse of infants by inadequate nutrition, and the forced use of drugs, should be vigorously controlled by existing criminal laws which find such practices so abhorrent that no serious "religious" claim can be entertained in their defense. Where funds are raised under false pretenses state and Federal criminal fraud statutes should be and are invoked.

Any further or special regulation seems unnecessary. Again, merely because the tactics of some groups seem offensive or bizarre they cannot be treated differently than conventional religious organizations without violating the neutrality required by the Establishment Clause.

It is also important to note that if recruiting practices were regulated it would not only violate the First Amendment rights of the religious organization to disseminate information, but also the First Amendment rights of the public to receive that information.

Defining the Truth or Falsity of Religious Claims The first cornerstone of the law of religious liberty, then, is that religious practices may be regulated only upon a showing of a compelling state interest of the highest order. The second foundation is that it is not permissible for governments to define the truth or falsity of religious belief. The key case involved allegations of mail fraud against the "I AM" movement. Although the Supreme Court affirmed that the "good faith" of the mail solicitors could be evaluated, it refused to permit jury consideration of the "truth or falsity of the religious beliefs or doctrines" of those on trial.

Once it is determined that an individual legitimately holds a religious belief, it is not proper for government to evaluate the origin of that belief. Critics of new religions frequently allege that the groups use "psychological coercion" on potential converts. For the Congress to adopt this conclusion would place them in a Constitutionally forbidden zone. In a case involving conservatorship orders for several Unification Church members in California the court wisely noted, in rejecting such orders:

> Evidence was introduced of the actions of the proposed conservatees in changing their life styles. When the court is asked to determine whether that change was induced by faith or by coercive persuasion is it not in turn investigating and questioning the validity of the faith?

Faith is by nature totally subjective. One cannot measure its presence or absence in any way in which a legislature may take official notice. Neither does the recanting of some adherents call into question the faith of an entire group.

"Deprogramming" "Deprogramming" raises serious questions about the right of individuals to practice their faith and associate with those they choose. This cherished right is vital for adults, who are generally the targets of this authoritarian method, yet even minors are increasingly becoming entitled to serious protection of their First Amendment interests in private decision-making.

So far, this has largely been a state matter. Nevertheless, proposals have been made by practitioners of this tactic that a 'justification" defense be explicitly added to the Federal Kidnapping Act. With it parents or their agents could legally "kidnap" their adult offspring if they had reason to believe it would prevent a larger harm. Such a defense, however, would invite a gigantic increase in the physical and emotional violence now done by "deprogrammers." Lest anyone feel that they will use great restraint, many of these charlatans now admit to the "deprogramming" of born-again Christians and even members of political groups with which they disagree. To explicitly add a "justification" defense would be an open invitation to bring back witchhunting and the Inquisition.

Congressional Investigation of Religious Activity   There are limits to the investigative power Congress may exert in regard to religious activity. Constitutionally, it is not within the power of Congress to act as a judge of specific instances of alleged criminal activity. Constitutionally, it is not within the power of Congress to act as a judge of specific instances of alleged criminal activity or as a prosecutor of unpopular causes or groups. If there is substantial evidence of a pattern of illicit behavior—be it arson for hire or fraudulent fundraising by organizations which claim to be religious—investigations may be cautiously conducted. Fundamental fairness and equity, however, require that any organizations cited as involved in misconduct must be given the opportunity to reply.

Conclusion   Mr. Justice Douglas, in 1944, reviewed the Constitutional history which is implicitly on trial here today. He wrote: "The Fathers of the Constitution were not unaware of the varied and extreme views of religious sects. . . . They fashioned a charter of government which envisaged the widest possible toleration of conflicting views."

If the Congress or state governments end up making any mistakes in response to the phenomenon of new religious groups, let those mistakes be on the side of religious tolerance. When our nation's leaders have done otherwise, and erred on the side of intolerance or hysteria, they have always plunged us into the darkest periods of our history.

The United Church of Christ is a 1957 union of the Evangelical and Reformed Church and the Congregational Christian Churches. The Congregational Church was the established church in Salem, Massachusetts, in 1692, and a Congregational elder presided at the infamous witchcraft trials. With that sense of history we are particularly troubled at any hint of governmental scrutiny of religious faith.

Testimony of John G. Clark, Jr., M.D.

Special Investigating Committee of the Vermont Senate: "Investigating the Effects of Some Religious Cults on the Health and Welfare of Their Converts," Summer 1976

In this statement to the committee established by the Vermont Legislature, I intend to present substantive conclusions drawn from 2 1/2 years of research on the effects of membership in some religious cults on personal health of their converts. My conclusions are rather grim: The health hazards are extreme! Though I will talk primarily of the absolute dangers to mental health and personal development, I must also as a physician draw attention to equally serious, often life threatening, dangers to physical health leaders.

I will state that coercive persuasion and thought reform techniques are effectively practiced on naive, uninformed subjects with disastrous health consequences. I will try to give enough information to indicate my reasons for further inquiries as well as review of applicable legal processes.

From the specific data gathered during the time of my investigations a rather accurate natural history of involvement in the cults can be now adequately described. In doing this I believe I can adequately demonstrate why I think there are major health hazards as well as many other social concerns directly caused by activities of the particular cults which we try to define as destructive. The destructive cults are numerous and include the very well known ones such as Hare Krishna, the Unification Church, the Scientologists, the Divine Light Mission, all of whom are utilizing the same basic techniques. The fact that I use the word techniques indicates that these investigations have delineated a series of technical aspects to these questions which need to be understood and can be explained.

All of the groups that we are talking about have living leaders who are demonstrably wealthy. The beliefs of all these cults are absolutist and non-tolerant of other systems of beliefs. Their systems of governance are totalitarian. A requirement of membership is to obey absolutely without questioning. Their interest in the individual's development within the cult towards some kind of satisfactory individual adult personality is, by their doctrines, very low or nonexistent. It is clear that almost all of them emphasize money making in one form or another, although a few seem to be very much involved in demeaning or self-denigrating activities and rituals. Most of them that I have studied possess a good deal of property and money which is under the discretionary control of the individual leaders.

Most of the cults of concern consider themselves purely religious; some others appear to be more political. One of the most important of the common properties of such cults is the presence of a leader who, in one way or another, claims special powers or may even allow himself to be thought of as the Messiah. Such leaders do have special personal qualities including a unique world view and a special willingness to effect drastic changes in the thinking and behavior of followers.

It appears that the techniques utilized by these cults are very similar overall although each one uses its own peculiar style. It would appear obvious that all of these cults have worked out ways of gaining access to susceptible individuals in order to have survived to any degree. Those who succumb to the enlisting efforts seem to be divided into two rather distinct groups. The first is composed of the "seekers," of whom we all know, popularly though incorrectly thought to constitute the entire population of susceptible people. They are schizophrenic, chronically so, or border-line personalities. It is quite clear that the existence of emotional or personality problems is a reason for becoming involved in the cults and that most mental health professionals consider only this reason at present. These inductees involve themselves in order to feel better because they are excessively uncomfortable with the outside world and themselves. Such motivated versions [sic] are "restitutive," in that the "seekers" are trying to restore themselves to some semblance of comfort in a fresh, though false, reality. We also see this attempt at restitution in the development of the so called secondary symptoms of schizophrenia and other forms of mental illness as the attempt of a troubled or damaged mind to put together a new, simplified mental world and style of reasoning in order to compensate for the terrible awareness or near awareness of personal vulnerability. Approximately 58 percent of inductees were found to be in this first group from my studies.

The remaining 42 percent of the examined sample, however, were found to be apparently normal, developing young people who were going through the usual crises of development on the way to becoming adults, who, for any of a number of reasons, had fallen into the trap laid by the cults and had been taken in. On examination they were strong growing students on the average who were facing the normal pains of separation from their families, the normal depressions therefrom, the new, clear, slightly feverish view of the complexity of outer reality which is part of early college life. I think of their joining the cult as being "adaptive"; that is, they are presented with certain problems by the cult and adapt themselves as pathological as those involved in the "restitutive" conversions. In some ways it is this more healthy "adaptive" group that is most alarming to the observer.

From a clinician's point of view the first or restitutive group under the influence of cult indoctrination and practices is very much at risk. In many ways it can be very easily shown from long experience within the mental health field how very much more damaged they may become by being given a thought disorder by a group that conforms to a prior tendency to this sort of thinking disability. Their chances of ever developing good relationships to outer reality and becoming autonomous individuals must, perforce, diminish with the passage of time. I am reminded of the chronic schizophrenics of some years ago whose psychotic style of thinking became totally institutionalized when placed in the back wards of hospitals for such a long enough time that they ultimately could no longer think at all effectively. The healthier second group, though theoretically less totally vulnerable, is more easy to identify with; their problems may be especially revealing as I will try to explain.

These people tend to be from intact, idealistic, believing families with some religious background. Often they had not truly made any of the major shifts toward independence, and so, left home at the appropriate time believing they were ready for freedom. When this belief was seriously challenged in this brave new world by their first real set backs or by any real crisis they became covertly depressed, thus enhancing their susceptibility to the processes of conversion.

For individuals in this state of vulnerability to be converted a series of circumstances, techniques and events must occur to bring about the complete subjugation of mind and person which I am attempting to describe. The first event is the gaining of access to these potential converts which is raised to a high art by all of the successful cults. Some even have printed manuals describing where to approach prospects, exactly what types of initial pressure to put on each of them and what the odds are that they will acquire a certain number of converts from a given amount of pressure well

applied. The general openness of manners of this age group adds
to the ease of access. Once such a prospect has agreed to investigate the rather simple propositions expressed by the representa-
tives of the cult he or she is brought into the next and highly
sophisticated activities of the conversion process. From the first,
intense group pressure, lectures, lies, false use of facilities and other
interpersonal pressures unexpected by the individual are brought
to bear. Singing, chanting and a constant barrage of the kinds of
rhetoric which catch the young idealistic minds are constantly in
play. So intense is this that individuals who are under such pressure and are susceptible tend to enter a state of narrowed attention, especially as they are more and more deprived of their
ordinary frames of reference and of sleep. This state must be described as a trance. From that time there is a relative or complete
loss of control of one's own mind and actions which is then placed
into the hands of the group or of individuals who have the direct
contact with the individual inductee. This induction period has
also been described as "coercive persuasion."

Once this state of passive, narrowed attention and willingness
to be influenced is achieved, the true work of conversion (or of
thought reform) begins in earnest. This is always a program of
unbelievable intensity! During this, all of the cults step up their
ideological reform pressures by increased group pressure, change
of diet, and the introduction of elements of guilt and terror. The
question of supernatural pressures that one must face in the future
are brought out more and more explicitly and concretely. Many
promises are made of redemption or safety, in the certainty that
the world will soon end at which time there will be enormous rewards or terrible punishments to believers or non-believers. The
threats may be implicit but are sometimes increasingly physical
and explicit physical threats. Preaching is constant from all sides;
supervision is absolute and privacy of body or of mind may not be
allowed for days or weeks into the future, even to use the bath-
room. All relationships to other people are organized and stereotyped and no chance is given for idiosyncratic expression. The
victims are induced rapidly to give up all familiar and loved past
objects—parents, siblings, home, city, etc.—and they are physically
and emotionally moved to as foreign an environment as is possible to imagine. Thus, it becomes increasingly hard for them to
reconstruct in imagination what one has once experienced some
time in the past. Reality becomes the present and includes in it
elements of the supernatural, magical, terrifying thought which
has been expressed constantly all around. There is no base left for
reality testing.

Perhaps as important a factor as any is that the base of each individual's language which has been part of the mind and the body function from the very early stages is slowly and deliberately changed. All words of any emotional importance have had some shifting of their meaning to an oversimplified, special sort of related definition. Each person is given more and more tasks to learn, to study, to grasp, and has less time to believe that the past ever existed. By this time the indoctrination has defined parents as being infected by Satan's influence and parenthood is reinvested in the leaders of the cults. The urge to go home has been replaced by the need for the absolute authority of the cult and its leaders and at the same time the value of education and the need to go to school has disappeared from consciousness. This much radical change of attitudes, loyalties and thinking style can occur and regularly does occur within a few days to a few weeks.

From this time the problem of maintenance of the state of mind is apparently rather simple. Leaving the old familiar life setting and renouncing it for a new communal theology, the accepting of a new family with new definitions of love and the denouncing of natural parents leads an individual to think all bridges to the past are closed and that a very brave move into a new world has, indeed, been made. In some cults members are taught intensive chanting and meditating procedures which in case of any attack on their beliefs can cover up all possible thoughts and doubts. Others can apparently reenter a trance state with a narrowed consciousness of reality the first moment that somebody questions or challenges their beliefs. They are then promoted to the next steps or stages in their cults usually as proselytizers, money raisers or in some cases garbage collectors.

In my opinion, the last stage of this process in both adaptive and restitutive groups probably may evolve after four to seven years. This would be "acculturation" and would be irreversible. This stage may be compared to that of the untreated person with a schizophrenic illness who slides without proper help into a kind of personal degradation which, if unchallenged or untreated, in time finally becomes acculturated and permanent. Anyone trying to nudge a person from this acquired style of thinking and behavior as we in the mental health field know very well is going to feel that he is the natural enemy of his patient. In my opinion, I repeat, by acculturation this new style of thinking may become irreversible.

Before this final state cult members seem to experience two forms of personality: the original and the imposed. The original is complex, full of love relationships, expectations and hopes and, especially, rich language. This reaction is appropriately panic! They recognize and correctly identify terrifying, sudden, unacceptable changes in the style of language and the style of relating as well as a narrowing and thinning down of the thought processes. Formerly bright, fluent and creative individuals are rendered incapable [of] the use of irony or a metaphor and they speak with a smaller carefully constricted vocabulary with cliches and stereotyped ideas. They also appear to have great difficulty using abstractions in their speech or arguments. They do not love except in cliches and established forms. Almost all of the charged, emotion-laden language symbols are shifted to new meanings. Parents notice this long before professionals because they do not need cumbersome and elaborate tools to analyze language patterns. Their memories and intuition are sufficient.

The evidence for what I call a shift in personality, which may be what we call in psychiatry "depersonalization," comes from several kinds of observations. The first is that, despite the appearance to very experienced clinicians of flagrant and classical schizophrenia in many converts the induced mental state being discussed does not respond to the most effective antipsychotic drugs or any of the methods of treatment customarily applied by mental health professionals to restore effective thinking. Thus, we are relatively helpless to restore thinking processes because, under the current interpretations of the laws, we cannot maintain physical control for long enough to bring about the confrontation therapies which might be effective in reestablishing the original personality style in the way it was done with the Korean war prisoners. On the other hand, antipsychotic medicines are still effective in treating acute psychosis in these same people though not affecting the state of conversion.

The second and rather compelling piece of evidence is that the thought reformed state is dramatically altered by the process of deprogramming about which, though I cannot legally advise it as a therapy under most circumstances, a great deal is known. The deprogramming process as it is now practiced effects, in a large numbers of cases, a fairly rapid return to the old organization of the mind, a "repersonalization," and brings back with it the old language skills and memories, original personal relationship patterns and of course the old problems. Furthermore, it is regularly observed that for some time after the deprogramming the affected individuals are very vulnerable for about a year and, especially during the first few weeks to two months, they feel themselves aware of, and close to, two different mental worlds. Their strong impulses to return to the cult are controlled by logical reasoning processes and the great fear of someone taking control of their

minds from the outside once again. During this time a former convert can quickly be recaptured either by a fleeting impulse or by
chanting or by a team from the cult. In general, however, after a
return to an original state of mind the individual's problems begin
to seem like ordinary health problems. Most of them are depressed
depleted people reminding one very much of the status of patients
who have recently recovered from acute psychoses who are able
to feel that for the first time in their lives they had lost a clear sense
of reality and of control. They feel ashamed of what they have done
and the pain they have inflicted, are very scared and for a while
unable to manage their lives effectively. To remain within the strict
mental and social confines of the cult experience for even a short
time is disastrous for some who have become psychotic or have
committed suicide. Continuing membership appears to invite a
deeper acceptance of the controlled state of mind and, in my opinion, leads to the gradual degradation of ordinary thought processes
necessary to cope with highly differentiated and ambiguous external life problems of the future. In this state after some time the
intellect appears to lose a great many I.Q. points; the capacity to
form flexible human relationships or real intimacy is impaired and
all reality testing functions are difficult to mobilize so that judge-
ment is poor. An individual with even moderate prior psychological disability is likely to be set back considerably and permanently
in his or her maturation to adulthood and will certainly be impaired in the ability and capacity to deal with the real world's opportunities and dangers. The loss of educational and occupational
experiences will confirm these losses beyond any doubts.

This is the rough picture of the phenomenon of thought reform as practiced by present day cults and the natural history of
this process and its effects on the involved individuals. Though
incomplete it is based on examination of 27 subjects at all stages of
involvement in six different cults as well as interviews with many
more interested and informed observers. I believe the overall outline is sound though, of course, incomplete. The fact of a personality shift in my opinion is established. The fact that this is a
phenomenon basically unfamiliar to the mental health profession
I am certain of. The fact that our ordinary methods of treatment
don't work is also clear as are the frightening hazards to the process of personal growth and mental health.

In this paper I have tried to describe the phenomenon of involvement of young people in destructive cults. The problems of
special vulnerability to conversion were described and two major
groups of susceptibles were identified. A natural history of ac-

cess, induction by coercive persuasion, the process of thought and attitude reform and the maintenance of conversion [were] described. An opinion that a permanent state of acculturation was likely to occur after a number of years was expressed. The rapidity of these catastrophic changes were emphasized as well as many of their qualities and these were related to mental health and maturational concerns.

Specific and important problems such as suicide, depression, psychotic reactions and psychosomatic disorders are most serious and deserve another discussion and much more study. It is also clear that the multiple, serious and often bizarre problems of physical illness need careful and official attention. Both the mental health and physical health problems presented by the activities of the cults

FIGURE 1
Growth of New Religions in the United States in the Twentieth Century

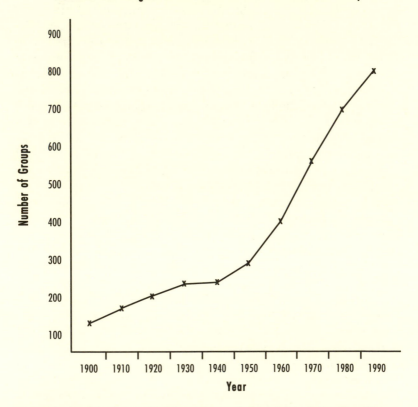

Source: Updated graph based on J. Gordon Melton, *A Directory of Religious Bodies in the United States* (New York: Garland, 1977).

should be investigated in much greater detail by official agencies. I believe that they merit active interest of such constitutive authorities as this Legislative body who, I trust, can see some greater implications of all that has been discussed and will be further revealed in these hearings.

Statistics

The statistics in this section represent selections from a wide variety of published studies of nontraditional religious groups. This section is particularly indebted to the compilation of such data found in J. Gordon Melton's "Modern Alternative Religions in the West," in John R. Hinnells, ed., *A New Handbook of Living Religions* (London: Blackwell, 1997).

Growth of Alternative Religions in the United States

Figure 1 indicates the growth in" the number of new religious bodies to come into existence between 1900 and 1990. The decisive

FIGURE 2
New Religions in 1990 in the Continental United States per Million Residents

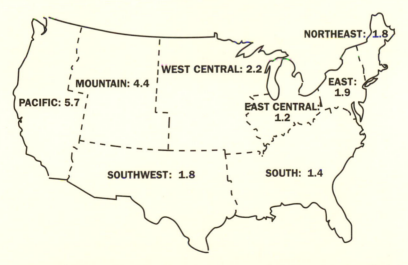

Source: J. Gordon Melton, "Modern Alternative Religions in the West," in John R. Hinnels, ed., *A New Handbook of Living Religions* (London: Blackwell, 1997).

upswing in the rate of expansion occurs between the mid 1950s and the mid 1960s, reflecting (1) an increase in religious experimentation corresponding with the social-cultural revolution of the 1960s, and (2) a sharp upswing in the number of Asian religions as a result of the lowering of immigration barriers in 1965.

Distribution of New Religions

Figure 2 examines the distribution of new religions in 1990 in terms of where they are headquartered in the United States. As one would anticipate, most groups are centered in the Pacific Coast states, especially California. The southeastern part of the country would have been the region with the least new religious activity had it not been for Florida—a state that is culturally more diverse than the rest of the south.

TABLE 1
New Religions in Europe and the United States in the Early 1990s

	Cult movements per million	No. cult movements
Switzerland	16.7	108
Iceland	12.0	3
United Kingdom	10.7	604
Austria	7.9	60
Sweden	6.8	57
Denmark	4.5	23
Netherlands	4.4	64
Ireland	3.9	14
West Germany	2.5	155
Belgium	2.4	24
Norway	1.9	8
Greece	1.5	15
Italy	1.2	66
Portugal	1.0	10
France	0.9	52
Finland	0.8	4
Spain	0.7	29
Poland	0.5	17
Europe*	3.4	1,313
United States	1.7	425

* Total based only on the nations listed in the table.
Source: Rodney Stark, "Europe's Receptivity to New Religious Movements," *Journal for the Scientific Study of Religion* 31 (1993): 389–397.

New Religions in Europe

Table 1 is derived from a 1993 article by Rodney Stark. According to Stark's figures, over three times as many alternative religions are headquartered in Europe as are in the United States. This data contradicts the conventual wisdom, which says that the United States is the source of most new religions in Europe.

Religious Backgrounds of Members of New Religions

Table 2 is taken from a series of different studies that collected data on the religious backgrounds of people who had joined new religions. This data sheds light on a number of hypotheses observers have held about alternative religions, especially the perception that individuals from Jewish homes are disproportionately represented in such groups. While the data supports this informal observation, none of these organizations are overwhelmingly Jewish, as some have suggested.

Another casual observation is that neopagans are predominantly from Catholic backgrounds, presumably because of their felt need for a "ritualistic" religion. This hypothesis is decisively disproven by the data, which indicate that the percentage of ex-Catholics in neopagan groups is actually less than participants raised in other faiths.

TABLE 2
Religious Backgrounds of Participants in New Religions (in percentages)

	Protestant	Roman Catholic	Jewish	Other
Unification Church (1976)	47.1	35.8	5.3	11.8
Soka Gakkai (1970)	30.0	30.0	6.0	34.0
Neopagans (1979)	42.7	25.8	6.2	25.3
Hare Krishna	35.5	18.0	14.5	32.0
Zen Center of Los Angeles	52.0	12.0	28.0	8.0
Church Universal and Triumphant (1994)	43.7	35.7	3.0	17.7
MSIA (1997)	51.2	27.0	14.2	7.6

Sources: J. Stillson Judah, *Hare Krishna and the Counter Culture* (New York: Wiley, 1974); McCloy Layman, *Buddhism in America* (Chicago: Nelson Hall, 1976); J. Gordon Melton, "The Neo-Pagans of America: An Alternative Religion" (paper presented to the American Academy of Religion, 1970); Constance Jones, "Church Universal and Triumphant: A Demographic Profile," in James R. Lewis and J. Gordon Melton, eds., *Church Universal and Triumphant in Scholarly Perspective* (Stanford, CA: Center for Academic Publishing, 1994); James R. Lewis, *Seeking the Light* (Los Angeles: Mandeville Press, 1997).

Postinvolvement Attitudes of Ex-Members

Table 3 reports the results of a 1984 survey of 154 ex-members of controversial religious groups. Respondents were divided into three treatment groups: no exit counseling (dropped out of group without intervention of anticultists), voluntary exit counseling (left group voluntarily, but experienced intervention of anticult counselors), and involuntary exit counseling (kidnapped and deprogrammed).

The questionnaire contains eight items that indicated how ex-members evaluated their former movement. Four of these measured cult-stereotypical attitudes, asking respondents if they felt (1) they had been recruited deceptively; (2) they had been brainwashed; (3) that their ex-leader was insincere; (3) the extent to which the worldview and beliefs of their ex-religion were false.

The other four items measured positive-negative attitudes in a less stereotypical manner. Respondents were asked if they would (1) discourage others from joining their former groups; (2) if they would repeat their membership (with few or many changes); (3) if they considered their membership a learning experience; and (4) if they felt they had grown as a result of their participation in their ex-religion. All eight items were highly correlated with the exit mode, as reported in Table 3.

What these figures show is that the tendency of ex-members of controversial religions to portray their membership period in negative terms is highly correlated with the extent of their contact with the anticult movement. In other words, people who were

TABLE 3
Relationship of Postinvolvement Attitudes to Anticult Socialization

Questionnaire Item	Correlation
Deception	.392
Brainwashing	.587
Leader	.407
Worldview	.551
Discourage joining	.522
Repeat membership	.465
Learning experience	.320
Growth experience	.503

Note: All values significant at the .001 level (two-tailed tests).
Source: James R Lewis, "Reconstructing the 'Cult' Experience: Post-Involvement Attitudes as a Function of Mode of Exit and Post-Involvement Socialization," *Sociological Analysis* 47 (1986): 151–159.

deprogrammed or otherwise counseled by anticultists are far more likely to accuse their former religion of having recruited them deceptively, brainwashing them, and the like. (See Chapter 1 for further discussion of the role of ex-member testimony in the cult controversy.)

The Cult Withdrawal Syndrome

As discussed in Chapter 1, anticultists have focused attention on the so-called syndrome that former members experience following removal from their religious communities in order to document the pathological effects of "cultic mind control." Of these studies, the one that conveys the most substantial appearance to casual readers is Conway and Siegelman's survey of 400 ex-members of controversial religions reported in a 1982 article published in *Science Digest* entitled "Information Disease: Have Cults Created a New Mental Illness?" Conway and Siegelman presented data on seven symptoms—floating/altered states, nightmares, amnesia, hallucinations/delusions, "inability to break mental rhythms of chanting," violent outbursts, and suicidal/self-destructive tendencies—for which respondents reported "long term mental and emotional effects." More particularly, Conway and Siegelman claimed that the psychological trauma cults inflict upon their members is directly related to the amount of time spent in indoctrination and mind control rituals.

While one could critique many aspects of this study, the decisive weakness of the "information disease" notion is that this supposedly new and unique syndrome is actually a response to traumatic stress, clinically designated the post-traumatic stress disorder (PTSD). The trauma of deprogramming, particularly a deprogramming of the classic "snatch" type, is a stressful event outside the range of normal human experience. And, because two-thirds to three-fourths of the samples used by anticult researchers are usually deprogrammed, it is reasonable to hypothesize that the difficulties these individuals experienced would be partially—if not entirely—a response to traumatic stress.

The survey referred to in the preceding section also asked respondents to compare their preinvolvement period (before joining their religious group) with their postinvolvement period in terms of the various symptoms described in anticult literature. For the sake of simplicity, using only the seven symptoms for which Conway and Siegelman presented quantified data in the "information disease" article and dividing the sample into the three treatment groups described in the preceding section, a distribution of "information disease" can be charted out (Table 4), which, as anticipated, clearly links the postinvolvement syndrome with deprogramming/exit counseling.

TABLE 4

Relationship between the Mode of Exit and Incidence of
Information Disease Symptoms (percentage of respondents reporting symptom)

	No Counseling	Voluntary Counseling	Involuntary Counseling	Correlation Coefficient
Floating	11	41	61	.414
Nightmares	11	41	47	.358
Amnesia	8	41	58	.482
Hallucinations	4	24	36	.337
Chanting	3	55	56	.530
Violence	9	31	42	.301
Suicidal	9	34	41	.270

Note: All correlations significant at the .001 level.
Source: Flo Conway and Jim Siegelman, "Information Disease: Have Cults Created a New Mental Illness?" *Science Digest* (January 1982): 86–92; James R. Lewis and David G. Bromley, "The 'Cult' Withdrawal Syndrome: A Case of Misattribution of Cause?" *Journal for the Scientific Study of Religion* 26 (1988): 508–522.

Organizations and Websites 6

Academic Organizations

American Academy of Religion
Scholars Press
P.O. Box 15399
Atlanta, GA 30333
The American Academy of Religion (AAR) is the largest association of academics in religion in North America. The AAR has a group devoted to new religious movements, the chairperson of which varies from year to year. One can reach the chair of this subsection of the AAR via Scholars Press in Atlanta.

CESNUR: The Center for Studies on New Religions
Via Juvarra 20
10152 Torino (Turin), Italy
39 (country code) 11-541950
www.cesnur.org
e-mail: cesnurto@tin.it

CESNUR is the only scholarly association devoted exclusively to the study of new religions. The group is international in scope and holds its annual meeting in various parts of the world. Because it is centered in Italy, it tends to focus on the cult issue in Europe. CESNUR was established in 1988 by a group of religious scholars from leading universities in Europe and the Americas. Its managing director is Professor Massimo Introvigne. CESNUR's original aim was to offer a professional association to scholars specializing in new religious movements.

In the 1990s, CESNUR became more proactive and started supplying information on a regular basis, opening public centers and organizing conferences and seminars for the general public in a variety of countries. Today CESNUR is a network of independent but related organizations of scholars in various countries whose goal is to promote scholarly research in the field of new religious consciousness, to spread reliable and responsible information, and to expose the very real problems associated with some movements, while at the same time defending everywhere the principles of religious liberty.

CESNUR's yearly annual conference is the largest world gathering of those active in the field of studies on new religions. Each conference normally features 50 to 80 papers. Conferences have been held at the London School of Economics (1993), the Federal University of Pernambuco in Recife, Brazil (1994), the State University of Rome (1995), the University of Montreal (1996), and the Free University of Amsterdam (1997). The website includes news on future CESNUR activities and a library of selected papers on a wide variety of topics.

Society for the Scientific Study of Religion
1365 Stone Hall
Sociology Department
Purdue University
West Lafayette, IN 47907-1365

The Society for the Scientific Study of Religion (SSSR) primarily attracts sociologists of religion. Sociologists were, for the most part, the first scholars to study new religious movements in North America. The society's quarterly journal, the *Journal for the Scientific Study of Religion*, regularly publishes articles and reviews books of interest to scholars of nontraditional religions.

Cult Information
Organizations and Websites

Over the past several decades, many organizations on both sides of the cult controversy have come and gone. A number still exist in name but have ceased to function actively, often for lack of funds. For many public issues, governmental agencies often provide information. Because, however, the nontraditional religions issue is perceived as a religious issue, the doctrine of the separation of church and state effectively blocks governmental bodies from becoming involved as long as the law is obeyed.

Because of the constant flux in this field, perhaps the best way to locate information centers on new religious movements is to search for "cults" or "new religions" on the Internet. This is also the best way to locate the relevant religious groups themselves, which move often enough to make any attempt at a comprehensive address list difficult.

Many of the website reviews listed here have been adapted from the reviews found at Jeffrey Hadden's website at the University of Virginia.

American Family Foundation
P.O. Box 2265
Bonita Springs, FL 34133
941-514-3081
www.csj.org

For many years, the American Family Foundation (AFF) served the U.S. anticult movement as its academic wing, leaving the Cult Awareness Network (CAN) to serve as a day-to-day information service and as a cult watchdog organization. Since CAN's demise, it is unclear whether or to what extent AFF will step in to fill the gap. It should be noted that members of this organization are generally opposed to the label anticult, preferring alternate designations such as cult critics, or some other, more nuanced label.

The American Family Foundation publishes two periodicals, the *Cult Observer*, a general audience publication, and *Cultic Studies Journal*, an academic publication. Both are invaluable for individuals interested in keeping up-to-date with developments in the anticult movement.

The AFF website also highlights the various outreach programs of the group, which include education about, study of, and assistance for those involved in groups determined by AFF to be cults. The group was founded in 1979. The organization offers information packets about the various groups by mail for a fee.

Becket Fund for Religious Liberty
2000 Pennsylvania Avenue
Suite 3200
Washington, DC 20009
800-BECKET 5
www.becketfund.org
e-mail: mail@becketfund.org

A diverse group of lawyers, professors, and civic leaders dedicated to the defense of religious liberty. The website covers up-to-date breaking news on religious freedom legal issues, including legislation and judicial decisions.

Bible Discernment Ministries
www.rapidnet.com:80/~jbeard/bdm

This extensive Christian anticult site run by Rick Meisel seeks to expose "false teachers and their teachings." The notebook section of the site offers information about groups and specific group leaders. It is divided into exposés, cults, and New Age groups.

Christian Research Institute
30162 Tomas
Rancho Santa Margarita, CA 92688-2124
www.equip.org

The Christian Research Institute was founded by Walter Martin, the most successful author of Christian anticult books. Martin's *The Kingdom of the Cults* is a guiding light for a substantial subset of the evangelical anticult movement. *The Kingdom of the Cults* is formatted like a Bible, with cult belief in one column and evangelical response, or "correction," of that belief in the other column. CRI's website primarily serves as an online store that sells the organization's books and other materials.

Cult Awareness Network
1680 North Vine Street, Suite 415
Los Angeles, CA 90028
800-556-3055
www.cultawarenessnetwork.org

When the Cult Awareness Network (CAN) name and number were acquired by the Church of Scientology, even the most sympathetic observers anticipated that CAN would become little more than a propaganda wing of Scientology. It was thus a pleasant surprise when the "New CAN" began functioning as a genuine information and networking center on nontraditional religions. The New Cult Awareness Network has established a working relationship with scholarly specialists and other professionals. When people in the CAN office are unable to adequately answer queries from callers, the callers are referred to the appropriate specialist. The New CAN also publishes a small newsletter.

Cult Information Service
Box 867
Teaneck, NJ 07666
201-833-1212
http://members.aol.com/shawdan/cis.htm

The Cult Information Service (CIS) is a new anticult group that has emerged to fill the vacancy left by the bankruptcy of the "old" Cult Awareness Network. It appears to have grown out of the Cult Clinic and Hot Line of the Jewish Board of Family and Children's Services in New York City. In addition to running a cult hotline, CIS has also begun to sponsor conferences. Whether CIS will be able to fill the old CAN's shoes remains to be seen.

Ex-Cult Archive
http://ex-cult.org

This site contains little substantive information but links together significant anticult resources. By no means comprehensive for anticult activity, this is nonetheless the best available resource for the novice interested in becoming familiar with anticult materials on the Internet.

Foundation for Religious Freedom
1680 North Vine Street, Suite 415
Los Angeles, CA 90028
800-556-3055
www.cultawarenessnetwork.org
e-mail: inform@cultawarenessnetwork.org

The Foundation for Religious Freedom runs the New Cult Awareness Network hotline and information service. Formerly a religious hate group, the New Cult Awareness Network runs an 800-number hotline, provides factual information, has an extensive list of qualified religious experts who act as professional referrals, and reconciles families through mediation.

Graduate Theological Union Library
http://aquinas.gtu.edu/library/LibraryNRMLinks.html

The new religious movements page from the Graduate Theological Union is not as well developed as other academic websites, but new materials are being added. The page consists mostly of links. Its specific utility is that it organizes groups following the structure of "families" found in J. Gordon Melton's *Encyclopedia of American Religions*.

Hadden Site at the University of Virginia
http://cti.itc.virginia.edu//~jkh8x

Jeffrey Hadden's homepage is easily the best academic website on new religious movements. The site contains overviews of many groups as well as a selection of papers on the cult controversy. Hadden also reviews and gives connecting links for relevant websites. Many of the website reviews in this section are adapted from his reviews.

INFO-CULT
5655 Park Avenue, Suite 305
Montreal, Quebec H2V 4H2
Canada
514-274-2333
ftp://triples.math.megill.ca/pub/rags/infocult.ic1.htm

Info-Cult (Info-Secte, in French) is the Canadian wing of the U.S. anticult movement and has functioned in much the same way as the Cult Awareness Network. Info-Cult has been less active in the wake of the demise of the "old" CAN, though this may be temporary.

International Association for Religious Freedom
576 Fifth Avenue, Suite 1103
New York, NY 10036
212-843-9493
www.interfaith-center.org/iarf
e-mail: iarfna@nywork2.undp.org

The International Association for Religious Freedom was organized in 1900 to affirm the right to religious freedom. The IARF welcomes into membership anyone who is committed to the fundamental right of religious freedom and includes religious groups from around the world. The organization runs interfaith conferences for groups of very diverse faiths working together for religious freedom.

International Coalition for Religious Freedom
7777 Leesburg Pike
Suite 307N-A
Falls Church, VA 22043
703-790-1500
www.religiousfreedom.com

The International Coalition for Religious Freedom's website includes a country-by-country report on religious freedom around the world. The coalition publishes a monthly update on religious freedom issues from around the world and sponsors religious freedom conferences to promote religious freedom.

Mandate Ministries
http://easyweb.firmware.com.au/mandate/index.htm

This is an Australian countercult site maintained by Mandate Ministries, an organization created by Fred and Barbara Grigg after they and their eight children left the Jehovah's Witnesses in 1978. Attractively created, this website provides a good example of a theological framework that has been geared toward opposition to cults as profane and spiritually and psychologically damaging to adherents. Grigg claims that post-traumatic stress disorder made him susceptible to Jehovah's Witness conversion after the Vietnam War. He converted along with his wife and children but soon realized he was not following the "true God," and moved to get his family out. He and his wife have now dedicated themselves to preventing other people from "falling victim" to cult conversion.

Margaret Singer Foundation
www.singer.org
www.irsociety.com/singer.html

Margaret Singer is a favorite speaker among anticultists and is often cited as a cult expert. She was regularly called in to testify in trials over conservatorship where she often succeeded in convincing the court that cults practiced brainwashing and mind control techniques that could only be countered if the individuals were forcibly removed from the group. Recently courts have rejected the brainwashing theory of conversion under pressure from academics, but Singer continues to dominate anticult literature and theory. The Margaret Singer Foundation is a site that is currently under construction but should provide additional information and insight into Singer's activities.

Ontario Consultants for Religious Tolerance
P.O. Box 514
Wellesley Island, NY 13640
Box 27026, Frontenac
Kingston, Ontario K7M 8W5
Canada
www.religioustolerance.org/acm.htm

Hosted by four individuals of diverse faiths, this website has factual information on 63 religions and over 500 essays covering both sides of many religious issues. Probably the largest and most frequently visited religious freedom website in existence with objective information covering both sides of many religious controversies. The Ontario Consultants for Religious Tolerance website is the most comprehensive and balanced presentation of information on new religious movements anywhere on the web.

reFOCUS: Recovering Former Cultists' Support Network
P.O. Box 2180
Flagler Beach, FL 32136-2180
904-439-7541
www.nwrain.net/~refocus/supporg.html

ReFOCUS is a network of referral and support for former members of nontraditional religions. As the name suggests, the perspective of this group is distinctly anticult. The group also publishes a quarterly newsletter, *reFOCUS Forum*.

Rick Ross Home Page
www.rickross.com

Ross is a deprogrammer deeply involved in the anticult movement who was involved in the court case that drove CAN into bankruptcy. He has been featured extensively in the media on programs such as "48 Hours." The site, although comprehensive and helpful in understanding Ross's own theories, is extremely slow to load because it contains extensive sound and graphics. Rick Ross is a highly visible entrepreneur who has carved out a niche for himself as a cult expert and counselor to families wishing to retrieve family members from new religions.

Spiritual Counterfeits Project
P.O. Box 4308
Berkeley, CA 94704
510-540-0300
www.scp-inc.org

The Spiritual Counterfeits Project (SCP) was a product of the student counterculture in the 1960s. The initial founders were former members of Eastern mystical religions. Its history is closely linked to the University of California and the 1960s free speech movement at Berkeley, specifically the People's Park. SCP members adhere to a conservative Christian faith today and seek to uncover the ways in which nontraditional religions fail to adhere to conservative Christian ideas. Early successes included a victory in court against transcendental meditation, forcing the removal of TM ideas from the public schools. The website offers information about the journal, hotline, and other materials offered by the group.

Steve Hassan Home Page
www.shassan.com
Resource Center for Freedom of Mind
www.fom.org

Hassan is an ex-member of the Unification church who has become a professional former member. He has recently created the Resource Center for Freedom of Mind to further his aim of providing information about mind control in cults based on Hassan's own writings. He rejects deprogramming in favor of exit counseling (noncoercive deprogramming) and provides links exclusively to anticult sites.

Thursby Site at the University of Florida
www.clas.ufl.edu/users/gthursby/rel/newrels.htm

This website is very useful as an analytical site because it provides links to academic journals for the study of religions and to other academic sites for the study of new religions. The site also includes an extensive bibliography. The site is in the process of adding information about specific groups.

Watchman Fellowship Inc.
http://www.watchman.org

This is far and away the most comprehensive Christian anticult site on the Internet. It includes at least some information on over 1100 groups. The site presents information on many groups that are not otherwise represented on the Internet. The information should be approached with an awareness of the fact that the authors' perspective is that of an Evangelical Christian. Each group is assessed from their theological perspective. While they strive for objectivity, and are often successful in being objective about much of the information they present, their theological perspective necessarily results in some bias in their presentation of groups that are not faithful to the Christian tradition as they understand it.

Resources 7

Mainstream Scholarship

There now exist so many good scholarly books on the general subject of new religious movements that it is difficult to choose from among those available.

Reference Books

Lewis, James R. *The Encyclopedia of Cults, Sects and New Religions.* Amherst, NY: Prometheus, 1998.

This is a comprehensive, up-to-date examination of minority religious groups in North America. This encyclopedia is illustrated, and many of the longer entries are written by specialists on specific groups.

Lewis, James R. *Peculiar Prophets: A Bibliographic Dictionary of New Religious Movements.* New York: Paragon, 1999.

An A-to-Z survey of the leaders/founders of some of the more important new religions. Almost all of the entries are short overviews. This book contains many photos of leaders and founders of alternative religious groups.

Melton, J. Gordon. *The Encyclopedic Handbook of Cults in America,* 2d ed. New York: Garland, 1992.

This is the best short reference book on the topic. The book contains an overview of key groups and discusses the controversy. Melton, a Methodist minister, includes a useful discussion of the distinction between the evangelical anticult movement and the secular anticult movement.

Melton, J. Gordon, ed. *Cults and New Religions: Sources for the Study of Nonconventional Religious Groups in Nineteenth- and Twentieth-Century America.* New York: Garland, 1990.

This is an important 22-volume set of original documents, mostly shorter pieces, from a wide variety of different religions and published by the groups themselves, from the Theosophical Society to Jonestown. Other groups and movements covered are spiritualism, Rosicrucianism, Jehovah's Witnesses, Mormonism, Christian Science, Unification church, Hare Krishna movement, and neopaganism. Most individual volumes are out of print. The most likely place to find this series is in major research libraries.

Textbooks and General Surveys

Barker, Eileen. *New Religious Movements: A Practical Introduction.* London: Her Majesty's Stationery Office, 1989.

A comprehensive overview of new religions by a leading British sociologist of religion. Barker's book is highly readable and, as one would anticipate, is particularly strong on the British situation.

Beckford, James A. *Cult Controversies: The Societal Response to the New Religious Movements.* London: Tavistock, 1985.

An examination of the cult controversy in Europe, focusing on the differences between the responses of England, France, and Germany. Beckford is a prominent British sociologist of religion, whose analysis of the interests of the various factions involved in the controversy is particularly strong.

Bromley, David G., and James T. Richardson, eds. *The Brainwashing/Deprogramming Controversy.* Lewiston, NY: Edwin Mellen, 1983.

An anthology of papers by leading scholars, organized according to historical, sociological, psychological, and legal perspectives. This is one of the few volumes to include papers from writers on both sides of the controversy, although the anticult perspective is underrepresented.

Bromley, David G., and Anson D. Shupe, Jr. *Strange Gods: The Great American Cult Scare.* Boston: Beacon Press, 1981.

An overview of the cult controversy by two sociologists. Although dated, this is still the best survey of its kind (often used as a supplementary text). While focusing on issues, the volume also draws examples from six specific groups—Children of God, Unification church, ISKCON, People's Temple, Divine Light Mission, and Church of Scientology.

Ellwood, Robert A., and Harry B. Partin. *Religious and Spiritual Groups in Modern America,* 2d ed. Englewood Cliffs, NJ: Prentice-Hall, 1988.

This is the earliest textbook on modern new religions. Revised in 1988, it is still a good choice for a general survey. While discussing the larger social situation and the cult controversy, the core of this book is a survey of specific groups. Included are brief readings from the literature of each group.

Miller, Timothy, ed. *America's Alternative Religions.* Albany, NY: State University of New York Press, 1995.

A compilation of short articles by a wide variety of scholars on specific religions or traditions, this book was initially offered as a reference book and recently issued in paperback. The book is weak on Buddhist traditions, but nevertheless one of the best of its kind.

Robbins, Thomas, and Dick Anthony, eds. *In Gods We Trust: New Patterns of Religious Pluralism in America,* 1st ed. New Brunswick, NJ: Transaction Books, 1981.

Although not focused exclusively on the cult controversy, there are a number of important chapters on the issue. Unfortunately, some of the better papers dropped out when this volume went into second edition. This book is often used as a supplementary textbook.

Saliba, John A. *Understanding New Religious Movements.* Grand Rapids, MI: William B. Eerdmans, 1995.

A recent overview designed as a general text, Saliba examines new religions in terms of a series of perspectives: historical, psychological, sociological, theological, and legal. Saliba's treatment is original and sophisticated. His theological chapter is particularly useful in a field of study dominated by social scientists with little theological training.

Specialized Studies

Levine, Saul. *Radical Departures: Desperate Detours to Growing Up.* New York: Harcourt Brace Jovanovich, 1984.

A Canadian psychiatrist, Levine has documented hundreds of young converts to new religions, discovering that, typically, the vast majority drop out voluntarily within the first two years of their memberships. This book is written in the form of a series of vignettes, making it particularly accessible to the general reader.

Richardson, Herbert, ed. *New Religions and Mental Health: Understanding the Issues.* Lewiston, NY: Edwin Mellen, 1980.

An early but still useful anthology that was published in response to the anticult laws that were being considered by state legislatures. The book contains a wide array of material, including the texts of proposed anticult legislation and public statements made against such legislation.

Robbins, Thomas. *Cults, Converts and Charisma.* Newbury Park, CA: Sage, 1988.

This is a comprehensive overview of new religions from a sociological viewpoint by an author widely recognized as one of the half-dozen or so top sociologists in the field of new religions.

Shepherd, William C. *To Secure the Blessings of Liberty: American Constitutional Law and the New Religious Movements.* New York: Crossroad, 1985.

A comprehensive, well-written overview of the cult controversy in the courts up through the conservatorship stage of the legal battle. The book also includes an overview of the history of religious liberty decisions that bear on the contemporary cult controversy. The volume is dated but still highly useful.

Shupe, Anson D., Jr., and David G. Bromley. *The New Vigilantes: Deprogrammers, Anti-Cultists, and the New Religions.* Beverly Hills, CA: Sage, 1980.

A sociological study of the early anticult movement by mainstream scholars. Shupe and Bromley examine the movement in terms of a resource mobilization perspective. Though dated, this book is essential for anyone wishing to acquire a thorough knowledge of the controversy.

Books on Specific Groups or Movements

Barker, Eileen. *The Making of a Moonie: Brainwashing or Choice?* Oxford, England: Basil Blackwell, 1984.

A comprehensive overview of one of the most controversial new religions. Barker's study of "Moonie" conversion is particularly important for undermining the notion that the Unification church possessed omnipotent techniques of mind control that could overcome the will of potential recruits.

Carter, Lewis F. *Charisma and Control in Rajneeshpuram: The Role of Shared Values in the Creation of a Community.* Cambridge: Cambridge University Press, 1990.

A number of interesting, semiacademic books have been written about Osho (Bhagwan Rajneesh) and his group's Oregon community. Carter's book is the most scholarly.

Lewis, James R., ed. *From the Ashes: Making Sense of Waco.* Lanham, MD: Rowman and Littlefield, 1994.

This was the first scholarly book on the Branch Davidian conflict to appear. It contains short essays, commentary, and original documents by scholars and others and served as a resource for the documentary *Waco: The Rules of Engagement.*

Lewis, James R., ed. *The Gods Have Landed: New Religions from Other Worlds.* Albany, NY: State University of New York Press, 1995.

A collection of articles on UFOs and religion. Some chapters deal with specific groups (e.g., the Unarius Society and the Raelian movement) while others deal with particular aspects of the phenomenon (e.g., the religious dimension of the abduction experience).

Lewis, James R., ed. *Magical Religion and Modern Witchcraft.* Albany, NY: State University of New York Press, 1996.

An anthology on the modern neopagan movement. Many of the contributors are academically trained neopagans. Essays are on the Goddess and the Wiccan worldview, the role of magic and ritual, history of the movement, neopagan ethics, and the relationship between Christianity and the neopagan movement. The volume concludes with overviews of the literature.

Lewis, James R., and J. Gordon Melton, eds. *Church Universal and Triumphant in Scholarly Perspective.* Stanford, CA: Center for Academic Publishing, 1994.

An academic anthology on one of the more controversial, yet one of the least studied, new religions. Chapters are on the organization's historical background, the controversy in which the church has been involved, psychological profile of members, sociological profile of members, and the church's legal battles.

Lewis, James R., and J. Gordon Melton, eds. *Perspectives on the New Age.* Albany, NY: State University of New York Press, 1992.

The first serious academic anthology dealing with the New Age movement. The book contains a series of essays on the historical roots of the New Age as well as a section on the international impact of the New Age movement. Other essays compare/contrast the New Age with the neopagan movement, the women's spirituality movement, and charismatic Christianity.

Lewis, James R., and J. Gordon Melton, eds. *Sex, Slander and Salvation: Investigating The Family/Children of God.* Stanford, CA: Center for Academic Publishing, 1994.

A comprehensive compilation on one of the most controversial new religions published just before the death of the founder. Subsequently the movement experienced a major transformation.

Richardson, James T., Joel Best, and David G. Bromley, eds. *The Satanism Scare.* New York: Aldine de Gruyter, 1991.

A series of essays examining the satanism scare of the late 1980s. This scare is treated sociologically—as a "moral panic," rather than as a response to an organized satanic threat. In other words, the

overall thrust of the volume is to debunk the idea that an organized satanic conspiracy exists.

Shinn, Larry. *The Dark Lord.* Philadelphia: Westminster, 1986.

One of the better studies of the Hare Krishna movement. Unlike
other people who have studied ISKCON, Shinn has a strong background in the Hindu tradition. The author is also interested in the
issue of conversion, so that parts of his discussion address the
cult controversy.

Weightman, Judith Mary. *Making Sense of the Jonestown Suicides: A
Sociological History of the People's Temple.* New York: Mellen Press, 1984.

Some twenty books have been written about the Jonestown tragedy. This book and John R. Hall's essay in *In Gods We Trust* (see
above) are two of the better treatments.

Wilson, Bryan, and Karel Dobbelaere. *A Time to Chant: The Soka
Gakkai Buddhist in Britain.* Oxford, England: Oxford University
Press, 1994.

The best book-length study of the most important new Japanese
religion to establish itself in Western countries. This book was
written not long after Soka Gakkai separated itself from the
Nichiren Shoshu sect of Buddhism and thus contains a comprehensive analysis of that split.

Wright, Stuart A., ed. *Armageddon in Waco: Critical Perspectives
on the Branch Davidian Conflict.* Chicago: University of Chicago
Press, 1995.

The definitive scholarly anthology on the Branch Davidian events.
The essays on the role of the media, law enforcement, and so forth
provide insights beyond this specific conflict and are thus useful
for people more interested in the larger cult controversy than in
the Waco tragedy.

Individual Articles

Balch, Robert W. "Looking Behind the Scenes in a Religious Cult:
Implications for the Study of Conversion." *Sociological Analysis* 41
(1980): 137–143.

Fisher, Barry A. "Devotion, Damages and Deprogrammers: Strategies and Counterstrategies in the Cult Wars." *Journal of Law and Religion* 9:1 (1991): 515–177.

Lewis, James R. "Apostates and the Legitimation of Repression: Some Historical and Empirical Perspectives on the Cult Controversy." *Sociological Analysis* 49:4 (Winter 1989): 386–396.

Lewis, James R., and David G. Bromley. "The Cult Withdrawal Syndrome: A Case of Misattribution of Cause?" *Journal for the Scientific Study of Religion* 26:4 (December 1987): 508–522.

Richardson, James T. "Conversion Careers." *Society* 17:3 (March/April 1980): 47–50.

Saliba, John A. "The New Religions and Mental Health." Pp. 99–113 in David G. Bromley and Jeffrey K. Hadden, eds. *Religion and the Social Order,* vol. 3B. New York: JAI Press, 1993.

Anticult Scholarship

Partially because the scholarship of cult critics tends to focus on the theme of the manipulation of members of certain groups, it is easier to lay out a more defined set of publications that the reader can consult to acquaint her- or himself with this perspective. The following list (though not the annotations) was provided by Dr. Michael Langone of the American Family Foundation.

Books

Cialdin, Robert B. *Influence: The Psychology of Persuasion.* New York: William Morrow, 1993.

An overview of manipulative techniques that bring about compliance—in advertising, human relations, sales, recruitment to groups, and other areas. Useful as a context for more specific discussions of cultic influences.

Enroth, Ronald. *Churches That Abuse.* Grand Rapids, MI: Zondervan, 1992.

An examination of churches—doctrinally orthodox as well as unorthodox—in which, the author asserts, abusive behavioral influence is exercised over at least some members of the congregation. Authored by an evangelical scholar, this has been a highly controversial book within the Christian community.

Langone, Michael, ed. *Recovery from Cults: Help for Victims of Psychological and Spiritual Abuse.* New York: Norton, 1993.

As the title indicates, this is an anthology focused on the problems experienced by former members of controversial groups. The contributors represent a wide variety of writers in the field.

Lifton, Robert J. *Thought Reform and the Psychology of Totalism.* New York: Norton, 1961.

Lifton, a scholar of Chinese communist brainwashing, restates his findings in terms of more general principles. This particular book has often been used by deprogrammers, who saw Lifton's descriptions of thought reform as parallel to the manipulative influences exercised over group members by cults.

Rudin, Marcia R., ed. *Cults on Campus: Continuing Challenge.* Bonita Springs, FL: American Family Foundation, 1996.

Almost from the very beginning of the controversy cults were accused of targeting idealistic young people for recruitment. This anthology brings that aspect of the controversy up-to-date.

Schein, Edgar H., Inge Schneier, and Curtis H. Barker. *Coercive Persuasion: A Socio-Psychological Analysis of the "Brainwashing" of American Civilian Prisoners by the Chinese Communists.* New York: W. W. Norton, 1961.

Contemporary critics of cults view the influence of leaders over their followers as bearing a family resemblance to communist brainwashing techniques.

Singer, Margaret T., with Janja Lalich. *Cults in Our Midst: The Hidden Menace in Our Everyday Lives.* San Francisco: Jossey-Bass, 1995.

A general book on cult as menace by one of the primary architects of the notion of cultic mind control. Singer discusses the controversy from the anticult perspective.

Articles

American Bar Association. "Cults in American Society: A Legal Analysis of Undue Influence, Fraud and Misrepresentation. A Report Prepared for the American Family Foundation and the Cult

Awareness Network." Reproduced in *Cultic Studies Journal* 12:1 (1995): 1–48.

Chambers, William, Michael Langone, Arthur Dole, and John Malinoski. "The Group Psychological Abuse Scale: A Measure of the Varieties of Cultic Abuse." *Cultic Studies Journal* 11:1 (1994): 88–117.

The Council of Europe's Report on Sects and New Religious Movements. Reproduced in *Cultic Studies Journal* 9:1 (1991): 89–119.

Langone, Michael. "Clinical Update on Cults." *Psychiatric Times*. July 1996.

Langone, Michael. "Secular and Religious Critiques of Cults: Complementary Visions, Not Irresolvable Conflicts." *Cultic Studies Journal* 12:2 (1995): 166–186.

Ofshe, Richard. "Coercive Persuasion and Attitude Change." Pp. 212–224 in Edgar F. Borgatta and Marie L. Borgatta, eds. *Encyclopedia of Sociology*. New York: MacMillan, 1992.

Ofshe, Richard, and Margaret Singer. "Attacks on Peripheral Versus Central Elements of Self and the Impact of Thought Reforming Techniques." *Cultic Studies Journal* 3:1 (1986): 3–24.

Singer, Margaret. "Group Psychodynamics." Pp. 1467–1471 in Robert Berkow and Andrew Fletcher, eds. *The Merck Manual of Diagnosis and Therapy*, 15th ed. Rahway, NJ: Merck Sharp and Dohme Research Laboratories, 1987.

Singer, Margaret, and Richard Ofshe. "Thought Reform Programs and the Production of Psychiatric Casualties." *Psychiatric Annals* 20:4 (1990): 188–193.

West, Louis, and Paul Martin. "Pseudo-Identity: A Form of Personality Change Seen in Victims of Captivity and Cults." In Lynn Rhue and Judith Rhue, eds., *Dissociation: Clinical, Theoretical and Research Perspectives*. New York: Guilford, 1994.

Zablocki, Benjamin. "The Blacklisting of a Concept: The Strange History of the Brainwashing Conjecture in the Sociology of Religion." *Rova Religio* 1:1 (1997): 96–121.

Zimbardo, Philip. "What Messages Are Behind Today's Cults?" *APA Monitor*. Washington, DC: American Psychological Association, May 14, 1997.

Popular Books

Numerous books have been written from the standpoint of cult as menace. Often these are authored by conservative Protestant Christians and published by evangelical presses. For many years, one of the most popular types of cult-related book was the apostate tale— former members who wrote exposés about the experiences they had had as members of groups. The demand for these appears to have waned.

It should also be noted that every group with more than a hundred members usually runs some sort of publishing operation, often printing high quality books and other materials related to their religion. Readers interested in specific minority religions will usually find abundant information readily available direct from the group itself. Because of the tendency for organizations to change addresses every few years, the reader is advised to consult the Internet for the latest address and phone number of a particular religious group.

Conway, Flo, and Jim Siegelman. *Snapping: America's Epidemic of Sudden Personality Change,* 2d ed. New York: Stillpoint Press, 1995.

This journalistic account of deprogramming and the cult menace puts forward the thesis that cult brainwashing techniques produce a unique mental illness—information disease.

Patrick, Ted, with Tom Dulack. *Let Our Children Go!* New York: E. P. Dutton, 1976.

Written by the one who invented the process of deprogramming, this book describes enough of the violence associated with the practice to make the reader aware that deprogramming is *not* "just talking to people." Though out of print, this book can often be found in public and university libraries.

Sherwood, Carlton. *Inquisition: The Persecution and Prosecution of the Rev. Sun Myung Moon.* Washington, DC: Regnery Gateway, 1989.

A fast-moving overview of the inside story behind Rev. Moon's conviction of tax evasion. The author concludes that, whatever else one might think of the man and his movement, Rev. Moon was framed by critics of the Unification church.

Underwood, Barbara, and Betty Underwood. *Hostage to Heaven.* New York: Clarkson N. Potter, 1979.

One of the many "ex-cultist" apostate tales, written jointly by a mother and daughter. This particular book is of more than usual interest because Barbara Underwood was one of the members of the Unification church to be deprogrammed as part of the *Katz* ("Faithful Five/Faithless Four") conservatorship case.

Nonprint Resources

Cults: Saying NO under Pressure
Type: VHS videotape
Length: 29 min.
Date: 1990
Cost: $33 ($39 outside the U.S.)
Source: American Family Foundation
P.O. Box 2265
Bonita Springs, FL 34133
941-514-3081

This educational videotape is designed for high school and college students and others. Hosted and narrated by Charlton Heston, this video was co-developed by the International Cult Education Program of AFF and the InService Video network of the National Association of Secondary School Principals (NASSP).

After the Cult: Recovering Together
Type: VHS videotape
Length: 25 min.
Date: 1994
Cost: $33 ($39 outside the U.S.)
Source: American Family Foundation
P.O. Box 2265
Bonita Springs, FL 34133
941-514-3081

Ten ex-members relate their personal stories, as well as how they went on to live their lives after leaving their respective groups.

What Is a Cult and How Does It Work?
Type: VHS videotape
Length: 56 min.
Date: 1995
Cost: $28 ($33 outside the U.S.)
Source: American Family Foundation
P.O. Box 2265
Bonita Springs, FL 34133
941-514-3081

Dr. Margaret Singer, a prominent anticult psychologist, provides a general overview of the cult phenomenon.

Leaving a Cult: Information about Exiting and Recovery
Type: VHS videotape
Length: 56 min.
Date: 1995
Cost: $28 ($33 outside the U.S.)
Source: American Family Foundation
P.O. Box 2265
Bonita Springs, FL 34133
941-514-3081

Dr. Margaret Singer provides advice for current and former members as well as for their friends and family.

Gods of the New Age
Type: VHS videotape
Length: 103 min.
Date: 1988
Cost: $29.95
Source: Jeremiah Films
Spiritual Counterfeits Project
P.O. Box 4308
Berkeley, CA 94704
510-540-0300
www.scp-inc.org

The focus of much recent Christian anticult material is the New Age movement, as reflected in this video.

The Pagan Invasion, Volume II
Type: VHS videotape
Length: 48 min.
Date: 1991
Cost: $29.95
Source: Jeremiah Films
Spiritual Counterfeits Project
P.O. Box 4308
Berkeley, CA 94704
510-540-0300
www.scp-inc.org

Among various new religions, Christians view neopagan religions as particularly dangerous.

UFOs: The Mystery Resolved
Type: VHS videotape
Length: 60 min.
Date: 1992
Cost: $25
Source: Reasons to Believe
Spiritual Counterfeits Project
P.O. Box 4308
Berkeley, CA 94704
510-540-0300
www.scp-inc.org

The view of UFOs in demonological terms.

Deprogramming: Understanding the Issue
Type: VHS videotape
Length: 28 min.
Date: 1985
Cost: $19.95
Source: Cult Awareness Network
1680 North Vine Street, Suite 415
Los Angeles, CA 90028
800-556-3055

Critical of the secular anticult movement, this video contains some startlingly brutal footage of actual kidnappings and follows the stories of parents who had hired deprogrammers, only to regret their decision later. A wide variety of professionals as well as people who had been kidnapped offer their comments at various stages of the presentation.

Waco: The Rules of Engagement
Type: VHS videotape
Length: 136 min.
Date: 1997
Cost: $25
Source: Reko
P.O. Box 4005
Joplin, MO 61803-4005
800-771-2147

An award-winning videotape (that was also nominated for an Academy Award) that brings up issues relevant to the controversy, this is a professional overview of events in Waco, Texas. It is a poignant presentation of the tragedy that left 4 law enforcement agents and 86 men, women, and children in the community dead. The video calls for the nation to recommit itself to the basic precepts of tolerance and freedom upon which American society is built.

Introduction to Scientology
Type: VHS videotape
Length: 58 min.
Date: 1990
Cost: $19.95
Source: Bridge Publications
4751 Fountain Avenue
Los Angeles, CA 90029
800-722-1733
www.bridgepub.com.

An exclusive filmed interview with L. Ron Hubbard, founder of Scientology, in the only filmed interview he ever granted. Hubbard answers the commonly asked questions about Dianetics and Scientology and explains how he made his discoveries and breakthroughs regarding the spirit, the mind, and life.

How to Use Dianetics (A Visual Guidebook to the Human Mind)
Type: VHS videotape
Length: 47 min.
Date: 1994
Cost: $24.95
Source: Bridge Publications
4751 Fountain Avenue
Los Angeles, CA 90029
800-722-1733
www.bridgepub.com.

This film explains the way that the reactive mind causes stress, nightmares, unhappiness, and negative emotions and shows the application of the procedures of Dianetics to another person.

Your Ever Well Wisher
Type: VHS videotape
Length: 120 min.
Date: 1987
Cost: $25 plus shipping
Source: ITV (ISKCON Television)
          P.O. Box 556
          Topanga, CA 90290
          800-551-0380

A biographical work about the life of Shrila Prabhupada, ISKCON's founder, by filmmaker John Greisser. This is a professional production about an amazing man.

A Hare Krishna World
Type: VHS videotape
Length: 120 min.
Date: 1985
Cost: $25 plus shipping
Source: ITV (ISKCON Television)
          P.O. Box 556
          Topanga, CA 90290
          800-551-0380

A general overview of the Hare Krishna movement worldwide, this video gives viewers a glimpse into the ISKCON lifestyle.

Introducing The Family
Type: VHS videotape
Length: 20 min.
Date: 1993
Cost: $15
Source: The Family
          2020 Pennsylvania Avenue, Suite 102
          Washington, DC 20006
          800-ForAFam

The practice of deprogramming as well as the first anticult organization were initially focused on this group.

The Family—Making a Difference
Type: VHS videotape
Length: 20 min.
Date: 1994
Cost: $15
Source: The Family
   2020 Pennsylvania Avenue, Suite 102
   Washington, DC 20006
   800-ForAFam

A fascinating overview of The Family, focusing on their social work worldwide.

A Living Faith: Insight into Education in The Family
Type: VHS videotape
Length: 30 min.
Date: 1995
Cost: $15
Source: The Family
   2020 Pennsylvania Avenue, Suite 102
   Washington, DC 20006
   800-ForAFam

This documentary takes the viewer inside the communal homes of The Family for a close look at their home-based approach to education.

Climb the Highest Mountain
Type: VHS videotape
Length: 19 min.
Date: 1993
Cost: $10
Source: Royal Teton Ranch
   Box 5000
   Corwin Springs, MT 59030-5000
   406-848-7441

A profile of the Church Universal and Triumphant. This is a very upbeat production, focused on the ideals of the church.

The Mandate of the Bright and Morning Star
Type: VHS videotape
Length: 60 min.
Date: 1995
Cost: $19.95

Source: Aquarian Concepts Community
P.O. Box 3946
Sedona, AZ 86340
520-204-1206

Aquarian Concepts Community is a small group in Sedona, Arizona, that in March 1998 was featured on a "Dateline" program. The community produces its own videos. This film provides a glimpse into Aquarian Concepts Community beliefs and worldview and gives a close-up of the founders.

There have also been some box office movies on the cult controversy, almost always presenting minority religions negatively. It is usually possible to find *Ticket to Heaven* or *Blinded by the Light* in large video stores.

Index

James R. Lewis is Professor and Chair, Department of Religious Studies, World University. He is an authority on non-traditional religious movements and has worked as a media consultant on cult-related events, including the 1993 crisis at the Branch Davidian complex in Waco.